INTERNATIONAL ORGANIZATION

Essays by

P. J. ALLOTT

J. F. McMAHON

IAN BROWNLIE

ROSALYN HIGGINS

OSCAR SCHACHTER

S. A. DE SMITH

ANDREAS J. JACOVIDES

MICHAEL HARDY

John McMahon

INTERNATIONAL ORGANIZATION

LAW IN MOVEMENT

ESSAYS IN HONOUR OF
JOHN McMAHON

EDITED BY
J. E. S. FAWCETT AND
ROSALYN HIGGINS

Published for
THE ROYAL INSTITUTE OF
INTERNATIONAL AFFAIRS
by
OXFORD UNIVERSITY PRESS
LONDON   NEW YORK   TORONTO
1974

Oxford University Press, Ely House, London W1

GLASGOW NEW YORK TORONTO MELBOURNE WELLINGTON
CAPE TOWN IBADAN NAIROBI DAR ES SALAAM ADDIS ABABA
DELHI BOMBAY CALCUTTA MADRAS KARACHI LAHORE DACCA
KUALA LUMPUR SINGAPORE HONG KONG TOKYO

ISBN 0 19 214998 9

JX 1954
I48

*Printed in Great Britain by
The Eastern Press Limited
of London and Reading*

CONTENTS

ABBREVIATIONS

ACMRR	Advisory Committee on Marine Resources Research
Afr. Aff.	*African Affairs*
AJIL	*American Journal of International Law*
ASIL	American Society of International Law
BYBIL	*The British Year Book of International Law*
ECLA	Economic Commission for Latin America
ENEA	European Nuclear Energy Agency
FAO	Food and Agriculture Organization
For. Aff.	*Foreign Affairs*
GAOR	*General Assembly Official Records*
GELTSPAP	Group of Experts on Long-Term Scientific Policy and Planning
GESAMP	Group of Experts on the Scientific Aspects of Marine Pollution
IAEA	International Atomic Energy Agency
ICAO	International Civil Aviation Organization
ICJ Rep.	International Court of Justice, *Reports of Judgments, Advisory Opinions and Orders*
ICLQ	*International and Comparative Law Quarterly*
ICSEM	International Commission for the Scientific Exploration of the Mediterranean
ILA	International Law Association
ILO	International Labour Organization
IMCO	Intergovernmental Maritime Consultative Organization
Int. Aff.	*International Affairs* (London)
Int. Org.	*International Organization*
IOC	Intergovernmental Oceanographic Commission
ISS	Institute for Strategic Studies
OAS	Organization of American States
ODAS	Ocean data acquisition systems
ONUC	Organization des Nations Unies au Congo
PCIJ	Permanent Court of International Justice
Recueil	Les Communautés Européennes, Cour de Justice, *Recueil de la Jurisprudence de la Cour*
SCOR	Scientific Committee for Oceanic Research
SCOR	*Security Council Official Records*
UKTS	United Kingdom Treaty Series

UNCITRAL	United Nations Commission on International Trade Law
UNEF	United Nations Emergency Force
UNESCO	United Nations Educational, Scientific, and Cultural Organization
UNFICYP	United Nations Force in Cyprus
UNIPOM	United Nations India-Pakistan Observation Mission
UNITAR	United Nations Institute for Training and Research
UNRIAA	*United Nations Reports of International Arbitral Awards*
UNTEA	United Nations Temporary Executive Authority
UNTS	United Nations Treaty Series
UNYOM	United Nations Yemen Observation Mission
WHO	World Health Organization
WMO	World Meteorological Organization

FOREWORD

THIS volume of essays is dedicated to the memory of John McMahon.
It is a tribute by his friends and by Chatham House, for which, when
he died in April 1969, he was writing a major work on decision-
making in the UN specialized agencies.

The volume contains a study by him of the judicial methods of
the European Communities Court, which was one of the steps towards
the larger work. The other essays all have themes that were close
to the interest and work of John McMahon, and the volume is offered
as a token of the book that was not to be finished.

We express our gratitude to Hertford College and Lincoln College
in Oxford, to the Trustees of the International Law Fund in Cambridge, to a number of John McMahon's colleagues and friends, and
to the McMahon family for contributions which have helped to meet
the cost of producing this work; also to the *Harvard International
Law Journal* for permission to include an essay originally published
in that journal.

JAMES FAWCETT
Director of Studies

Royal Institute of International Affairs
Chatham House, London
January 1973

JOHN McMAHON

AN APPRECIATION BY

P. J. ALLOTT*

JOHN McMAHON died on 12 April 1969 at the age of 32. He will be remembered for what he was as a person and for what he was and would have been as an international lawyer.

He was a Fellow and Dean of Hertford College, Oxford, having previously been Lecturer in Law at Lincoln College, Oxford. He read law at Christ's College, Cambridge, and took a further degree at Cambridge and a master's degree at Harvard University, in both cases specializing in international law. He took part in the student interne programme with the Office of Legal Affairs of the United Nations Secretariat in New York and did research work in Geneva principally on matters relating to international organizations. He had recently completed a period of some eighteen months as a Legal Officer in the Office of Legal Affairs of the United Nations Secretariat. After his return to Oxford he had continued as a Consultant to the United Nations in the preparation of studies on the sea-bed question and he was in New York on that business at the time of his death. His published work included four articles for *The British Year Book of International Law*.[1]

His career as an international lawyer was thus already exceptionally well founded and no one doubted that it would continue as well as it had begun. But it is as a representative of, and an inspiration to, what might be called a new wave of international law that it is perhaps most appropriate to remember him here. He was one of a group of lawyers who studied international law at Cambridge in the late 1950s and who believed themselves to be somewhere near the beginning of such a new wave of international law. They were of many nationalities and they had come to Cambridge (or stayed on at Cambridge) because, as a result of some notably forward-looking thinking on the part of those who arrange such matters, the possibility

---

* Legal Counsellor, Foreign and Commonwealth Office. With minor modifications, this appreciation is taken from *The British Year Book of International Law*, 1968–9. © P. J. Allott 1970.

[1] ' The Court of the European Communities: Judicial Interpretation and International Organization ', 37 (1961), p. 320; ' Legal Aspects of Outer Space ', 38 (1962), p. 339; ' The Legislative Techniques of the International Labour Organization ', 41 (1965–6), p. 1; ' Legal Aspects of Outer Space: Recent Developments ', ibid. p. 417.

existed (and exists) to study international law in an academically serious but practical sort of way such as to enable the graduate to move on, with a deep personal commitment to international law, into any field where such a commitment can be put to use, whether in the diplomatic service, as a government legal adviser, in the academic world, in an international organization, or in private practice. The members of the particular group to which John McMahon belonged at Cambridge are now distributed throughout the world. Their paths cross from time to time and very often those paths were found to meet in the company of John McMahon. It was as if he had become the centre of an international network of younger international lawyers who had been with him at Cambridge or Harvard or the United Nations and who all counted him as a friend and gained from his enthusiasm and optimism.

He had concentrated on outer space law, on the law of international organizations, and, more recently, on the regime to govern the sea-bed of the high seas. It is no coincidence that these are all topics where the role of international law is primarily positive and creative—law as the principle of functioning of an organism rather than as a body of rules. It is easy to forget that this aspect of international law is not new but there is no doubt that it has gained extraordinary momentum in recent years as a result of many contributing factors (among others, the emergence of the new nations with internationalist ideals but suspicious of a 'class-interest' in traditional international law, the so-called ideological conflicts between nations which weakened the self-confidence of value-based law, the new facts of international power stemming from new weapons and new relationships, the emergence of the managerial and cybernetics approaches to a wide range of problems). In this new context international law had to be treated differently, as something organic, inevitable, everyday, practical, and natural rather than as something artificial or super-natural. John McMahon typified this Reformation or Enlightenment. He was an internationalist not merely by conviction but as an expression of his personality. His internationalism was communicated in his person as well as in his work. It is not only those who knew him personally who have suffered by his untimely death. But it is to his close friends and his family in particular that we express our sympathy, knowing, as we do, something of what has been lost.

THE COURT OF
THE EUROPEAN COMMUNITIES:
JUDICIAL INTERPRETATION AND
INTERNATIONAL ORGANIZATION *

J. F. McMAHON †

INTRODUCTION

IT is customary, in the constitutive instrument of an international organization, to vest in an appropriate body jurisdiction concerning questions involving interpretation of that instrument. In the case of the European Communities the appropriate body is the Court, whose function is to ensure the rule of law in the interpretation and application of the basic treaty of each of the three Communities.[1] However, judicial interpretation of the charter of an international organization is the exception rather than the rule. The Charter of the United Nations, following the example of the Covenant of the League, contains no provisions for the authoritative interpretation of its basic instrument.[2] Many of the specialized agencies, although they may make a small genuflection in the direction of the International Court,[3] will usually refer disputes concerning their charter to a non-judicial organ such as the Executive Directors,[4] the Board of Governors,[5] the Council,[6] the Assembly,[7] the Congress,[8] or the General Conference.[9]

The reasons for such lack of enthusiasm among states for referring every dispute concerning the basic instrument of an international organization to a judicial organ are not difficult to discover. Sometimes, as with the International Monetary Fund, the technical nature of the organization may render it unsuitable for judicial control.[10] More often, however, it is the acute need for an informal, flexible and an expeditious method of interpretation that will militate against the concept of judicial control. Nor, in this context, should one underestimate the political sensitivity of states, especially where their vital interests are concerned. As most disputes concerning the interpretation of such an instrument as the United Nations Charter will

* © J. F. McMahon 1962. With minor modifications, taken from *The British Year Book of International Law*, 1961.

† LL.B. (Cambridge), LL.M. (Harvard), Lecturer in Law, Lincoln College, Oxford.

involve important political considerations (for example, the *Admissions* cases or the question now pending concerning the financial obligations of members), it is not surprising that states are unwilling to commit themselves in advance to submitting such questions for an authoritative judicial decision.

Many conflicts of opinion concerning the meaning of a particular provision of the basic instrument of an international organization will be settled by informal discussion and consultation without the necessity for an authoritative interpretation. It is also important to note that the routine, day-to-day application of the contents of a constitutive instrument will inevitably involve its interpretation, as was indeed pointed out at the San Francisco Conference:

In the course of the operations from day to day of the various organs of the Organization, it is inevitable that each organ will interpret such parts of the Charter as are applicable to its particular functions. This process is inherent in the functioning of any body which operates under an instrument defining its functions and powers. . . . Accordingly, it is not necessary to include in the Charter a provision either authorizing or approving the normal operation of this principle.[11]

It is by means of such practical application and interpretation that the charter of any international organization becomes a viable instrument responding to the needs of an evolving international society and providing scope for change and adaptability. One need only refer to the Uniting for Peace Resolution, the creation of a United Nations Emergency Force, the increasing power of the Secretary-General, and the concept of absence and abstention [12] in the Security Council to realize to what an appreciable extent the text of the charter of an international organization may be modified or extended by its operation in practice.[13] How far such practice, if not embodied in a formal amendment, is legally binding is an interesting question. It might be difficult to maintain that because the Security Council had followed a certain practice on two or three occasions, such practice should constitute a binding precedent. In two or three cases, however, the International Court of Justice has referred to ' subsequent practice '[14] when interpreting a provision of the United Nations Charter. Such practice or conduct might also raise some interesting points concerning the applicability of the doctrine of estoppel [15] and the growth of customary law within an international organization.

The above remarks presuppose the necessity of interpreting the basic instrument of an international organization and such a necessity always exists. The words used in the drafting of the instrument are rarely precise or susceptible of a single meaning; nor is it possible to envisage and provide against every situation in which the charter of an organization will have to apply.

It is frequently stated that the object of interpretation is to discover the intentions of the parties.[16] However, Judge Lauterpacht has indicated [17] at least five different situations when it could be said that no such intentions existed and had to be ' implied ', ' imputed ', or ' presumed '. Even if such intentions exist, the fact that a dispute arises as to what they are indicates that they cannot have been expressed in an unambiguous manner. Nor is it clear to whom the word ' party ' refers in this context; the plenipotentiaries who drafted the constitutive instrument, or the governments that ratified it. In any case, one is likely to be dealing with forty or fifty parties. It is also pertinent to ask where one is to find the intentions of the parties if not in the text itself. Nor is there only one ' true ' interpretation of a disputed text. As Kelsen says:

The function of authentic interpretation is not to determine the true meaning of the legal norm thus interpreted, but to render binding one of the several meanings of a legal norm, all equally possible from a logical point of view. The choice of interpretations as a law-making act is determined by political motives. It is not the logically ' true ', it is the politically preferable meaning of the interpreted norm which becomes binding.[18]

However, a judge does not have unlimited legal discretion in this matter, and traditional jurisprudence distinguishes various principles of interpretation which will normally be invoked. One may mention the plain, ordinary, ' natural ' meaning principle, the effective principle, the restrictive principle, the teleological principle, the integration principle, the subsequent practice principle, the emergent purpose principle, and the use of *travaux préparatoires*.[19] It will be readily appreciated that an astute merger of any two of the above principles may substantiate almost any conclusion the judge has reached independently of their assistance and that the application of the effective or the restrictive principle may well yield a contradictory result. As Lauterpacht says, such principles will frequently only be the form in which the judge cloaks a decision already reached by other means:

It is elegant—and it inspires confidence—to give the garb of an established rule of interpretation to a conclusion reached as to the meaning of a statute, of a contract, or of a treaty.[20]

The hollow fiction of the intentions of the parties is all the more difficult to sustain in regard to the constitutive instrument of an international organization. Such a treaty, if it is to prove effective, must inevitably develop a life of its own, often totally different from the concept of its founders. The teleological principle of interpretation is ideally suited to this purpose. One may now turn to the jurisprudence of the Court of the European Communities to examine by what principles that Court has been guided in interpreting the constitutive instrument of each Community.

THE NATURE OF THE COURT OF JUSTICE OF THE EUROPEAN COMMUNITIES

The Court of the European Coal and Steel Community was replaced in October 1958 by the Court of the European Communities. The present Court, like the European Parliament, is an institution common to all three Communities; a sort of pledge of more unity to come.[21] As, at the time of writing, the only cases decided under the European Economic Community Treaty have been two appeals lodged by public servants against their dismissal, this article is principally concerned with the jurisprudence arising from interpretation of the European Coal and Steel Community Treaty, concerning which nearly one hundred judgments have been rendered.[22] However, there can be little doubt that a court, now responsible for interpreting the three constitutive treaties, all of which are concerned with closer European integration, will seize the opportunity to strengthen such efforts towards integration by the unity of its jurisprudence in their interpretation and by the formulation of a Community law.

The function of the Court, as already stated,[23] is to ensure the rule of law [24] in the interpretation and application of the basic treaty of each of the three Communities. Parties who may appear before the Court are: states, the High Authority, the Commissions and Councils of Ministers,[25] enterprises, associations, and individuals.[26] The four grounds of appeal,[27] namely incompetence, violation of a substantial procedural requirement, violation of the Treaty or of any rule of law concerning its application, and *détournement de pouvoir*, are the same as the grounds which may be alleged in the French Conseil d'État against a French administrative action. This similarity to French administrative law is no mere chance, for it is precisely as the administrative tribunal of the Communities, reviewing the legality of the legislative acts of the High Authority, the two Commissions, and the three Councils of Ministers, that the importance and principal task of the Court is to be found.[28] However, this task is not exclusively an administrative one, for the treaties, more particularly that of the Coal and Steel Community, also vest jurisdiction in the Court concerning matters of discipline,[29] the use of the veto,[30] imposition of pecuniary sanctions,[31] revision of the Treaty,[32] delictual and contractual liability,[33] assessment of economic facts and circumstances,[34] and points involving international law.[35] This brief survey of the competence of the Court should quickly dispel any idea of classifying it under one of the traditional headings of international law.[36]

The domestic courts of the various member countries will also have occasion to interpret the Community Treaties. By virtue of their ratification of the Treaties (some member states such as the Netherlands and Luxembourg even amended their constitutions to avoid future constitutional difficulties), the Community law embodied in these Treaties is now a part of the municipal law of each member state and thus falls within the competence of the domestic courts. This competence is, however, a limited one. In the Coal and Steel Community the domestic courts are obliged by Article 41 of the Treaty to refer to the Court of Justice of the Communities for a ruling on the validity of resolutions of the High Authority or of the Council, should this be contested before them. On the other hand, the domestic courts are competent to interpret the Treaty and the acts of the common institutions directly. This lacuna has been filled in the other two Communities. Article 177 of the European Economic Community Treaty —to which Article 150 of the Euratom Treaty corresponds exactly— provides for reference to the Court of Justice for preliminary determination of questions raised before a domestic court or tribunal in connection, not only with the validity of the acts of the common institutions, but also with the interpretation of the Treaty. However, such reference is only imposed on domestic courts from whose decisions no appeal lies under municipal law. It is interesting to note that municipal courts have already made an appreciable contribution to the elaboration of Community law and that about fifteen cases have so far been the subject of decisions before them, some of which have not yet become executory.[37]

The Community Treaties make frequent references to municipal law [38] and there is no doubt that the treaties involve a substantial penetration into the municipal sphere.

On certain matters at least, the Common Market requires really common rules known to all people and enterprises concerned, and each Member State cannot remain free to decide whether, when and how its national law should be modified . . . the Member States have agreed to lay down on specified matters a law of the Community, directly binding and applied as national law within each Member State and subject to sovereign interpretation by the single Court of Justice of the Communities. As aforesaid, the basic law of the Communities, more or less detailed, is laid down in the Treaties themselves. But it has to be completed, possibly adapted, anyhow implemented and applied to individual cases. Within the limits of competence and under the conditions of procedure determined by the Treaties for each matter, the Council and the executive bodies are entitled to do so. They are empowered to make regulations which bind everyone in the community.[39]

Such regulations may be issued under Articles 58, 79, and 85 of the European Economic Community. Most of the provisions, however, are not self-executing and merely oblige the member states to take appropriate measures in their municipal law for the fulfilment of their obligations. Only in very rare cases will the Court apply municipal law directly [40]; nor will it attempt to decide whether a particular regulation of the High Authority violates municipal law or the constitution of one of the member states.[41]

An important effect of the Community Treaties in the municipal sphere will be the necessity to rationalize and harmonize the principles of law in the various member countries. This fact is recognized in the European Economic Community Treaty which devotes two of its articles to what it calls ' approximation of laws '.[42] It is interesting to note in this respect that there was a meeting of non-governmental experts in Paris, in June 1960, which resulted in the formulation of concrete proposals for a convention on the formation of a company of European type.[43]

This gradual approximation of law, however, will have to take place both in the field of legislation and in the jurisprudence of the courts. The Court of the European Communities is not itself concerned with private international law and that question has only been invoked on one occasion before the Court.[44] In this connection one might refer to Article 215 of the European Economic Community, which provides that:

The contractual responsibility of the Community shall be governed by the law applying to the contract in question. As regards non-contractual responsibility, the Community must, in conformity with the general principles common to the laws of Member States, make good any damage caused by its institutions or by its agents in the discharge of their duties.

Some measure of harmonization of private international law will, of course, be required on the municipal level. If, for example, a person is regarded as French in Italy he will then enjoy the status of a national of a member state and, as such, will benefit from all the advantages of the Common Market. But if under the German law of nationality this same person may be declared to be Swiss and so barred from these advantages in Germany, an absurd and intolerable discrimination will arise.[45]

In striking contrast to the Statute of the International Court of Justice,[46] none of the Community Treaties refers to the sources of law which the European Court must apply when interpreting each basic treaty. It would be unreasonable to presume that such omission was due to mere negligence; a more likely explanation is that the three Communities were such an unprecedented and complex legal venture that it was thought expedient not to fetter the Court in advance but, ' laisser le droit de la Communauté puiser aux sources dont il aura besoin avec assez de liberté '.[47] Nor, according to either international law or municipal law, may the Court pronounce a *non liquet* and so dismiss the case.[48] In fact, however, an analysis of the practice of the Court reveals that there is no danger that it will ever be at a loss for a ' source of law '; the richness and diversity of the sources it has drawn upon are remarkable.

Of course, the three constitutive treaties themselves [49] are the fountain-head of the Court's law. Together with these treaties one must mention the regulations, decisions, and directives issued by the Councils, Commissions, and the High Authority; on the occasions when such regulations are self-executing they too will constitute a source of law. Thirdly, the municipal laws, municipal decisions (especially the decisions of the Conseil d'État),[50] and textbook writers [51] of the member states form a fertile and most vital source of law for the Court. Such laws and decisions are not applied directly. However, faced with the necessity of interpreting in the treaty such a concept as *détournement de pouvoir*, the Court examines the jurisprudence of the member states relating to this concept and extrapolates those principles common to most of the states. This common denominator then becomes the Community law.[52] International law is rarely cited.[53]

Quant aux sources de ce droit, rien ne s'oppose évidemment à ce qu'on les recherche, le cas échéant, dans le droit international, mais normalement, et le plus souvent, on les trouvera plutôt dans le droit interne des divers États membres. . . .[54]

The laws of municipal systems other than those of the member states are equally seldom mentioned; only one reference has been made to English law [55] and one to American law.[56] Finally, the Court frequently refers to its own jurisprudence, as formulated in previous decisions. However, there is no law of precedent and the Court, being a court of last instance, is at liberty to change its opinions, although it will rarely acknowledge that it is doing so.[57]

It is interesting to note that in the very first case the Court decided concerning the European Economic Community Treaty, many of the above sources of law were invoked:

Les parties ont exposé de façon approfondie leurs conceptions divergentes en matière de droit applicable; elles invoquent le traité instituant la C.E.E., le statut du personnel et le règlement général de la C.E.C.A., les décisions de la Commission économique européenne et du Conseil de ministres, la jurisprudence de la Cour dans les affaires de personnel, le droit belge du travail en tant que *jus loci* et les principes généraux de droit en vigueur dans les États membres.[58]

It is an altogether idle pursuit to attempt to characterize the three Communities as a federation [59] or as supra-national [60] organizations; to ascertain their true nature one must examine the exact powers given and reserved in each case, and the use of emotive words will not help to solve the problem. It is pertinent, however, to ask to what extent the Court of the Communities is an international court of justice. The origins, powers, and objectives of the three Communities are all to be found in international treaties. It is the function of the Court to interpret these international treaties. The Communities themselves are international organizations, possessing international personality,[61] and are subjects of international law. States may be parties before the Court and the Court has jurisdiction in ' any dispute among member States concerning the application of this Treaty . . .' [62] De Visscher, recognizing these international aspects of the Court, refers to it as applying a ' droit international spécial ',[63] somewhere in between traditional international law and municipal law.

However, although the Communities were brought into being in the form of an international treaty, one should not allow the circumstances of their birth to obscure their real nature as organs of economic legislation, nor the function of the Court as an administrative tribunal. The Court of the European Communities more closely resembles the French Conseil d'État [64] and the four grounds of appeal are the same as the grounds which may be alleged in the Conseil d'État against a French administrative action. It will be recalled that the principal parties appearing before the Court are the High Authority, the Councils and Commissions, associations and enterprises, and individuals. The competence of the Court includes civil, constitutional, and disciplinary as well as administrative matters. Reference has also been made to its limited competence to assess and evaluate economic facts and circumstances, and the extent to which it draws upon the municipal laws of the member states for its sources of law. One is not surprised, therefore, to read in the jurisprudence of the Court that ' notre Cour n'est pas une juridiction internationale, mais la juridiction d'une Communauté créée par six États. . . .' [65] Nor does the operation of the Court much resemble that of the International Court of Justice:

Peut-être suffit-il de rappeler encore une fois la situation de notre Cour: elle ne connaît ni juges ad hoc, ni nationalités, ni opinions dissidentes, mais seulement des juges de notre Communauté européenne dont les arrêts sont immédiatement exécutoires sans procédure d'exequatur portant sur le fond, et elle impose ainsi le respect du droit de la Communauté.[66]

In its work the Court is assisted by two court advocates. Their function is patterned after the French Commissaire du Governement at the Conseil d'État. Court advocates are neither judges nor public prosecutors; nor do they participate in the deliberations of the Court or vote. Their principal function is to prepare an opinion for the Court on the legal aspects of any questions submitted to it. Such opinion is not part of the judgment itself; nor is it bound to be accepted by the

Court.[67] However, there is no doubt that such opinion strongly influences the Court and the development of the law of the Community and we shall frequently have occasion to refer to it.

DOCTRINE OF THE COURT OF JUSTICE OF THE EUROPEAN COMMUNITIES AND INTERPRETATION (A)

In the judgments of the Court one rarely finds any theoretical discussion concerning the principles of interpretation to be applied. No doubt the Court wishes to avoid taking any doctrinal position which might severely limit its freedom of action in the future. However, in contrast to the austerity of the Court's judgments, one may find an elaborate and fertile source of speculation in the conclusions of the Advocate-General.

In accordance with the usual canons of interpretation, the Court will not attempt to interpret a text which is quite clear: 'Mais, toute la question est précisément de savoir si le texte est clair et n'a pas besoin d'interprétation '.[68] And again:

Mais, Messieurs, il nous paraît inutile d'engager une discussion doctrinale sur ce point, car, qu'il s'agisse de. . . . Traités internationaux ou de lois internes, il est un principe communément admis et auquel nous nous sommes déjà référés, c'est qu'il n'y a lieu à interprétation et à recherche de l'intention présumée des auteurs du texte qu'en cas d'obscurité ou d'ambiguité et que la lettre lorsqu'elle est formelle doit toujours prévaloir.[69]

Apart from the classical remark, ' En effet, d'une part la volonté commune (la commune intention des parties) qui doit être le fondement de l'interprétation . . .',[70] one finds few references to the ' intentions of the parties'. This fact is not to be altogether regretted, for as mentioned in the introduction to this article, the Court and the parties may adopt one of several possible interpretations, whichever one serves them best, and may then maintain that such interpretation ' conforme à la volonté de ses rédacteurs '[71] or that ' l'intention des auteurs paraît donc incontestable ',[72] whilst maintaining at the same time that the interpretation of the other party ' contreviendrait manifestement aux intentions des auteurs de ces textes '.[73] It is for this reason that the occasional references in the jurisprudence of the Court to ' the intentions of the parties ' are meaningless.[74] One case in particular expressly refers to the great difficulties attached to an attempt to ascertain the intentions of the authors of a multilateral treaty.[75]

There is a good deal of interesting discussion to decide whether the fact that the Court is interpreting an international treaty means that it should adopt a restrictive interpretation:

Enfin, la méthode d'interprétation stricte ainsi défendue serait celle qui doit toujours prévaloir lorsqu'il s'agit de traités internationaux suivant les usages des juridictions internationales, telles que la cour de La Haye.[76]

Another argument (well known to international lawyers) pleaded before the Court in favour of a restrictive interpretation, concerned ' derogations from State sovereignty ' and the principle that restrictions on such sovereignty cannot be lightly presumed [77] unless they are formally embodied in the text.

Le Traité repose sur une délégation de souveraineté consentie par les États membres à des institutions supranationales pour un objet strictement déterminé. . . . Le principe juridique qui est à la base du Traité est, un principe de compétence limitée. La Communauté est une personne morale de droit public, et à ce titre elle ' jouit de la capacité juridique nécessaire pour exercer ses fonctions et atteindre ses buts ' (Art. 6), mais de celle-là seulement.[78]

Thus, the exact powers and limitations of the various organs of the Community are carefully prescribed.[79]

However, one may find an equal number of statements in favour of a flexible, effective and dynamic approach to interpretation by the Court. One of these,[80] whilst acknowledging that as a matter of form the Community is based on an international treaty, goes on to maintain that in fact its sources of law are taken from municipal law and therefore the rules of municipal law concerning interpretation ought to apply. Such rules will be less restrictive.

In another case [81] we find the Advocate-General arguing strongly in favour of a teleological approach to interpretation. One of the parties had invoked international law as the appropriate law to interpret the Treaty; to fortify this invocation, the party referred [82] to those cases where individuals had been considered subjects of international law, and secondly to those aspects of the Treaty, particularly the requirement of unanimity of the Council of Ministers, which seemed to reflect international law. The Advocate-General rejected both examples as embodying the exception rather than the rule. Instead, he strongly urged the Court to look to municipal law for its principles of interpretation, and secondly to avoid any rigid or literal interpretation of the Treaty which would result in frustrating its whole object:

. . . il fait appel au droit des différents États membres dont il faut tenir compte dans une mesure décisive pour l'interprétation de notre droit communautaire. . . . Dans le problème que vous avez à trancher ici, il s'agit sans aucun doute d'appliquer le droit économique qui est à la base du Traité . . . Le Traité est allé particulièrement loin dans le domaine de la codification juridique des faits économiques . . . Il en résulte que, dans l'application et dans l'interprétation du Traité, il serait dangereux de ne s'en tenir qu'à la lettre de son texte. Pour découvrir les objectifs économiques assignés à telle ou telle disposition particulière, il faut se reporter aux objectifs et aux principes fondamentaux du Traité. Tout récemment dans ses premiers arrêts, la Cour a relevé tout spéciale- ment la portée de ces objectifs généraux et mon éminent collègue Lagrange a insisté dans ses conclusions sur le fait que dans l'exercise de ses pouvoirs, la Haute Autorité ne doit perdre de vue aucun des objectifs du Traité et que, pour atteindre le but visé par une disposition particulière, elle doit éviter de sacrifier un objectif général plus important; il a fait observer que les mêmes principes doivent guider la cour dans l'interprétation du Traité.[83]

Finally, one may recall what has already been said concerning the need for a dynamic interpretation of a charter and the constitutive instrument of an international organization. It is submitted that the following statement is an excellent illustration of what must be the guiding principle of interpretation for any constitutive treaty:

Mais d'abord il n'est pas certain que le Traité doive être interprété restrictivement. Ce principe, déjà discutable lorsqu'il s'agit d'un véritable Traité international, l'est plus encore lorsqu'il s'agit comme en l'espèce, de la charte créant un organisme supranational. Dans ce cas, les sacrifices de souveraineté consentis par les États signataires ne correspondent pas au strict équilibre synallagmatique du ' do ut des ' habituel : c'est une mise en commun, une construction nouvelle, dont la vocation, comme celle de toute institution vivante, est de s'épanouir, de croître à partir du germe initial. Le Traité est, en somme, la constitution de l'organisation fédérale embryonnaire qu'il crée. Une constitution ne s'interprète point strictement.[84]

In now examining the practice of the Court, we may perceive just how far it has interpreted the constitutions in question restrictively.

PRACTICE OF THE COURT OF JUSTICE OF THE EUROPEAN COMMUNITIES AND INTERPRETATION (B)

(a) Travaux préparatoires

Although in theory the use of *travaux préparatoires* has been fre- quently condemned by the International Court of Justice and its predecessor, in practice it has been equally frequently invoked.[85] The problem is largely related to the question whether the ultimate object of interpretation is to discover the intention of the parties or the meaning of the words which they used. Both Judge Alvarez and Judge Azevedo [86] consider the expression ' the intention of the parties ' to be a mere figure of speech to which little attention should be paid, and they regard it as a fruitless task to look for such intentions in the negotiations leading to the Treaty: '. . . the said conventions must not be interpreted with reference to the preparatory work which preceded them; they are distinct from that work and have acquired a life of their own '.[87] However, even those who subscribe to the view that the object of interpretation is to discover the intentions of the parties will sometimes deprecate the use of *travaux préparatoires* as unreliable, confused, confusing, inconclusive, and merely reflecting the views of the more articulate. Such arguments are all the more cogent in the case of a multilateral treaty establishing an international organization purporting to continue for an unlimited period.[88]

Turning to the practice of the Court of the European Communities, we find, at least concerning the Coal and Steel Community: ' En ce qui concerne le Traité du 18 avril 1951, les travaux préparatoires du Traité lui-même sont pratiquement inexistants . . . ou secrets (ce qui revient au même).[89] In one or two cases the Court readily admits the validity of access to *travaux préparatoires*,[90] even though such preparatory work must be used with prudence [91] and must not be allowed to contradict the text if it is clear.[92]

The ghost of the intent of the parties still continues to exist in a modified form by resort to the governmental reports which accompanied and explained the text of the Treaty when it was submitted to the various parliaments for ratification. These reports, especially the French one,[93] are frequently cited and taken note of: ' A notre avis, la Cour devra tenir compte des exposés des motifs des lois de ratification soumises aux Parlements des autres pays.' [94] And again:

'. . . nous pourrions invoquer un passage de l'exposé des motifs de la loi luxembourgeoise de ratification qui est ainsi conçu . . . L'intention des auteurs paraît donc incontestable.' [95] Thus *travaux préparatoires*, in the guise of the ratification debates, do play a limited role in the interpretative work of the Court.

(b) Community law

Many of the legal concepts embodied in the treaties, such as *faute de service, recours en annulation*, and *détournement de pouvoir*, are borrowed from municipal law. It is natural therefore that the Court should turn to the jurisprudence of the member states [96] when interpreting such concepts. It will be convenient to call this process of interpretation ' Community law '.

In its broadest sense the term ' Community law ' will connote the law contained in the treaties themselves, the regulations of the High Authority, Councils and Commissions, and all the previous decisions and jurisprudence of the Court. These precedents are not binding. However, one frequently finds such statements as ' selon la jurisprudence constante de la Cour ';[97] or ' La possibilité d'attaquer par voie de recours cet avis non formel de la Haute Autorité est reconnue par la jurisprudence de la cour (affaires 8–55 et 9–55) . . .';[98] or 'A plusieurs reprises déjà, la Cour a eu à se prononcer sur l'interprétation de la notion de détournement de pouvoir. Elle a adopté une formule de ce genre. . . .'[99] It is to the whole of this repertoire of legal principles that the Court refers when it invokes ' le droit des Communautés européennes . . .'[100] to interpret some ambiguous provision.

One may, however, use the term ' Community law ' to characterize the process by which the Court conducts an analysis and synthesis of the municipal law of the member states. The result of this analysis and synthesis is a ' common law ' or ' Community law ' which the Court then applies to interpret an ambivalent provision. Given its broad meaning, therefore, ' Community law ' includes the whole law of the Community: in its narrower meaning it refers to the process of synthesis by which those principles of law common to the member states become part of the law of the Community. In both its meanings it may be used to interpret the treaties. However, it is with the narrower meaning that we are principally concerned here.

This narrower concept, which really means the general principles of law common to the member states of the European Communities, should be distinguished from the general principles of law recognized by civilized states mentioned in Article 38 of the Statute of the International Court of Justice. The former is confined to Europe; the latter includes legal systems outside Europe. Occasionally one finds the Court referring to ' principes généraux du droit, applicable même sans texte ',[101] or saying ' il faut inclure les principes généraux du droit dans les règles relatives à l'application du traité '[102] without making it clear to which general principles it is referring. Usually, however, the Court will explicitly state that it is referring to the general principles of the European Communities: ' Il s'agit là des principes juridiques élémentaires communs à tous les États de la Communauté, et qui doivent donc être également accueillis dans le droit communautaire '.[103] It is also interesting in this respect to note the provision of Article 215 of the European Economic Community Treaty, that concerning non-contractual responsibility, the Community must, ' in conformity with the general principles common to the laws of Member States ', make good any damage caused by its institutions.

The Advocate-General in his conclusions often refers to decisions of municipal courts and textbook writers. Reuter [104] is particularly favoured. The decisions of the French Conseil d'État [105] are frequently invoked, and mention is also made of the decisions of Italian [106] and German courts.[107]

It should not be thought that the Court always refers to the law of all the member states. If it regards a particular concept as peculiar to one or two countries, then it will only examine the jurisprudence of those two countries.[108] Sometimes it will only refer to French law [109] and to no other. In only a few cases,[110] however, will the Court ever apply municipal law directly:

. . . il ne s'agit pas ici d'appliquer le droit italien ni le droit français ni celui de tout autre pays de la communauté, mais le droit du Traité, et c'est uniquement pour parvenir à l'élaboration de ce droit du Traité que l'étude des solutions juridiques nationales doit être entreprise, chaque fois qu'elle apparaît nécessaire à cette fin.[111]

Nor is it the function of the Court to decide if a particular regulation of the High Authority violates municipal law [112] or the fundamental law of the municipal constitution.[113] However, without applying them directly, the Court will sometimes have to take cognizance of the laws in operation in a particular country. If, for example, it is necessary to know whether or not a certain German company has been dissolved, the Court will ascertain those rules of German law governing the dissolution of companies.[114]

A few examples may now be given of the manner in which the Court extracts, refines, and applies those legal principles common to some of the European countries, as the Community law. The best example is that of *détournement de pouvoir*, concerning which, as the Advocate-General says,

. . . l'appel aux droits nationaux nous paraît s'imposer. La notion de détournement de pouvoir n'a évidemment pas été inventée par les auteurs du Traité et, pour essayer de se former une opinion sur ce que doit être le détournement de pouvoir dans l'application du Traité . . . il faut d'abord savoir ce qui en est dans le droit respectif de nos six pays.[115]

Twenty-six pages later the Advocate-General comes to the end of his brief incursion into domestic law! Other examples of this process of comparative law are to be found concerning ' le principe de l'égalité ',[116] ' l'exception d'illégalité ',[117] contracts of employment,[118] the revocability of certain administrative acts,[119] a comparison of the powers of verification under Article 47 of the European Coal and Steel Community Treaty,[120] and the posting rules concerning letters.[121]

The application, by analogy, of rules of municipal law to international law is by no means a new phenomenon.[122] However, it has now achieved a new intensity and dimension in the jurisprudence of the Court of the European Communities.

(c) Teleological interpretation

According to the teleological principle, a treaty must be interpreted by reference to its objects, principles, and purposes: in this way, gaps can be filled and texts expanded or supplemented, so long as this is consistent with the objects and purposes in question.[123] Such a principle of interpretation is particularly well suited to the needs of an international organization. In this respect it has frequently been invoked by the International Court of Justice [124] and that Court, in its recent Judgment interpreting the constitution of the Intergovernmental Maritime Consultative Organization, expressly stated that:

The interpretation the court gives to Article 28 (a) is consistent with the general purpose of the Convention. . . . The Court cannot subscribe to an interpretation of ' largest-ship-owning nations ' in Article 28 (a) which is out of harmony with the purposes of the Convention.[125]

Articles 1–8 of the European Economic Community Treaty and Articles 2–5 of the European Coal and Steel Community Treaty contain the general objectives and purpose of the Treaty. Theoretically, it would be possible for the Court to place great emphasis on these general objectives and to attempt to justify any extensive and dynamic interpretation of the Treaty by reference to them.

In practice the Court has certainly recognized their importance:

Les articles 2, 3 et 4 du Traité, mentionnés en tête du paragraphe 1 de l'article 60, constituent des dispositions fondamentales établissant le marché commun et les objectifs communs de la Communauté. Leur importance résulte clairement de l'article 95. En autorisant la Haute Autorité à définir les pratiques interdites, le Traité l'oblige à tenir compte de tous les buts prescrits par les articles 2, 3 et 4.[126]

The reference here to Article 95 serves to confirm the importance of the fundamental provisions, for Article 95, although it allows for an amendment of the rules proposed by the High Authority and the Council, stipulates that such amendments may only be made ' provided that they do not modify the provisions of Articles 2, 3 and 4 '. This special emphasis on the general provisions of the Treaty has led some writers to conclude that such provisions may well occupy a special juridical position in the Treaty. However, the better view would seem to be that all the articles in the Treaty possess an equal juridical value.[127]

In one of the early cases decided by the Court, there is a most forceful statement by the Advocate-General in a passage which has already been cited but bears repeating to the effect that, when interpreting the Treaty, the Court must pay particular attention to its general objectives:

Il en résulte que, dans l'application et dans l'interprétation du Traité, il serait dangereux de ne s'en tenir qu'à la lettre de son texte. Pour découvrir les objectifs économiques assignés à telle ou telle disposition particulière, il faut se reporter aux objectifs et aux principes fondamentaux du Traité. Tout récemment, dans ses premiers arrêts, la Cour a relevé tout spécialement la portée de ces objectifs généraux et mon éminent collègue Lagrange a insisté dans ses conclusions sur le fait que, dans l'exercice de ses pouvoirs, la Haute Autorité ne doit perdre de vue aucun des objectifs du Traité et que, pour atteindre le but visé par une disposition particulière, elle doit éviter de sacrifier un objectif général plus important; il a fait observer que les mêmes principes doivent guider la Cour dans l'interprétation du Traité.[128]

Several questions arise from a consideration of the general provisions of any of the three Treaties. May one refer to such provisions when they are not expressly mentioned in one of the specific provisions? What happens if there is a conflict between the specific provisions of the Treaty and the general provisions, or between the general provisions themselves? [129] The answer to these questions is that the Court has tended to interpret specific provisions in the light of the purpose of the whole Treaty and so avoid an approach which would be too literal and confined.

Lorsque la Haute Autorité est appelée à exercer un pouvoir tel que celui qui lui est conféré par l'article 60. paragraphe 2, de fixer les conditions de publicité des barèmes, elle ne doit perdre de vue aucun des objectifs du Traité et, pour atteindre celui ou ceux qui sont plus spécialement visés par la disposition à appliquer, éviter d'en sacrifier d'autres peut-être plus importants.[130]

An equally well-balanced and integrated approach is illustrated by the Court's statement that all the general objects and principles of the Treaty

... doivent être considérés dans leur ensemble et simultanément appliqués; .... ces objectifs étant des principes généraux, vers la réalisation et l'harmonisation desquels il faut tendre dans toute la mesure du possible.[131]

The Court recognized that facts and economic circumstances may sometimes necessitate the emphasis of one particular general article and consequent lack of attention to the others.[132] Such general articles may also be invoked, even if not expressly referred to in a specific provision.[133]

In the early cases decided by the Court, the general articles and purpose of the Coal and Steel Community Treaty were frequently mentioned.[134] In more recent years, however, less express reference is made to them,[135] and one may note at least one of the early judgments of the Court upholding a literal interpretation of a specific provision, even though this was manifestly in conflict with the clear guiding principle enunciated in Article 4.[136]

As the purpose of a treaty is usually closely interwoven from one provision to another, especially in the Community treaties,[137] a teleological interpretation of such provisions is both necessary and desirable.

(d) Implied powers

Apart from the express powers conferred on it by its constitutive instrument, it is inevitable that any international organization will require a certain measure of implied powers in order to discharge its functions effectively. Such has been the experience of the International Labour Organization,[138] the International Monetary Fund,[139] the United Nations, and the European Coal and Steel Community. One may refer in this connection to the well-known statement by the Court in the *Reparation for Injuries* case: '. . . under international law, the Organization must be deemed to have those powers which, though not expressly provided in the Charter are conferred upon it by necessary implication as being essential to the performance of its duties ' [140] The same view was again expressed by the Court concerning the power of the United Nations to establish a tribunal to decide disputes between the Organization and its staff. As the establishment of such tribunal '. . . was essential to ensure the efficient working of the Secretariat and to give effect to the paramount consideration of securing the highest standards of efficiency, competence and integrity. Capacity to do this [i.e., to set up the tribunal] arises by necessary intendment out of the Charter.' [141]

Such a rigorous application by the Court of the principle of effectiveness must almost bring the above statements within the category of judicial legislation. In this respect it is pertinent to note the more cautious remark of Judge Hackworth in his Dissenting Opinion that, ' Powers not expressed cannot freely be implied. Implied powers flow from a grant of expressed powers and are limited to those that are necessary to the exercise of powers expressly granted.' [142]

As the Court of the European Communities has also had occasion to give a decision on this point, its jurisprudence on this matter will be of some interest.

The case concerned a dispute between the *Fédération charbonnière de Belgique* against the High Authority involving the interpretation of section 26 of the Convention containing the transitional provisions. These provisions were designed to regulate the gradual integration of the coal and steel of the six countries, and section 26, in particular, to assist the Belgian coal industry, since its costs of production compared unfavourably with those of the other countries. A detailed system of compensation was therefore adopted to facilitate the integration of Belgian coal, to harmonize prices in the Common Market generally, and to reduce Belgian prices to a level near that of the estimated costs of production at the end of the transition period. However, as section 26 gave no precise indication as to who was to be responsible for operating the ' rapprochement des prix ', a dispute arose.

The Belgian Coal Federation alleged that the Treaty had envisaged a kind of market in which the enterprises would be free to fix the prices '. . . sauf dérogation expresse, ce sont donc, en l'espèce, les entreprises elles-mêmes qui fixent les prix . . .'; [143] and that any intervention by the High Authority in this matter must be limited '. . . à des cas expressément prévus au Traité, notamment à l'article 61 de celui-ci '.[144] However, the Court found itself unable to accept this submission and stated that such an interpretation would defeat the whole object of the convention.[145] On the same ground it rejected the argument that the High Authority must be confined to the powers already granted to it to fix prices under Article 61 of the Treaty.[146] The Federation, tenacious as ever, then argued that the High Authority could still achieve the purpose of the Transitional Convention by indirect means. It could do this by taking sanctions against the enterprises which had failed to observe the obligation to lower their prices in accordance with the Convention. However, this argument also found no favour with the Court.[147]

One may notice the determination of the Court to reject any interpretation which would not fulfil the object of the Convention. This is confirmed by the interpretation which the Court finally accepted: ' Dans ces conditions, il faut constater que seule l'intervention directe de la Haute Autorité est de nature à garantir la réalisation immédiate de l'abaissement des prix qui doit obligatoirement accompagner la péréquation '.[148] It follows from this, that if the object of the Convention is to be implemented and this can only be achieved by the direct intervention of the High Authority, yet there is no express power permitting this direct intervention, then it must of necessity be implied.[149] The Court then invokes the principles of municipal law and international law to justify such an interpretation:

De l'avis de la Cour, il est permis, sans se livrer à une interprétation extensive, d'appliquer une règle d'interprétation généralement admise tant en droit international qu'en droit national et selon laquelle les normes établies par un traité international ou par une loi impliquent les normes sans lesquelles les premières n'auraient pas de sens ou ne permettaient pas une application raisonnable et utile. En outre, la Haute Autorité est chargée aux termes de l'article 8 du Traité d'assurer la réalisation des objectifs fixés par le Traité dans les conditions prévues par celui-ci. Il faut conclure de cette disposition, principe directeur des attributions de la Haute Autorité définies au Chapitre I du Traité, qu'elle jouit d'une certaine autonomie en vue de déterminer les mesures d'exécution qu'appelle la réalisation des objectifs visés au Traité ou à la Convention qui en fait partie intégrante. Comme il s'agit en l'espèce de réaliser l'objectif du paragraphe 26 de la Convention, la Haute Autorité a le pouvoir, sinon l'obligation, de prendre . . . dans les limites tracées par cette disposition

. . . les mesures susceptibles d'assurer l'abaissement des prix du charbon belge.[150]

It will be noticed that the Court here is formulating a limited [151] and severely circumscribed doctrine of implied powers. There is no attempt to impute a new power to the Organization. Powers will only be implied to implement a power already expressed in the Treaty and then only to achieve the limited purpose of that express power and to permit it a reasonable and useful application. In two recent cases the Court has again referred to the above views [152] and it is submitted that the attitude of the Court is to be welcomed. Subject to and within the above limitations, the doctrine of implied power will always be necessary for the effective functioning of any international organization.

(e) Effective and restrictive interpretation

The principle of effective interpretation or *ut magis valeat quam pereat*, has been a consistent feature of the jurisprudence of the International Court of Justice, especially when construing the constituent instrument of an international organization.[153] The principle involves, when a provision is doubtful, giving it an extensive interpretation and one that will be most conducive to the proper functioning of the organization. In other words there is no presumption that the constituent instrument of an international organization involves a derogation from State sovereignty and so must be restrictively [154] interpreted; rather one presumes that States intended to impart some measure of meaning to the text and that it is the function of the Court to give full effect to this meaning without doing violence to the words used. Sometimes, of course, a restrictive interpretation will be the most effective in that it will be the most efficacious for the organization.

A brief survey will now be made of the approach to this question adopted by the Court of the European Communities, with the preliminary caution that it will inevitably be selective and will only serve as a tentative and limited indication of the Court's attitude.

One thread of continuity is to be found in the manner in which the Court has given extensive interpretation to those provisions concerning the protection of enterprises. In one case an attempt was made to distinguish between coal and steel enterprises in the sense that only coal enterprises affected by an act of the High Authority dealing with some aspect of the coal industry could appeal to the Court. Thus a steel enterprise, even though affected by such an act, would have no right of appeal. However, the Court refused to restrict the appeal of enterprises to the nature of the subject involved in the dispute: [155]

. . . considérant, conformément aux conclusions de l'avocat général, qu'aucune disposition du Traité n'exige que la spécilisation des producteurs soit liée à la spécialité du litige; que le silence du Traité, sur ce point, ne saurait être interprété au détriment des entreprises et associations.[156]

In another case [157] the Court had to determine whether an enterprise engaged in making iron castings was an enterprise within the terms of the Treaty. Although it was agreed that iron castings fell outside the definition of 'steel' contained in the annex to the Treaty, yet the annex did mention 'raw pig-iron' and the plaintiff used liquid pig-iron in the manufacture of the iron castings. The Court had to decide, therefore, whether the plaintiffs' liquid pig-iron fell within the term 'raw pig-iron' and whether the plaintiffs, in making liquid pig-iron as the initial step in the production of iron castings, could be held to be 'engaged in an activity of production' of pig-iron within the meaning of the Treaty. The Court answered both questions in the affirmative.

In an equally extensive approach, the Court has interpreted the meaning of a decision of the High Authority. It considered that a letter of the High Authority addressed to the Belgian government and officially published [158] was an individual act subject to appeal. A welcome lack of formalism on the part of the Court was again apparent in the statement that, ' cette thèse doit être rejetée, en effet une décision individuelle camouflée reste une décision individuelle, le caractère d'une décision ne dépendant pas de sa forme mais de sa portée.' [159] Concerning decisions of the High Authority, one may also note that the Court willingly extended the right granted to enterprises to appeal against decisions of the High Authority, to enable enterprises to appeal against decisions of one of the administrative bodies established by the High Authority to run a subsidy fund.[160]

Finally, a good illustration of the effective approach of the Court and its readiness to provide legal rights of appeal against executive action is its judgment allowing enterprises to appeal against a general decision under which an individual decision has been passed. Such an appeal, even against the general decision, may be brought on all the four grounds set out in Article 33, paragraph 1; and this in spite of the fact that the article only expressly grants a right to enterprises to challenge general decisions on the ground of their being vitiated by a *détournement de pouvoir* having effects with regard to them.[161]

One may now turn to a consideration of those cases where the Court has adopted a more restrictive approach. The powers embodied in the Treaty are already extensive and it is understandable that on occasions the Court is cautious not to extend these powers too far. Such judicial caution is not necessarily inimical to fulfilling the object of the Treaty; too expansive and vigorous an interpretation may sometimes do more harm than good. Nor is it the function of the Court to attempt to revise the Treaty.[162]

Such a restrictive approach was taken by the Court in one of the very first cases it decided.[163] The point involved an interpretation of Article 60, paragraph 2, which stated that ' price-lists and conditions of sale applied by enterprises within the common market shall be published to the extent and in the form prescribed by the High Authority. . . .' The Court held that such price-lists must indicate the exact prices and that the High Authority, under its power to determine the ' extent' and ' form' of the obligation, could not authorize the steel producers to deviate up to 2·5 per cent upward or downward from their published prices. The High Authority had only attempted to make some provision for the inevitable fluctuation of prices. However, the Court was adamant that the Treaty would allow for no such flexibility, no matter how desirable such flexibility might be: ' La Cour doit s'abstenir de se prononcer sur l'opportunité de ce régime; elle ne peut constater qu'il a été consacré par le Traité qui . . . à tort ou à raison . . . ne contient pas de texte permettant une certaine souplesse des barèmes en cas d'oscillations mineures ou passagères.'[164]

A rather interesting case concerned the attempt by the High Authority to delegate certain of its powers to the Caisse, an organization in Brussels which had been set up by the High Authority to run a system of subsidies.[165] It was held in the circumstances that such a delegation was not possible and constituted a violation of the Treaty. However, the Court did envisage that an express delegation of power might be possible provided that it did not upset the carefully balanced institutional structure of the Treaty and that the High Authority would still exercise effective control over the powers delegated.[166]

Two more decisions may be noted. The first [167] related to the power of the High Authority under Article 70, paragraph 3. This power—to require governments to publish or to bring to the knowledge of the High Authority transport rates, prices, and tariff provisions—was challenged before the Court by the government of the Netherlands. The Court, noting that the powers of the Community were greater than those recognized by traditional international law, adopted a restrictive interpretation.[168] After an analysis of Article 70 it concluded that the High Authority had no authority to prescribe the manner in which the obligation incumbent upon the Netherlands government to publish prices was to be carried out.

Finally, in a case concerning steel manufacturers in Luxembourg,[169] the Court took a rather restricted view of the general articles of the Coal and Steel Community Treaty and allowed them to be limited by one of the specific articles. The plaintiffs requested the Court to hold that a special duty placed on coal by the Luxembourg government constituted a violation of Articles 4 (*b*) and 4 (*c*) of the Treaty. However, after a discussion of Article 67 of the Treaty, the Court held that the clear terms of Article 4 of the Treaty abolishing tax-barriers, subsidies, and restrictive practices did not constitute the overriding principles of the Community, but rather that they were principles which were circumscribed by the provisions in later articles.

This brief survey of a few cases concerned with an effective or restrictive approach on the part of the Court illustrates that, although the Court may occasionally err on the side of timidity, on the whole its approach will be conducive to an effective functioning of the organization.

(f) *Other principles of interpretation*

(i) *Comparison of the three European Community Treaties.* In its more recent jurisprudence, the Court, after interpreting a provision, will sometimes add, ' que ce raisonnement est confirmé par les traités instituant la C.E.E. et la C.E.C.A.'.[170] A precedent for this particular principle of interpretation is to be found in the Advisory Opinion of the Permanent Court of International Justice concerning the employment of women during the night.[171]

This principle of interpretation will normally be used only to sustain a conclusion already reached by other means. It is most frequently invoked by the parties themselves,[172] and the Advocate-General in his conclusions emphasizes its limited value.[173] Although this approach to interpreting the Community treaties may become more frequent in the future, it will never be decisive.

(ii) *A contrario.* It is sometimes argued that the express reference to a principle in one provision will exclude the application of such a principle whenever it is not expressly mentioned.[174] However, the Court has clearly stated that such an approach to interpretation is only to be used as a last resort:

... l'on ne saurait trouver dans la mention expresse figurant à l'article 36 un argument excluant *a contrario* l'application de la règle énoncée dans les cas où elle n'a pas été expressément mentionnée, la Cour ayant décidé, dans son arrêt no. 8/55, qu'une argumentation *a contrario* n'est admissible que lorsqu'aucune autre interprétation ne s'avère adéquate et compatible avec le texte, le contexte et leur finalité.[175]

(iii) *Subsequent practice and interpretation.* It is a reasonable principle of interpretation to observe how a party in practice has interpreted and applied a particular provision. Such a principle is recognized by the International Court of Justice [176] and was applied by the Court of the European Communities in one of its earliest cases: ' C'est du reste dans ce sens que la Haute Autorité, aussi bien dans ses décisions antérieures que dans la décision 2–54, semble avoir toujours interprété le Traité. . . .' [177] Although this is the only example of its application, it would seem to be a more reliable guide towards ascertaining the meaning of a provision than many of the other principles.

(iv) *Interpretation by reference to the context.* Words must be given their ordinary [178] plain, reasonable meaning.[179] If, however, their meaning still remains unclear, the Court will place them in their context: ' On a dit, il est vrai, à juste titre, qu'une simple interprétation littérale ne peut rien apporter de décisif sur le critère de charge spéciale. Il faut donc placer cette interdiction dans le cadre d'ensemble de l'article 4 et se demander quel est son sens et quel est son but.' [180] If its meaning is still obscure then the Court will sometimes refer to other parts of the Treaty: ' La lecture du texte de l'article 70, alinéa 1, donne lieu à des doutes. Une comparaison avec d'autres passages du Traité et l'examen du système du Traité dans son ensemble . . . doivent contribuer à éclaircir cette question.' [181] Such a method of interpretation is unexceptional and calls for no comment.

CONCLUSION

Bearing in mind the jurisprudence of the Court of the European Communities and that of the International Court of Justice relating to the interpretation of the constitutive instrument of an international organization, some general conclusions may be tentatively advanced.

Lord McNair has urged that we should

free ourselves from the traditional notion that the instrument known as the treaty is governed by a single set of rules, however inadequate, and set ourselves to study the greatly differing legal character of the several kinds of treaties and to frame rules appropriate to the character of each kind.[182]

The charter of an international organization creates something organic and permanent and would seem to demand recognition as falling into a special category of treaty.[183] In a sense such treaties are analogous to documents embodying a written constitution such as that of the United States.[184]

' One must remember this is a constitution we are interpreting! ' This type of statement may be frequently found in judgments of the Supreme Court when interpreting the constitution. The reason ' one must remember ' is given by Chief Justice Marshall in *McCulloch* v. *Maryland*,[185] when he says that a constitution should never ' partake of the prolixity of a legal code ', and by Chief Justice Hughes's pronouncement in the famous *Mortgage Moratorium Case* in 1934:

It is no answer to say that this public need was not apprehended a century ago, or to insist that what the provision of the Constitution meant to the vision of that day it must mean to the vision of our time. If by the statement that what the Constitution meant at the time of its adoption it means to-day, it is intended to say that the great clauses of the Constitution must be confined to the interpretation, which the framers, with the conditions and outlook of their time would have placed upon them, the statement carries its own refutation.[186]

Similarly, the basic instrument of an international organization calls 'into life a being the development of which could not have been foreseen completely by the most gifted of its begetters'.[187] Flexibility and adaptability will be its essential desiderata to enable it to respond to a future full of uncertainty and change. Such a treaty is not to be construed as a contract [188] or statute in municipal law and incantations concerning state sovereignty and restrictive interpretation [189] will be totally unrealistic. Equally unreal will be any reference to the intentions of the parties. Such intentions, always difficult to discover, become even more elusive in the case of a multilateral treaty establishing a permanent state of affairs.[190] Indeed, in the case of the United Nations Charter, less than half the present members even participated in drafting the constitutive instrument. It is useful to note in this respect that with the advent of the multipartite instrument, less attention is being paid to the contractual aspects [191] and more attention given to the legislative element involved.

The teleological [192] and effective principles of interpretation suggest themselves as being best suited to the needs of an international organization.[193] In this respect one may note a variation or extension of the teleological principle called the 'emergent purpose' principle.[194] This is an extreme and dynamic form of the teleological approach according to which the object or purpose of the treaty is itself not a fixed or static one, but is liable to change or develop as experience is gained in the operation and working of the convention. The intentions of the framers of a constitutive treaty are exhausted once they have given it birth; it then acquires a new dimension of its own.

This special case of constitutive treaties and their need for a dynamic and flexible interpretation raises the whole question of the nature and limits of the judicial function. The judges are not legislators, even though their activity may well involve a quasi-legislative element; nor is it their function to rewrite or revise a basic treaty. They will be limited to the text and should not seek to impart to it a meaning completely incompatible with the words used. Such an approach would only serve to empty the text of all reasonably ascertainable meaning and to alienate the good will of the member states.

However, the choice facing the Court will rarely be one of full effectiveness or utter frustration; it will usually be a question of a higher or lower degree of effectiveness. It is submitted that, when interpreting a constitutive treaty, a court should adopt as a guiding principle that the bias should be in favour of higher effectiveness.

THE UNITED NATIONS AS A FORM OF GOVERNMENT *

IAN BROWNLIE †

I remember John principally as a very amiable colleague, whether dispensing hospitality in his rooms at Hertford (my own college) or approaching the chores of academic life, such as examining. Though he took his law seriously, he enjoyed it and carried his learning lightly. One of his main concerns was the law of organizations, and his attitude to these and to the United Nations in particular was one of constructive scepticism. My belief is that both the theme and treatment of this essay are not out of accord with John's view of the United Nations.

I. INTRODUCTION

In law school we are told that the society of states has law but no government. The organs of the United Nations do not constitute an executive or legislature of the world and were not intended to function as such. The International Court is not in the same position as the supreme court in a national constitutional structure. Moreover the doctrinaires of jurisprudence adopt the national legal system in a somewhat idealized form as the paradigm case of law and then on the basis of a modification of their theories, by concession as it were, recognize that international law has some title to recognition as law.[1] Logically, there are objections to making national law the measure of the validity of international law within a theoretical system. However, for present purposes, the intention is to examine the United Nations on the assumption that it is a form of government. If the realities of national systems and constitutional structures are referred to (and not some theoretical Austinian model of efficient statism and docile subjects), it is both practical and also fruitful in terms of understanding, to regard the United Nations as substantially a form of government.

In spite of the lessons we learned in law school, the problems of the United Nations system have much in common with the problems

* © *Harvard International Law Journal* 1972. With minor modifications, from that *Journal*, vol. 13, no. 3 (1972).
† Fellow and Tutor, Wadham College, Oxford.

of government in national systems. As a matter of description it is much *less* accurate to say that the United Nations is *not* a form of government than to say that it is. Before I try to explain what I have in mind when I prefer the latter assertion as a general proposition, it is necessary to notice an obstacle which lies even in the way of the more intellectual members of a society in regarding the United Nations system objectively. It is particularly the populations of states with relatively high standards of government and education that are best conditioned to the acceptance of the state (and the political system) in general, and 'the law' in particular, as important, sufficient, effective, reliable, just, and, in some cases, an object to be venerated. The inculcation of internationalism is sporadic and the faults of national systems are inadequately reported and overlaid by historical alibis and myth making. Thus even the more able student will readily refer to the relative invulnerability of the Smith regime in Rhodesia after UDI in terms of the 'ineffectiveness of the United Nations' and will find it difficult to accept that the situation could also be said to be a test of the efficacy of the legal system of the United Kingdom.[2]

If the mind can be cleared of conventional frameworks and a great deal of conditioning about the role of the state, it can be seen that the United Nations and national governments have much in common. Many governments have a legitimacy, a political standing with the people as a whole, which is in various degrees superficial or provisional. Many governments work on a very small budget in relation to the tasks which, formally speaking, are on the agenda. Governments are frequently weak financially and politically in face of special interests, foreign corporations, and powerful minorities with a dominant position in the system. It is not uncommon for governments, out of wisdom, to approach major conflicts of interest and social crises by something more positive than mere police action. 'Effective' action may lead to civil war, genocidal viciousness, secession, or a combination of these. Inaction may sometimes be simply a product of weakness. On some occasions the reality of national government is seen to be a consensus, sometimes fragile and unstable or intermittent, and not always reflected in the formal structure of the political system, that is, the constitution. In many systems, in contrast to the rather unusual position of the United States,[3] judicial activity is peripheral to major issues and may be constitutionally indecisive if the system permits legislative or executive veto of judicial decisions. Most governments find the making of rules to be easier than effective promulgation and implementation. Even in advanced systems major legislative programmes and constitutional principles may stand as unfilled frameworks, which as time goes by embarrass the promisors and provoke the promisees.

Are not these statements of a type frequently made as if they applied uniquely to the United Nations and its organs? The object of the present exercise has been to establish a more relaxed and less sour perspective. In what follows further evidence will be advanced for the thesis that it is more realistic to accept that the United Nations is a form of government than not. The thesis can only be sustained in general terms and the United Nations system, like many political systems, has special features. As a paradox, certain aspects of the United Nations system create a situation in which some types of criticism have a certain plausibility which should not rank with justification. Thus matters, which in some systems would be within executive discretion, are the object of rules of competence and procedure. As within certain political systems, some but not all federal in character, a great deal is made subject to law and the general level of ' justiciability ' is raised. In such a system apparent shortcomings are less susceptible to interpretation as forms of executive discretion and sheer policy and are held up as infringements of the constitution. The whole political process becomes in constitutional terms a matter of precise canalizing. The result in some national systems has been the development of reliance on political structures outside the constitution and the production of great strains on the constitution itself as the substance of the political organism developed in shapes and volumes unrelated to the container provided by the constitution.[4] The United Nations has survived surprisingly well in this particular light. In all this it will not do to forget that the United Nations is not unconditionally an ill-funded and rather amiable monster dependent on consensus and unable to gaol tax evaders. If by a political accident the permanent members were a firm faction, the Security Council could launch a variety of violent actions to shape the world in the image shared by the coalition: the European directorate of the nineteenth century would be but a mild precedent for such a new order. Again, when the system of financial ' assessment for tax ' is looked at in the light of the *Expenses* Opinion,[5] it will be seen that, in the absence of a right to seek judicial review by individual members, the subjects of the system face a budgetary and appropriation system not unlike a federal taxing system.

II. THE PRINCIPLE OF UNIVERSALITY

A particular mark of the political system of a state is its independence and its exclusiveness within its own sphere. Individuality may be accommodated by a federal system, a quasi-federal union (the United Kingdom), an autonomous regime for certain areas, and so on: in such cases the diversity is allowed on terms set by the system as a whole. On the international plane the United Nations system has some similarities to the more thoroughgoing federal systems: items on the ' state list ' constitute the reserved domain of domestic jurisdiction and the right of self-defence. At any rate the United Nations is in principle a body with exclusiveness ' in its own sphere ' and that sphere by prescription and the practice of organs includes (a) the maintenance of international peace and security; and (b) the principle of self-determination and its implementation. For this purpose, universality is not simply a question of membership. Thus an excluded state, and a non-self-governing people aspiring to statehood, are still within the jurisdiction of the organs of the United Nations for certain purposes.

In a political sense a major limitation on universality in terms of membership of the United Nations was the absence of Communist China. Legally, the issue was that of the political non-recognition policy of the United States and its associates leading to a refusal to allow the Nationalist Chinese representation of China (as a state) to be displaced. The question was thus one of representation and not statehood. On 25 October 1971 the General Assembly adopted a resolution which recognized the representatives of the People's Republic of China ' as the only legitimate representatives of China to the United Nations '. Consequential action was taken by the Security Council, the International Labour Organization, GATT, and other institutions. Efforts by the United States to prevent what the press called the ' expulsion of Taiwan ' were almost bound to fail. No state was expelled, of course, since the *locus standi* of the authorities in Taiwan had depended on their role in representing China *as a state*. Indeed, the view adopted by the United Kingdom government has been that Taiwan is territory the title to which is undetermined. Reference to the special status of the Ukraine and Byelorussia is not particularly pertinent, since they were founder members and in any case the status they were accorded depended on the agreement of the Soviet Union.

The principal omissions of independent political entities from the United Nations are (i) the divided states; (ii) certain miniature states, like Western Samoa, which have opted not to apply for membership; (iii) Switzerland. The small non-members and Switzerland are accorded membership of specialized agencies and other bodies. The divided states raise problems which are substantially political. The political position of the Western group in the United Nations has made possible the granting of certain privileges to the German Federal Republic in specialized agencies. In the League period such agencies were less politicized. The issue of discriminatory treatment of

East Germany, North Korea, and North Vietnam in the form of exclusion from various institutions and from conferences sponsored by the General Assembly has arisen in connection with the prepara- tions for and convening of the United Nations Conference on the Human Environment.[6] It seems that the Communist group will boy- cott the conference unless East Germany is allowed to participate.

Apart from the divided states, the issue of membership amounts to the question as to which entities, if any, are too small to qualify (except on the grounds of their ability to contribute to peace and security). In spite of some interesting proposals for associate membership, the General Assembly has shown no real interest in adopting precise criteria of membership. Several existing members are ' small ' geo- graphically, demographically or economically.[7] Furthermore, the issue has become entwined with the question of implementing Resolution 1514 (XV), the Declaration on the Granting of Independence to Colonial Countries and Peoples. Aside from Southern Africa, the Colonial agenda is reduced to various smaller territories. By Resolution 2869 (XXVI) [8] the General Assembly affirmed the application of Resolution 1514 to American Samoa, Bermuda, the British Virgin Islands, Brunei, and various insular possessions such as the Seychelles and the Solomon Islands. Among other points in the resolution, the General Assembly reaffirmed ' its conviction that the questions of territorial size, geographical isolation and limited resources should in no way delay the implementation of the Declaration with respect to these Territories '.

A further development has been the concession of procedural *locus standi* to liberation movements. The background of principles may be discovered in Resolution 2625 (XXV),[9] the Declaration on Principles of International Law Concerning Friendly Relations and Co-operation Among States in Accordance with the Charter of the United Nations. By Resolution 2878 (XXVI) [10] the General Assembly endorsed the proposal of the Committee of 24 ' to take steps, in consultation with the Organization of African Unity, to enable rep- resentatives of national liberation movements in the colonial territories in southern Africa to participate . . . in its deliberations relating to these Territories '. In Resolution 2852 (XXVI) [11] there was a reaffirmation that ' persons participating in resistance movements and freedom fighters in southern Africa and in territories under colonial and alien domination and foreign occupation who are struggling for their liberation and self-determination should, in case of arrest, be treated as prisoners of war in accordance with the principles of the Hague Convention of 1907 and the Geneva Convention of 1949 '.

The theme of universality embraces two other matters. In the first place the General Assembly has adopted an amendment to the

Charter which, subject to ratification by the member states, will increase the membership of the Economic and Social Council from 27 to 54.[12] The cause of the change was a feeling on the part of many members that the Council, lacking broad representation, was unable to discharge its functions effectively. A number of states, including the Soviet Union, abstained. France and the United Kingdom voted against the proposal.

Finally, it is useful to notice the countervailing effects of certain fundamental principles of the law of the Charter and general international law.[13] There is pressure in the General Assembly to exclude Portugal and South Africa from participation in the Specialized Agencies.[14] Rhodesia, which would otherwise qualify for recognition as a state, cannot be recognized except in contravention of various General Assembly and Security Council resolutions which, apart from establishing sanctions, characterize the Smith regime as objectively illegal as a racialist minority government. These tendencies relate to the membership question: the universality of jurisdiction is not merely unaffected but positively expressed in the process of characterization, pressure, and sanction.

III. THE INHERENT LIMITATIONS IN THE UNITED NATIONS SYSTEM

The United Nations system has certain inherent features which, according to taste, may be regarded as inevitable, detrimental, or a source of desirable flexibility. The so-called veto was built into the system at the start. Its existence diverts attention from the fact that, even when in accord, the permanent members might conscientiously take the view that compromise or inaction was the better course in a given situation. This discretionary element is a characteristic of government and law enforcement everywhere.[15]

The performance of the political organs is to be judged, in part at least, with these points in mind. The Indian invasion of Goa in 1961 is a memorable example of exercise of the discretion not to prosecute. The failure of the Security Council to agree on a resolution relating to the Indian action in Bangladesh and the Indo-Pakistan hostilities in general has similar features. The possible explanations for this are all equally compatible both with the view that the United Nations is ineffective and lacks significance and with the view that it is a form of government. The choice of reasons for inaction are (a) a failure by the principal units in providing support for the executive to agree, a happening by no means unknown in national life; (b) a view on the part of some of the decision-makers that, in all the circumstances, exercise of the 'discretion not to prosecute' India for aggression was positively the best course: to interpose would support the insupportable, namely the policies and actions of Pakistan in East Bengal; (c) an appreciation by some members that the notion of major 'sanctions', of 'decisive action', in the particular context may be naive and even lunatic. In the event the United States, which tended to regard the Indian action simply as an invasion of Pakistan and to be treated as such, and had seen its resolutions vetoed by the Soviet Union, employed the procedure of the Uniting for Peace resolution to bring the matter before the Assembly. The outcome was a call for a cease-fire [16] on terms which left open the main issue: the fact of secession as a consequence of external intervention.[17] The fact is, of course, that certain types of problem (as in Cyprus, Ulster, or Bangladesh) cannot be seen merely as narrow issues of public order. In the event, even after withdrawal of Indian troops from Bangladesh there could be no possibility of a restoration of the status quo.

The twenty-sixth session witnessed a continuance of the tension in the Middle East. The divergence of approach, evidenced at the previous session,[18] between the Security Council and General Assembly remains apparent. At one level there is uniformity of approach. The forcible occupation of territory which may mature into annexation and outright annexation (of Jerusalem) is not an acceptable basis of title. This principle has been maintained both in General Assembly and Security Council resolutions relating to the Middle East. On 25 September 1971 the Security Council adopted a third resolution concerning Israeli measures purporting to affect the status of Jerusalem.[19] This principle of non-acquisition of territory by force is qualified in practice and probably also in principle (a) if there is general acquiescence in the change of status; and (b) if the result accords with the principle of self-determination. The level at which a divergence of approach has appeared between Council and Assembly is apparent from resolutions of the latter during the latest session.[20] The Assembly is more insistent on the rights of refugees, has asserted that Palestinian Arabs have the inalienable right of self-determination, and regards Israel as in default in the face of recent peace initiatives and Egyptian proposals. The United Nations posture is roughly this. At the level of principle and the standards of the Charter system, the rules have been applied: declarations have been issued and goals set. At the level of implementation, there is an absence of consensus beyond a desire to avoid taking steps which will make things worse and risk global conflict. In the writer's view, the problems of programme and policy are on a scale similar to those faced by national governments dealing with major aberrations in public order, particularly when in a coalition or otherwise consensus-based apparatus, one or more of the large groups involved in the confrontation have representation in the government or support from an influential section of the population. Thus the organs of the United Nations have not responded to Egyptian urging to institute sanctions against Israel. Lastly, the inherent limitations on the United Nations in the financial sphere must be chronicled. The last session of the General Assembly witnessed a decision by the United States to try to cut its annual contribution to the Organization, which amounts to 25 per cent of the budget, and also the rejection by the Senate of the foreign aid authorization bill. A significant proportion of the costs of the United Nations and its associated programmes—for example, the Development Programme —is borne by voluntary contributions. Such operations are clearly vulnerable to donor changes of mind and scaling up or down of payment on the basis of a political view of cost effectiveness.

In general terms the Organization has a chronic financial disability. Since the period 1955–60 the United States has had serious reservations about the United Nations as a political investment. The Soviet Union, the United Kingdom, and France have also had their own reasons for a cautious commitment to the Organization. A desire to reduce the commitment or a readiness to withhold assessed contributions has been in evidence. On 22 December 1971 the General Assembly decided to establish a Special Committee on the Financial Situation of the United Nations. The special problem of financing peacekeeping operations remains unsolved.[21] The hard truth is that the relation between funding and constitutional questions cannot be ignored. Majority decisions may be implemented by the General Assembly and, in the budgetary sphere, the system of appropriation and assessment apparently converts recommendations into legally binding financial burdens.[22] Since there is no proper means of review to check *ultra vires* action it could be that, perhaps unwittingly, the Organization was provided with a structure which was closer to the super-state concept than is generally believed, given the ambitious programme of action based upon the General Assembly.

IV. MAJOR CHARTER POLICIES

The calendar of business at the twenty-sixth session of the General Assembly, an agenda of 97 items, reveals the major Charter policies of the time. These appear to be: (a) the economic and social development of the poorer states; (b) the protection of human rights; (c) disarmament, with particular emphasis on non-proliferation of nuclear weapons and other restriction on use and deployment of weapons carrying a high risk for states in general if they are used; (d) the implementation of the principle of self-determination with particular reference to colonial situations; (e) support of modest peacekeeping operations, as in Cyprus, on a consensus basis; (f) maintenance of the principle of non-acquisition of territory by conquest.

These items overlap in practice. Moreover certain objectives may be incompatible or at least require careful matching. Thus developed states are keen on anti-pollution programmes, whilst under-developed states may not see these as a priority. Self-determination and balkanization may seem at odds with planned development on a regional basis. At any rate the General Assembly has set the priorities and the richer states are now being urged to fund programmes on conditions set by the General Assembly. In general the Assembly's concerns are those of the smaller states and not necessarily merely the under-developed states. Much comment in the press of the developed states on the ' ineffectiveness ' and ' paper resolutions ' of the Organization stems from a feeling that for the first time, in the economic and social sphere particularly, the United Nations is the institutionalized form of the world beyond the Foreign Offices and immediate influence of the Great Powers.

V. CONSTITUTIONAL STRUCTURE: CHANGES OF FORM AND CHANGES OF CONTENT

It is well known that changes in political facts may be reflected in constitutional amendments, the process of interpretation, and the generation of conventions of the constitution. The increase in the importance of the General Assembly has been evidenced in various ways. Quite often the restraint of Article 12 (1) has been disregarded.[23] The membership of organs has been expanded by Charter amendment. The majority of Afro-Asian states has provided the impetus for the creation of UNCTAD. The new emphasis on the economic and social aspects of the Charter has resulted in the creation of the Committee of 24 and the implication and, or, emergence of powers relating to non-self-governing peoples. In 1971 the constitutional practice of the Assembly, based principally upon Resolution 1514, and the tendency to assume the existence of powers not expressly prohibited, were legitimated by the Advisory Opinion of the International Court in the *Namibia* Case.[24] That Opinion tells us essentially that the Organization has a reservoir of necessary powers by no means confined to Chapter VII purposes and resulting in legal duties for states generally when matters of *jus cogens* are involved.

This situation is not without its difficulties,[25] and no amount of constitutional development can entirely avoid the problem of dealing with significant dissenters. This is particularly the case when the dissenter believes or asserts that he is justified in his position on constitutional grounds. The Security Council has now adopted a resolution [26] implementing the Advisory Opinion in the *Namibia* Case. None voted against the resolution, but the United Kingdom and France abstained. The representative of the United Kingdom explained the legal objections his government had to the Advisory Opinion.[27] The main point in his exposition was the extent and status of the powers of the General Assembly which, with certain exceptions, were recommendatory only. A similar stand had been taken by the Soviet Union in the *Expenses* Case in the context of peacekeeping.

VI. AREAS OF CONSENSUS AND EMPIRICAL ADVANCES

Even the most flexible and fragmented political systems may produce legislative reforms on practical matters of common concern. After a rather dramatic early period, the United Nations has been particularly successful in this respect. The work of the International Law Commission and, more recently, of UNCITRAL, provides good examples of this capacity. The United Nations has played a leading role in examining means of tackling racial discrimination.[28] Other subjects of recent concern are narcotics,[29] hijacking, and pollution in its various forms.

The empirical approach produced some interesting results in the field of disarmament during the twenty-sixth session. The General Assembly has commended the Convention on the Prohibition, etc., of Bacteriological (Biological) and Toxic Weapons and on Their Destruction.[30] The General Assembly Committee on the Peaceful Uses of Outer Space produced a Convention on International Liability for Damage Caused by Space Objects.[31] By Resolution 2816 (XXVI) [32] the General Assembly laid the basis for contingency planning for assistance in cases of natural disaster and other disaster situations. The resolution calls on the Secretary-General to appoint a co-ordinator with powers set out in the resolution. There is a need for regional food banks, related to local diets and customs. The scheme of the resolution would allow this, though no express provision is made.

VII. THE ROLE OF THE GREAT POWERS

The leading issue for the future is the role of the leading developed states and especially the Great Powers. Though weakened by the changes of 1965 the role of the Great Powers remains institutionalized in the Security Council and the attendant voting privilege. In political coalition they have a major constitutional role. At the same time individually they play, and are permitted to play, the role of the powerful dissenter. As in the federal situation, too great a pressure on dissidents may result not in conformity but either in civil war or secession. As in national life major events may take place off the parliamentary and, or, legal stage. Thus the Vietnam War, its ramifications for Laos and Cambodia, and the financial crisis of the developed states of 1971, leading to the United States import surcharges, have been events determined outside the United Nations system. Within the system the Great Powers are no longer certain of satisfaction in pursuit of their objectives. The success of the effort to seat a delegation from Peking is evidence that even the Power with greatest influence on votes can no longer obtain the support it needs for its own purposes.

It may be that the Great Powers still pursue a substantial number of objectives through the channels of multilateral and parliamentary diplomacy provided so well by the United Nations Organization. It is the case that on some occasions individual Powers fail to make the best use of the United Nations in this respect.[33] More significant is the situation in which individual Powers openly challenge United Nations decisions and standards. Two current examples relate to Rhodesia. The British government has used the veto [34] in the face of a Security Council proposal to oppose the settlement between the United Kingdom and Ian Smith. The United States government has shown a readiness, subject to the outcome of the negotiations between the United Kingdom and Mr Ian Smith, to accept the decision of Congress to break the mandatory sanctions by permitting the import of Rhodesian chrome. Individual Great Powers have challenged the view of the majority on other occasions, of course: and it is not the case that the majority is necessarily ' right ' on a particular issue. Nevertheless, two special features are present. First, these events involve reneging on actions and decisions in which the United Kingdom and the United States participated and which they have hitherto supported. Secondly, this and other issues centre on a matter which the vast majority of states regard as an ultimate test of credibility for claimants to status of law-abiding in the world at large, namely, the issue of racial discrimination, particularly in the form of apartheid or apprentice apartheid regimes.

THE DESIRABILITY OF THIRD-PARTY ADJUDICATION: CONVENTIONAL WISDOM OR CONTINUING TRUTH? *

ROSALYN HIGGINS †

John McMahon and I were contemporaries at Cambridge. From 1955 to 1958 we both read for our B.A. in Law; but we met for the first time in the autumn of 1958 in the smaller grouping of candidates reading international law for the LL.B.

That year at Cambridge was to forge lasting friendships. There were probably well over a dozen candidates for the LL.B., but a smaller group—including John McMahon, Andrew Jacovides, Philip Allott, and myself—met constantly. For all of us international law was by then our chosen subject: the thing we were best at, and the thing we most wanted to do. The Cambridge LL.B. course entailed—even in retrospect—an extraordinarily heavy workload. And this common pressure that we felt upon us, our intellectual interest in the subject matter, and indeed the amicable rivalry that existed between us made strong bonds of friendship. In addition, a fourth year at university can be an intense and formative period in any young person's life; and we were no exception.

In a curious sense John McMahon was always at the centre of that group; we were all attracted by his brand of high good humour, by his wit, by his love for art and classical music and eighteenth century literature. As a Catholic he could also be relied on to continue a stimulating theological discussion until the small hours of the morning. To be sure, he could on occasion be anxious or depressed, and he had the reputation of being some-what disorganized, but he had a tremendous joie de vivre. He cared for his friends; and he cared about international law.

After Cambridge he went to Harvard and I went to Yale. It was clear, upon meeting at Thanksgiving or at Christmas, that John was tremendously enjoying Harvard, and exhilarated by his association with, among others, Professor Louis Sohn and Professor Richard Baxter. He returned to a fellowship at Oxford; but our work

---

* © Rosalyn Higgins 1973. This essay is based on a lecture given to the International Law Association at University College, London, on 18 May 1970.

† Specialist on international law and United Nations affairs at Chatham House.

*continued to bring John, Andrew Jacovides, and me into contact
at the United Nations in New York. John mixed with an easy
ebullience among peoples of all races and religions. His circle of
friends, like his interests, was wide. His death was therefore a keen
personal loss to many of his contemporaries, for whom he was a
very special friend, as well as to the world of international law.
He had begun so well, and his work held so much promise.*

*John McMahon had a very real interest in the work of inter-
national tribunals—not only in the decisions they hand down but
in the way they operate and in the assumptions we make about
use of them. The ensuing essay looks at some of these matters.*

I

THERE is one point on which virtually all leading lawyers are agreed:
the desirability of third-party adjudication as a method of settling
international disputes. Some, it is true, are more pessimistic than
others about the possibility of increasing the use of the International
Court of Justice. Some point to real shortcomings in the operation
of the Court, and suggest improvements. Yet others point to psychological factors inhibiting parties to the Court's Statute. But all are
agreed, it would seem, that greater reliance on judicial or arbitral
settlement is a goal to which all international lawyers should direct
themselves.

The United Nations Charter lists, in effect, the traditional means
of pacifically settling disputes. Article 33 refers to ' negotiation,
enquiry, mediation, conciliation, arbitration, judicial settlement, resort
to regional agencies or arrangements, or other peaceful means of their
[the parties'] own choice '. Most international lawyers would, I
believe, acknowledge the primacy of negotiations, but would urge
that there are contexts and occasions (such as dispute settlement
clauses in multilateral instruments) where this is not an appropriate
method; and they would further contend that, of the other methods,
there is much to be said for judicial settlement.

The arguments in favour of judicial settlement are closely related to
the customary search of international lawyers for impartial standards.
The argument for judicial settlement is essentially the same as that
advanced for international law itself: namely that notions of order
in the affairs of nations require an acknowledged code *inter se*; that
claims by disputants about this code necessarily run the risk of being
partisan, and that one must have a court for an authoritative pronouncement; and that the smaller nations can only be protected from
the power of the greater if both are obliged to heed a common code
of conduct, overseen by an impartial judiciary. Thus the requirements

of both order and justice militate in favour of an international law system of which judicial settlement is an integral part.

In the *Report of a Study Group on the Peaceful Settlement of International Disputes* (under the chairmanship of Sir Humphrey Waldock), prepared by the David Davies Memorial Institute, Philip Allott has contributed a thoughtful and detailed paper which is a classical statement on the desirability of judicial settlement. He advances two reasons why negotiation is not the most satisfactory way of settling disputes. In the first place, he says, ' like the use of force, negotiation remains a means of asserting interests. Secondly, it necessarily carries the implication that what is within the discretion of States to agree is within the discretion of States to repudiate.'

I must at once admit that I find neither of these reasons very convincing. With regard to the second, I would need some empirical evidence that states regard themselves as more free to repudiate agreements freely arrived at *inter se* than outcomes indicated by an international body. And as for the first point, I do not see why the ' assertion of interests' should be regarded as undesirable in the context of conflict-resolution. Legal claims, too, are advanced as a particularized method of asserting national interests. I do see, however, that in bilateral negotiation (though by no means necessarily in multilateral negotiation) the weaker party may be at a disadvantage in respect of the stronger one. The corollary is also true: that a state whose political and legal culture represents a minority view in the world community is protected, by the device of negotiation, against a majority consensus. Third-party forms (including judicial settlement) may represent this majority consensus. It is a commonplace that the Soviet Union prefers negotiation to adjudication for this reason.

But there are, of course, more positive reasons for adjudication which commend themselves to lawyers. Speaking of the advantage of law generally, and of the need for impartiality (and these twin themes, as I have already said, run through much that is said in support of judicial settlement), Mr Allott notes that:

Arbitration brings together the concepts of third-party settlement and the application of rules of law. Courts of law take the matter a step further and formalise these concepts into a complete system.[1]

Courts, he suggests, symbolize the rule of law. And, moreover, a permanently established court removes the difficulty of convening, organizing, and agreeing upon the composition of a court. A further justification of a permanent court is that:

the existence of a court declaring the law in a series of cases means that the law itself not only tends to become more objective and autonomous but may be developed by the Court in its jurisprudence. As the habit of judicial settlement and the scope of the Court's jurisprudence grows, the foundations of law itself become more solid.[2]

Others, equally concerned to promote judicial settlement of disputes, have taken the opposite point of view. C. W. Jenks, for example, refers to those who tend

to regard fortuitous adjudication between particular parties as an inappropriate method of evolving rules of law of more general application in a society in which unique situations are as common as they are in the mutual intercourse of States.[3]

Jenks also implies that the price that one has to pay for the building up of a solid body of case law by one court is a certain inflexibility in the structure of the court. To be able to create a tribunal *ad hoc*, or to use regional or other specialized chambers which could be devised as an integral part of the International Court of Justice, could greatly add to the attractiveness of the judicial process, he believes.

Support for judicial settlement is not, of course, restricted to this side of the Atlantic. The Connolly Amendment notwithstanding, the United States favours, in principle at least, recourse to the Court. The present Secretary of State actively opposed the continuance of the Connolly Amendment when he was Attorney General.[4] The United States is party without reservation to more than twenty bilateral and innumerable multilateral instruments which incorporate clauses providing for automatic reference to the Court in case of a dispute as to their terms. American academics are united in their disapproval of the Connolly Amendment, and in their desire for a greater use of the International Court. Professor Thomas M. Franck, of New York University, in an interesting and provocative book contends that:

The failure of the international community to develop a system of third-party law-making comparable to that of the national community may well prove to be the fatal error of our civilization.[5]

American writers are, I would venture to suggest, much more concerned than their British colleagues with the structure of international law. They observe that international law is essentially a horizontal (that is to say, decentralized) system, and note the consequences for law enforcement. Those who apply and (if you accept some initial jurisprudential premises) 'make' law are not in the main judges, or even international officials, but foreign offices and governments. Over much of international law this is of little consequence—the understanding of the advantages of mutual restraint and reciprocity serve as encouragement to law observation. But there are certain areas, and especially those where an initial illegality appears legally to permit what would otherwise be another illegality (the reprisal or counter-intervention syndrome), where the absence of an effective judicial system is very damaging. The exchanging of claims and counter-claims by states intervening in a civil war situation is a case in point. Professor Falk has correctly contended that, given the absence of any vertical structure, the decentralized claims by outside states to treat a civil war as rebellion, insurgency, or belligerency make it impossible to standardize what is forbidden with sufficient clarity to enable a protesting party to identify a violation. Thus international law cannot do much to promote non-intervention, or self-determination by distinguishing authoritatively among various types of internal wars.[6] Yet *everything* in the problem of internal war depends upon the classification of status. Falk is among those American writers deeply concerned by the attempted reach of American power, whether the issue is Vietnam, the Dominican Republic, or extra-territorial legislation. But his belief in the necessity of more third-party adjudication is shared by Professor McDougal, whom we would *not* recognize as concerned about these things. It is interesting that one so closely associated with the lawyer's role in decentralized decision-making— that is to say, the making of legal decisions by governments—should so strongly support unfettered reference to judicial settlement.

In the context of a judicial settlement clause in the Convention on the Law of Treaties, Professor McDougal urged that the relevant legal tasks which might arise—the exploration of the facts and the precedents, the compatibility of the claim with *jus cogens,* and even the projection of a future policy in the making of the choice—are ' more likely to be made in terms of common interest through the assistance of third-party decision than by unilateral, naked-power decisions of either party '.[7] Part of the answer, of course, is that Professor McDougal envisages a very flexible and policy-oriented method of reaching judgments in the International Court. But he is not waiting upon that eventuality, but urges here and now the essentiality of reliance upon third-party adjudication.

II

I have so far been writing of the general consensus among lawyers on the desirability of third-party adjudication, and the differing views advanced to support this proposition.

The near-unanimity, in the Western world at least, concerning the desirability of third-party adjudication does not, as many international relations scholars seem to think, necessarily reflect a naïveté as to the significance of judicial settlement in conflict resolution. Lord McNair, in his Ludwig Mond Lecture for 1956, warned against exaggerating the significance of what courts could do in relation to the whole canvas of international problems. Increased adjudication would not, he suggested, contribute substantially to the peace of the world.[8] He pointed to three factors which necessarily limited the usefulness of resort to adjudication. The first he termed 'intrinsic', by which he meant that the Court can only deal with legal, and not with political, economic, or social disputes. This is not the occasion to enter into a discussion of this particular question, but I have elsewhere suggested [9] that it is virtually impossible sharply to distinguish these elements in a dispute; that furthermore, the Court's own practice shows that it has dealt with disputes with strong political and economic factors; and that the relevant question is the appropriateness of a legal form of decision-making in regard to the dispute, and not the nature of the dispute itself. Of the other limitations to which Lord McNair pointed, I shall want to say something in another context a little later. My wish here is to emphasize that it is frequently the most learned and distinguished of commentators who have cautioned against exaggerating the Court's role. Frequently it is the international relations scholars who put into the mouths of lawyers exaggerated claims concerning the Court, in order to demolish them. Sir Hersch Lauterpacht acknowledges (and he is speaking of the Permanent Court as well as its successor) that 'it would be an exaggeration to assert that the Court has proved to be a significant instrument for maintaining international peace'.[10] And Jenks, writing of power politics, ideological controversy, cultural diversity, and sharply divergent economic standards, says:

In none of these contexts is international adjudication the key to peace, progress and prosperity. But in all of them continuing progress presupposes developments in international organisation to which further progress in international adjudication can make a significant contribution.[11]

Rosenne writes with an equal sense of perspective, emphasizing time and again the essentially political function of adjudication. This is not, of course, to suggest that the Court makes political decisions, but rather to appreciate that legal decisions have their proper place in the political arrangement of things. A reference to the Court is a matter of political choice, though legal advice will be taken. The very existence of an international court of law often acts as a spur to finding other, non-adjudicative methods of settlement. The lists of withdrawn cases attest to this.[12] Rosenne does not even share with Allott the view that adjudication is the preferable way of conflict settlement. He thus regards the withdrawn cases as falling on the credit side of the Court's ledger; and, further, regards it as entirely healthy that judicial settlement today is merely one among a variety of possible methods of pacific settlement, without any primacy.

The allegations of certain international relations scholars are, therefore, not very impressive. Yet some other aspects of their work, as I shall suggest later, should give us pause in our thinking on third-party adjudication.

III

Over the last few years, although enthusiasm in the West for the increased use of the Court has continued unabated (and, as I have tried to indicate, from a wide variety of unlikely bedfellows), there has grown up a body of literature which reveals keen awareness both of real shortcomings in the workings of the Court, and of state attitudes —realistic or psychological—which limit the effective use of the Court. The most basic limitation within which the Court works is that it is a Court of Law, and not of Economics, Politics and Social Problems. This proposition is beyond the scope of this paper, but it is, at the very least, subject to different interpretations. The Court has, on many occasions, taken the view that if the interpretation of a treaty is involved, its task is a legal one even if the subject matter contains political or economic elements. This has been so at least so far as the advisory jurisdiction of the Court is concerned—the *Admissions* Case [13] of 1950 had the strongest political overtones, as did the Case of *Certain Expenses* [14] in 1962; but these entailed the interpretation of the United Nations Charter. And political and social questions were clearly present in the request for the Advisory Opinions on South West Africa—though these two related to legal instruments (the Charter and the Mandate) and called for legal tasks to be performed. In the *Customs Union* Case [15] the Court was concerned with issues that were economic—but again within a treaty context. Only on rare occasions the Court will decide that, even where there are legal frames of reference, the political or social aspects overwhelm the legal to such a degree that the Court ought properly not to adjudicate. The 1966 Judgment on *South West Africa* [16] affords such an example. But it is an unclear precedent on this point, and the proposition that the Court is concerned with law and not politics will continue to provide the most flexible of guidelines as to its task. We have also seen that specially constituted Courts of Law, or quasi-judicial bodies, can perform legally tasks within a strongly economic and political framework. The Court of the European Communities is an example— the intertwining of the legal considerations with the political and economic ones is almost complete. The Restrictive Trade Practices Court and the Industrial Relations Court in this country are further examples, and of course such bodies as the Securities and Exchange

Commission and the Interstate Commerce Commission in the United States. There are no inherent limitations upon the relevance of the legal function in non-legal contexts, at least where the issue does not arise in the form of contended jurisdiction. But, having said this, I am aware that a series of different problems arises in relation to the same point. If we reject the problem as one of jurisdiction or propriety, there still remains the problem of skills. Most lawyers, clearly, do not have the skill to be entrusted with economic decisions. Yet in the Restrictive Practices Court the legal function is meaningless without a full understanding of the economic context. Expert witnesses are available to guide the Judge through unfamiliar waters. They have not much been used by the International Court. ' Experts ' were of course heavily relied on by Counsel in the *South West Africa* Cases, though the Court in the event did not rely on them, in that it did not adjudicate the substantive issues. And, perhaps, one may be forgiven for regarding ' political experts ' as more partisan and less scientific creatures than economic experts, even where there is a clash of opinion among the latter. The judicial function can operate much more effectively in related technical fields in small, specially constituted courts, where the Bench over a period of time becomes immersed in the surrounding non-legal context in which its legal role must be carried out. A Bench which deals solely with restrictive trade practices or securities or wage claims is not constantly brought up against the problem of where the frontiers of its formal skills end and acquired knowledge begins. The inadequacy of the International Court of Justice as court for interpreting legal questions from many of the more technical of the Specialized Agencies is clear. Not being a specialist court, it does not have these skills, and the *ad hoc* introduction of expert witnesses would be an inadequate device. Arbitration often avoids this problem, of course, for the *ad hoc* formation of a tribunal can enable the necessary non-legal expertise to be found among the arbitrators.

Specialist courts deal with a plethora of personal, social, welfare, and economic problems. The role of the courts in family questions is now fairly well established and clearly demarcated so far as alternative and supplementary systems—such as the welfare services and probation work—are concerned. Some controversy still exists over the usefulness of the legal function in respect of economic questions. Lawyers and economists alike [17] have examined the workings of the Restrictive Practices Court in this context. What is clear beyond doubt is that where there is a non-specialist court—such as the International Court of Justice—it is very easy for the ' law not politics ' argument not only to be facile within its own terms, but also to mask and blur the need to address the problem in terms of skills possessed by the court as an institution and by the judges as individuals. One could imagine, on the international level, a range of specialist courts dealing with a variety of technical problems, in which legal tasks would still be thought helpful. These could either be in the form of special chambers within the ICJ (Art. 26) or separate from the ICJ.

This crossing of functions between the lawyer and the specialist can, of course, lead one entirely in the opposite direction. Thus the Indus Waters Treaty of 1960, which establishes the means for compulsory decision-making in technical disputes not solved by negotiation, assigns ' a highly qualified engineer' to carry out quasi-judicial functions, either alone or as a member of a Court of Arbitration. Another area of difficulty so far as third-party decision-making is concerned is one relating to cultures rather than to specialist skills. Where the legal rights at issue are based on a cultural and political affinity, regional courts again might be a more appropriate method of judicial settlement than a truly universal court.[18] Treaties establishing certain regional systems, such as the EEC, LAFTA, and the European Human Rights Convention, do of course already provide for courts. But these tentative beginnings could be extended, and suggestions to that effect have been made by several persons, including Julius Stone [19] and C. W. Jenks.

It can further be argued that judicial bodies are singularly ill suited to decide upon questions of fact, and that most assertions of a legal claim rest upon a disputed set of facts. For example, part of the United States legal position in Vietnam rests on the assertion that North Vietnam was sending troops and arms into the South *before* the US intervention. The quasi-judicial body of the International Control Commission has been too divided in its findings on the facts, and—as Thomas Franck puts it—' the World Court, with its large, distinguished and senior judiciary, is scarcely suited for tramping about the jungles of SE Asia.' [20] The Court did use a fact-finding Commission in the *Corfu Channel* Case,[21] but not in the *Preah Vihear* [22] Case, where the facts were much in dispute, and it has not undertaken the travel envisaged in its statute. The evidence seems to be that, so far as fact-finding is essential to the weighing of any legal claims, fact-finding commissions are likely to be more effective than a judicial body.

A cause for concern sometimes voiced is the time factor in the handing down of decisions. Allott, in the useful *Report* to which I have already referred, contends that a detailed examination makes a charge of dilatoriness hard to justify. In the main, he would seem to be right. Delay is usually due to the length of time given to parties to prepare their pleadings, and is at their request. The appearance of dilatoriness further occurs when, as in the *South West Africa* Cases,[23] no judgment on the merits is given after a litigation and judgment on preliminary objections and prolonged litigation on the merits; or when, as in the *Barcelona Traction* Case,[24] one or more of the preliminary objections are joined to the merits, and eventually find favour with the Court. Other than these two cases, the length of time seems more reasonable (though still very costly to smaller nations). The *Right of Passage* Case [25] took four years and five months from first application to judgment; but the *Certain Frontier Land* Case [26] took only one year seven months, *Interhandel* [27] one year six months, *Preah Vihear* [28] two years nine months, and *Northern Cameroons* [29] two years six months. Mr Allott, by taking a random sample of the last five civil cases in the Law Reports at the time he wrote, effectively showed that the wheels of domestic law move more slowly than those of international law.[30] And it is common knowledge that the British legal system enjoys a reputation for speed as compared with its European and American counterparts. The Court can also act speedily in the case of interim measures, as it has shown in the *Anglo-Iranian, Anglo-Icelandic*, and *Nuclear Tests* Cases; and in theory at least summary procedure is available under Article 29 of its Statute.

Various proposals could of course be made—and have been made —to improve and streamline the procedure of the Court. Jenks, Stone, and Allott have all tackled this problem, and no doubt, in the context of possible revisions of the Statute, studies have been initiated in foreign offices for consideration at the UN. The American Society of International Law, at its Sixty-fourth Annual Meeting, had a practitioners' panel on this, and their proposals for procedural reform of international courts—arbitral bodies as well as the ICJ—are no doubt useful and interesting.[31]

Questions of jurisdiction form another cluster of difficulties so far as effective third-party adjudication is concerned. The jurisdiction of the International Court is based on consent. This can be given *ad hoc*, or in advance through the use of the so-called Optional Clause. This Clause (Article 36 of the Statute of the Court) allows reservations, and these may arise *ratione temporis, ratione materiae*, or *ratione personae*. Clearly, no useful recommendations can be made about the Optional Clause *per se*, for its use is a reflection of confidence or lack of confidence in other fields. There have been numerous exhortations to nations to withdraw or severely limit their reservations to the Optional Clause. Suggestions are also periodically heard that the Court would be used more effectively if there were created a *locus standi in judicio* for international organizations. At the moment, of course, only states parties to the Statute can make a declaration of acceptance under Article 36. Certain international organizations clearly have acquired sufficient international personality for such a *locus standi* to be contemplated, and it would regularize certain anomalies which exist at present (for example, in claims procedures regarding UN forces, or in settlement of dispute clauses in bilateral agreements between international organizations and states). However, it is probably a mistake to assume that this is likely much to increase the reliance placed upon the International Court. The experience of the *Expenses* Opinion—in which an Opinion of the Court, though formally accepted by the Assembly, has in fact not been implemented because the dissenting minority soon became a tacit majority[32]— has caused observers to suggest that, in the present political climate at least, the Court should not be asked for an Advisory Opinion unless the request is unanimous. Although if the Assembly had a *locus standi* before the Court, the compliance with a judgment would presumably be binding, the same sorts of considerations still obtain. The Assembly, a political body whose smooth functioning is essential, might still have to face the prospects of a non-complying section of its membership, which could, if the obligation were an ongoing one, become a majority failing to comply.[33]

Indeed, if the basis of jurisdiction were substantially widened, whether by this or other means, the problem of compliance would be greatly increased. The more jurisdiction is based on full consent, the less is the compliance problem.

We have pointed to some of the real problems which an international adjudicative body faces, and briefly touched on some of the suggestions advanced to improve the situation. The obverse side of the coin is, of course, the attitude and psychology of states who are potential users of the International Court. Many of us have over the last decade followed, and tried to write about, the emerging views of the newer nations on the use of the Court, as well as of the Communist countries. There has been an ample literature[34] on this theme, and the main points which emerge need no labouring here. A fairly high percentage of the Western European countries have accepted the compulsory jurisdiction of the Court, though often with reservations. The old Commonwealth also (save for South Africa, which in April 1967 withdrew its acceptance) is well represented. But only ten Latin American countries have made declarations under Article 36 (2) (and of these, three were for a fixed duration which has expired). Of the Afro-Asian or newer nations the most recent listing includes only Botswana, Cambodia, Gambia, India, Israel, Japan, Kenya, Liberia, Malawi, Malta, Mauritius, Nigeria, Pakistan, the Philippines, Somalia, Sudan, Swaziland, Uganda, and the UAR. The Communist nations retain their doctrinal objections to adjudication by the Court, and there is no prospect for a change in their attitude.

Everything that I have so far said has been connected with the commonly held belief among Western lawyers of the desirability of

third-party adjudication. The brief survey of the real problems which
the present system of adjudication presents, and the further psychological hurdles which states erect, has been based on the tacit assumption that the goal is a desirable one, worthy of our efforts for reform.
Those who doubt that the Court will be much used in the next few
years do so with regret; their reasons are usually to be found among
those which we have touched on, a realistic appraisal of the contemporary international mood.

But it is possible to have doubts about the desirability of the goal
itself. Arguably, in our advocacy, as lawyers, of the merits of third-
party adjudication, we are being altogether too simple-minded about
the causes and resolution of conflict. We constantly assert that the
international community would be better off if there were wider
acceptance of the compulsory jurisdiction of the Court, and we assume
that our task is to help remove the obstacles to this objective. But
are we in fact not being rather parochial, and are we not in our zeal
for third-party adjudication ignoring much of what has been happening
in the academic world of international relations in the last few years?
To put my point another way: shall we not have to understand that
the appropriateness of a controversy for adjudication goes beyond the
traditional distinction made by courts between political and legal
issues? It is perhaps somewhat *simpliste* to assume that all disputes
are suitable for adjudication, so long as they are ' legal ' rather than
' political '. This ignores work being done both as to typologies of
conflict and the causes of conflict, and it assumes that settlement by
third parties on the basis of international law is a suitable remedy in
each case. There are indeed some international relations scholars
who contend that third-party settlement cannot, by definition, resolve
conflict in the sense that they understand those terms. Thus Dr John
Burton of University College, London, has developed a theory of
international relations which entails the view that conflict occurs
because of non-systemic behaviour due to misperceptions between the
protagonists. The termination of conflict situations can therefore only
be achieved, in his view, by the removal of such misperceptions by
trained personnel assisting the parties—who would then be in a
position to make the necessary changes and compromises *inter se*.
Dr Burton says, speaking of conflict:

The remedy is not to introduce an outside agent or set of ' normative
laws ' to control such behaviour, but to provide States with the theories,
insights, and rules that enable them to achieve their goals without running
into the self-defeating conflicts inherent in non-systemic behaviour.[35]

International law is not based on these behavioural theories, and the
imposition of legal solutions by a court introduces a static and in-
flexible element into a situation that calls—if conflict is to be properly

resolved—for entirely another approach. Now, we may view this argument with some caution. In the first place, the identification of what is or is not systemic behaviour seems less than scientific. Second, I take a more flexible view than some on the proper role of the judiciary, and the extent to which they can concern themselves with policy considerations. So I do not view the judicial system as a rigid one, as does Dr Burton. Third, Dr Burton seems to me to under-state the element of consent in recourse to international courts. The very fact that the jurisdiction of the International Court is essentially based on consent, presupposes a *volens* on the part of the parties to have their conflict resolved in this way. And this *volens* is surely a large part of resolving a conflict.

Nonetheless, I do not think that we can or should dismiss these international relations views out of hand. The judicial process often does seem to provide too clear-cut and sharp answers, where the instinct of the diplomats concerned is for a blurring of the edges of the dispute.[36] And, although jurisdiction is essentially by consent, preliminary objections to jurisdiction are often entered, and it is only in the most formal of senses that the Court can be said to be resolving a conflict in accordance with a method desired by both of the parties. The more marginal is consent the less likely, perhaps, is judicial settlement to *resolve* a dispute in the commonly understood sense of the term. In neither the *Corfu Channel* nor *Preah Vihear* Cases can the conflict have been said to have been resolved. In the former the judgment was not carried out by one of the parties; in the latter the acceptance of the Court's findings has not prevented occasional further outbreaks of hostilities between the parties. What judgments have done, perhaps, more modestly is to indicate a future line of options which are shut to the contending states, and removed controversy from those potentially likely to cause violence.

This point is closely linked to that of the inadequacy of international courts in the question of peaceful change. Again, a flexible view as to the role of the judge does allow one to believe that the judiciary is more than a mere protector of the *status quo*. ' applying the law as it is '. The function of law application to specific decisions inevitably carries with it the seeds of law development too. I would accept the Jenks' view that:

International, like national, adjudication consists in large measure of wrestling, by procedures of recognised impartiality and within a frame-work of commonly accepted principles, with a succession of dilemmas, the answers to which can be found only in morality and policy.[37]

But a hard core of both remains in Lord McNair's comment[38] that courts can only state the law, not help a party in its rejection of the *status quo*; and, as he points out, it is this very rejection of the *status quo* which gives rise to many disputes. The Indian invasion of Goa was clearly a rejection of the *status quo*. The judicial process, so far as title to Goa was concerned, would not have provided India with a realistic alternative to the use of force.

By the same token, the International Court can take no account of the international relations distinction between functional and dysfunctional conflict. Dysfunctional conflict is conflict that is non-systemic. But functional conflict may be directed towards the necessary protection of systems [39] (and not just of states) and to the achievement of social justice. The occasions when international law approves the use of force (in the self-defence of states, or when authorized by the UN) are clearly much narrower than the international relations notion of functional conflict, and do not overlap with it at all points.

Equally, international courts have before them as parties states, and not international systems. The judicial process can take little account of systems theory, and thus often, in the view of international relations scholars, fails to identify the *real* parties to a conflict. Perhaps even more importantly, the forms of the judicial process require the issue often to be phrased in slightly false terms. The *Right of Passage* Case affords a clear example: in final terms, it was about the interpretation of a treaty. But in *real* terms it was about a whole set of relationships and attitudes going beyond the treaty. The *South West Africa* Cases also come to mind: the Court was asked to pronounce upon a series of obligations by which the Plaintiffs alleged that South Africa was bound. But they were not so much interested in the fulfilment of those obligations (though they might have been in the 1950s) as in finding a legal basis for the removal of the Mandate from South Africa.

The problem of appropriateness for adjudication is usually, as I have already said, tackled by international lawyers in crude terms of ' political ' and ' legal ', the latter being appropriate, the former being beyond the pale. Thomas Franck has sought to go beyond this and suggests that recourse should be had to international adjudication only when the issues put to the Court are fully dispositive of the real issue. He has written:

The test ought not to be whether the issue is too big, or the defendant too stubborn, but whether the question posed is one a court is properly equipped to answer. The words merit stressing: to *answer*, not to *enforce*. In deciding whether to decide, a court must look to the *issues*, not to the *clients*. . . .[40]

The Brazilian-French lobster war is, says Professor Franck, very suitable for adjudication. Are lobsters fish, or are they ' sedentary species '?

A court is splendidly equipped to answer such a question, after hearing expert advice and argument on the locomotive proclivities of lobsters, and perhaps, evidence on the state of mind of the negotiators of the treaty. It is even conceivable that other interested states might ask to be heard on the larger economic implications of the issue. But, in the end, the court need only say ' yes ' or ' no '. . . .[41]

There is no undistributed middle ground, no complex work of inter-relation. But what if there are three possible solutions to what is the ' real problem '? Or ten? Or a thousand? There is a whole range of legal questions which a court could be asked about Berlin, including the present status of the London Agreement, the status of the Mem-orandum on Air Corridors, etc. But there will always remain more unanswered questions, going to notions of ' how much ', ' in what manner ', and ' under what circumstances '. And it is highly doubtful whether any questions which the Court could be asked would really contribute to a viable solution of the essential problem. Certainly the questions asked of the Court in the *Expenses* Case—good legal questions—have not; and nor, one imagines, would any answers which the Court might have given in the *South West Africa* Cases.

A further factor should, it seems to me, give us pause concerning the overall suitability of third-party settlement. The structure and func-tioning of international society over the last few years have revealed that bargaining is often a more promising conflict resolution device than clear adjudication in favour of one party. Certainly in most international disputes there is a bargaining factor present: that is to say, there are possible small adjustments which can be made without essential values being lost by either side, and neither side has a priority on behavioural rectitude, even though one may have the better legal case. And certainly international institutions like the United Nations have found, with very few exceptions, that it is preferable to address their directives to both parties to a dispute rather than to attempt the quasi-adjudicative function of indicating who has acted illegally. Clearly, the trend away from the originally intended enforcement to-wards peacekeeping by consent is evidence of this tendency. And the same pattern has been followed in resolutions directed at the parties to a dispute, but not concerned with UN peacekeeping. It has been found a preferable pattern so far as compliance is concerned. Only in those cases where the international community has long since given up real hope of compliance—such as apartheid in South Africa—is the quasi-adjudicative method of identifying the law breaker used.

International relations scholars are, of course, heavily engaged in an examination of industrial disputes and bargaining for any lessons that may be useful for the international field.

Elsewhere, we see a variety of third-party functions which have emerged from the growing institutionalization of international relations, which are by no means limited to third-party judicial settlement: middlemen and mediators of various kinds, commissions, and conciliation boards.[42] And of course, UN forces are a comparatively recent form of third-party intervention in conflict situations which have had some success at least in removing conflict from the stage of actual hostilities.

What is clear is that we are in urgent need of serious work to produce a typology of conflict, and to seek to relate it to various alternative types of settlement. If I believe that an international court still has some role to play, I am by no means sure that adjudication is even a desirable goal in certain types of conflict. Who would doubt that the Indus waters dispute was more effectively resolved through technical suggestions for a mutually improved situation than it would have been before the Court? At the moment we have international relations scholars working, often separately, on simulation, quantitative theory, systems and analysis bargaining; and international lawyers proclaiming the desirability of greatly increased international adjudication. Surely the time has come for us to join hands and to work to see if any pattern emerges between types of conflict and viable forms of settlement. Only then shall we see the proper place for our particular skills in the resolution of conflict.

SOME REFLECTIONS ON
INTERNATIONAL OFFICIALDOM *

OSCAR SCHACHTER †

It seems fitting to include some reflections on the international civil service in a volume dedicated to the memory of John McMahon. He was not a career official but was drawn into the secretariat of the United Nations, initially as an interne, fresh from law school, and later for two longer periods as an assistant legal adviser, while on leave from Oxford. It may have seemed strange that he should for some years have chosen to give up Oxford for the hectic environment of the United Nations in New York. Yet to those who knew him it was no surprise that he should have been strongly attracted to the United Nations.

This may be put down to youth and idealism, and it would not be wrong to do so. However one may discount the high-flown rhetoric in praise of the United Nations, it should be remembered that to many that organization has remained the focus of aspirations for world peace and justice. This is perhaps especially the case for those influenced by the ethical teaching of a great religious tradition. But along with ethical idealism, there are other components in the attraction of international organizations. There is excitement and stimulation in a multinational service made up of people diverse in interest, background, and values yet compelled to face up to common problems and to work together. John McMahon moved easily among those of different backgrounds and in a remarkably short time had a wide circle of friends of varied nationality and professional interest. He responded to new acquaintances as to new ideas with characteristic warmth and sympathy. In that milieu, he could find not only the interest of variety but the spice of intellectual challenge. The ' frontier ' problems attracted him—outer space, the sea-bed, mini-states; they opened wide vistas and the opportunity to develop new laws to serve the general welfare. It is no great wonder that he, like many others, should have found a reward, and even a fascination, in serving with an international secretariat.

Of course, any officialdom must have its dull and bureaucratic side.

* © Oscar Schachter 1973. This essay was written in 1970.
† Director of Studies, United Nations Institute for Training and Research.

For more than a few there is only a routine to follow, a narrow place to fill. They seem to be mainly concerned with the objectionable characteristics of their superiors and the obstacles to promotion. There are those who do not care what they do as long as they are at the centre of it. Others welcome or resign themselves to assignments which demand little and seem secure. As in any administration, many are engaged in ' busywork ', displaying (in Lasswell's neat phrase) an infinite capacity to make ends of their means. These are common features of bureaucracy and there is no good reason to expect an international organization to be free of them. To be sure, an international organization adds its distinctive flavour. That could hardly be otherwise in an administration made up of officials who lack a common tradition and training and even a common language, and, more important, one that is the creature of governments deeply divided among themselves on many subjects. Not the least of these is the question of the proper role and function of an international secretariat.

This essay attempts to convey some of the flavour of an international bureaucracy though it does not purport to offer more than personal reflections. The impressions on which the comments are based come from more than twenty-five years of international service in United Nations organizations. One could, I suppose, classify the writer as a ' participant observer ' but that might mislead the reader to expect social science. No such claim is made. Nor are any proposals put forward; at most there is a trace of hope that what is said might possibly have some practical implications for developing more effective international administration.

CIRCUMSPECTION AND INHIBITION

Yeats once remarked that ' the practical man cannot afford to be sincere '. Diplomats and international officials hardly need to be reminded of the perils of sincerity. Unlike poets or artists they have no licence for self-expression and good reason for self-control. No matter how much they appear to resemble one another, how convivial their social occasions, how easy their small talk, they cannot but remain aware of the currents of differences that run among them and sensitive to the risk of giving offence. Certain topics are off-limits, personal reactions are subdued, and the burning subjects, if at all discussed, are treated with the cool detachment of the professional.

The international official, even more than the diplomat, must be conscious of the need for restraint. Unlike the delegate, who has at least a position or point of view to present, the international official will generally have none—or, one might say, all—since it is his role to comprehend all while supporting none. A classic formula expressed first in the early days of the League of Nations is that the first duty of the secretariat is ' to collate the relevant documents and to prepare the ground for decisions without suggesting what these decisions should be '. In line with this oft-repeated formula, the secretariat at a governmental meeting normally adopts a ' low profile '. Only exceptionally would they take issue with a statement of a delegate. Such suggestions as they may make, even on procedural matters, are, more often than not, accompanied by expressions of deference to delegates. Papers or oral statements which indicate solutions or decisions tend to indirection and circumlocution. A direct and positive style might after all be considered as too assertive. Perhaps that is one reason, though not the only one, why United Nations documents exhibit that ' pompous, polysyllabic and relentlessly abstract style ' (to quote Edmund Wilson) which characterizes written ' bureaucratese '.

It is also one of the reasons, possibly the main one, why oral statements by officials sometimes seem so full of inflated compliments to government representatives and self-deprecatory observations about their own role or their suggestions. This public display of deference towards delegates is not infrequently accompanied by private expression of condescension. The transparent manœuvres, vanities, and ambitions of delegates, the not uncommon gaps in their knowledge are unfailing sources of secretariat shop-talk. Experienced officials will, by and large, take all this in their stride, as part of the system. However, newer and younger secretariat members tend to be more restive. Many of them will be inclined to contrast the inhibitions placed on their initiative with the opportunity for participation given to equally young and sometimes less qualified delegation members. A recent unofficial survey of a sample of secretariat members reports that most of those interviewed ' are frustrated by the vow of silence under which they are obliged to remain mute in conferences while former fellow students and friends who are part of the diplomatic community dominate the spotlight in the verbal area '.

The inhibitions placed on international officials are also felt outside the ' verbal areas ' of conference and committee work. There is certainly some feeling—one cannot say how widespread or intense it is—that the organization prizes the negative virtues—prudence, conformity, restraint—more highly than the positive qualities—initiative, creativity, vigour. It can be said this merely exemplifies the classic model of bureaucracy as first described by Max Weber in which the most valued traits of officials are strict subordination, precision, regularity, skill in technical or administrative routine, and the like. By the same standards, the bureaucracy shows uneasiness, if not outright hostility, when new ideas are advanced or independence and non-conformity manifested. No doubt these are characteristics of most large administrations and we have no hard evidence to enable us to rank international organizations as better or worse. But, putting comparisons aside, there are fairly obvious reasons to support the impression that international organizations tend to favour the more passive and more bureaucratic qualities. What we have already said about circumspection and restraint tells us in part why this is so. Underlying this is the political fact that the international civil service, by and large, operates under a far more limited conception of delegated authority than do national civil services.

It would be surprising if the restraints and inhibitions described above did not have substantial effects on the behaviour and attitudes of the individuals. One hesitates to generalize, since conditions, motivations, and personalities vary so widely. We do not have systematically organized data on this and indeed little in the way of scientific research has been attempted in this area. Still, some impressions may be of interest with the caveat that they should not be over-generalized.

I would suppose that the adjustment of individuals to the system is accomplished in large part through the ' natural selection ' of recruitment and duration of service. Those who find the conditions unpalatable do not enter or soon leave. Once in, many find it easier to resign themselves to, than from, their relatively well-paid positions. Some treat their jobs as secondary and look to other sources of personal satisfaction. They perform their tasks with limited interest and little enthusiasm. It is not unusual for older secretariat members to comment on how they, or others, have lost their drive or have been reduced to apathy. This does not necessarily mean that they express active dissatisfaction. Many will find support for a self-image of dedication by identifying with the goals of the organization, even if in an abstract way, rather than through their direct personal role. On that basis they may adjust to sitting through long and tedious committee meetings in which their role is marginal and barely requires attention. Others will adjust to preparing reports and studies which are no more than compilations or summaries of other published material, sometimes relevant to preparing the way for decisions, more often honoured by ritualistic praise and little more than that.

Those who have joined the international organization with a strong professional motivation may have more difficulty in adjusting to the inhibition and frustration of their jobs. They will have come in to further their careers as experts, challenged by the apparent opportunities in fields like economic development work, international law, social research, political analysis, or the variety of other disciplines represented in the organization. Mere bureaucratic approval is much less important for them than the approbation of experts in their field and acceptance of their ideas. They do not take so easily to the prevailing rule of anonymity under which their papers are presented by, or in the name of, a senior official who has made little if any personal contribution without any attribution to the actual writer. In addition the restrictions placed on scholarly contributions by staff members and an impression that such individual effort is deplored by higher officials are further reasons for dissatisfaction and reluctance to enter the international service. Such ' role oriented ' professionals are not likely to regard dedication to the aims of international organization as an adequate substitute for a satisfactory professional experience, nor do they tend to think of themselves as civil servants in the usual sense of a career in administration without regard to their particular expertise.

The inhibitions which affect the more scholarly sections of the secretariats probably do not have the same impact on those engaged more directly in operations. These include the thousands engaged in the execution of economic development projects around the world, in the regulatory activities of the specialized agencies, or in the relief activities for refugees or children. I would suppose that the restraints most keenly felt by operational personnel are those imposed by the complicated tangle of authority governing their activity. In an official study, Sir Robert Jackson described the development activities of the United Nations system as ' probably the most complex organization in the world '.[1] This may be an overstatement but the existence of formidable jurisdictional complexities cannot be doubted. What is distinctive, in comparison to national bureaucratic overlap and conflict, is that the international system lacks the ultimate centralized authority of the national state. There is no single overall parliament, no chief executive, no supreme court to lay down final rules or decisions. The various international organizations involved in the development pro-grammes have their own constitutions and are answerable to no other international authority. ' Co-ordination ' and consultative procedures permeate the international development process. International develop-ment officials feel at times that they are in a morass of inter-agency meetings, endless clearances, and continuous uncertainty as to who decides what.

Contributing to the complexity and pervasive ambiguity is the always uncertain line between the responsibility and authority of the international agency and that of the national government receiving development aid. That the national government is the final authority on what it needs and how to administer it is axiomatic in these pro-grammes, but the injunctions and restraints imposed on the inter-national agencies by their collective bodies cannot be automatically subordinated to individual national decisions. It is apparent that under this complicated system, individual officials must carry out their tasks with circumspect regard for the procedures laid down, and, even more important, with regard for the sensibilities of those in other international bodies and in national governments. One can easily see that the price for this system of fragmented authority may be high in individual frustration—to say nothing of time and energy expended. But while the reasons for this are not difficult to ascertain, it is not enough to convince the officials that the division of authority is inevitable. They must also be persuaded that it is possible for them to carry out the job for which they were hired. At least those with a conscience will need that conviction. There will always be others who can remain satisfied with meetings on co-ordination and with the endless movement of papers from office to office.

IDEAS AND ACTION

The house-broken official will rarely question the need for restraint. He may, however, share the sentiment expressed in verse by Roy Campbell:

> You praise the firm restraint with which they write,
> I'm with you there, of course.
> They use the snaffle and the curb all right
> But where's the bloody horse?

Even a government strongly in favour of the snaffle and curb for international officials will complain of lack of action on matters which it wishes to have pursued. Numerous resolutions are adopted which entrust the international staff with tasks that demand initiative, judgement, and vigour. There are ' bloody horses ' to be ridden, even if they have to be kept under tight rein. International organizations have long since shown that they cannot be confined to conference diplomacy and that, gradually or precipitately, they are required to take on tasks that go beyond the traditional functions of conference secretariats.

Certain of these tasks, described as operational or as executive action (a phrase favoured by Mr. Hammarskjöld), have acquired a lustre of their own. The international official appears as a man of action, directly engaged in moving men, materials, and funds to places where they are needed: the use of troops for policing, the transport of food for refugees, the sending of technical experts to discover natural resources, the transfer of capital to finance construction. In these cases, he has moved from words to deeds or at least the appearance of deeds. The official can feel that his work is closer to results—the relief of hunger, the suppression of violence, the establishment of a new school, a new road. As a consequence his own role—whatever his echelon—will seem concrete, less concerned with verbal resolutions, more with events. It is not surprising that many of the international officials should find their true vocation in the operational areas and that executive action should be seen by them as the high-water mark of a dynamic international organization.

But there are many mansions in the house of world organization and not all are dedicated to executive action. Nor do all international officials see their role as carrying out operations. If someone drew their attention to the classic fable of Menenius Agrippa about the body politic and its parts, many would regard themselves not as the hands or feet doing what is bidden but as the brain or at least the central nervous system. This would not mean that they question the competence of the intergovernmental organs to determine policy; only that they appreciate the extent to which secretariat studies and reports can mould that policy when issues are complex and difficult.

It is usually good tactics for the staff to present its reports as purely factual, served up to a policy-making body for decision. But it must be borne in mind that policy-makers are rarely interested in the facts as such. The knowledge they need for policy decisions is knowledge geared to specific goals, institutions, and acceptable solutions. The typical study produced in academic institutions would not, as a rule, meet these conditions. Indeed, studies based on rigorous scientific methodology and precise in their conclusions are generally not suited to the requirements of the policy-maker. An international secretariat cannot afford that kind of intellectual rigour; its sights have to be kept on the ends it serves and on practical necessities. It has a built-in bias because the knowledge which it obtains and conveys must be linked to policy and action. Officials are not paid to waste their efforts or to purvey knowledge for its own sake. They must concern themselves with felt needs and articulated demands. Their product has to meet the tests of feasibility and acceptability. That is a far cry from the kind of independence and flexibility enjoyed by universities and research institutions.

Studies and ' background papers ' have been used by the international secretariats to initiate or stimulate far-reaching programmes of action. In these endeavours style, strategy, and ' organizational ideology ' have played important parts. An interesting example can be found in the history of the United Nations Economic Commission for Latin America (ECLA) under the leadership of Raoul Prebisch. In a ten-year period Prebisch and his colleagues presented to the Commission a steady stream of explanations, predictions, objectives, and measures designed to bring about reform in economic policy on both the international and national levels. A principal element was a conception of international stratification, exemplified by a ' centre' of industrialized countries and a ' periphery' of agricultural raw material producers, the latter suffering from long-term decline in the terms of trade and from short-term fluctuations in the export price for raw materials. Also put forward was a set of functional goals, principally industrialization, the ' technicalization' of agriculture, and central planning and programming for the national economy. A third component was a series of specific means to achieve these goals of industrialization: for example, import substitution, protectionism, agrarian reform, and income redistribution.

Whatever the economic merits of the ECLA theory and programme of action (and many economists have been critical of both) Prebisch did win considerable support among the member governments of the region and among their national elites concerned with economic policy. The criticism (which was probably greater outside than in the region) did not greatly weaken the image of rationality and planning projected by the secretariat. Their ideas seemed a welcome contrast to the usual policies of stop-gap measures forced by political pressures. What is interesting for our present purpose is that the secretariat proclaimed its innovative and heterodox approach. Prebisch declared ' ECLA is heretical by nature' and that its thinking had to depart from accepted canons. He called for boldness and originality, often in dramatic and emotional language. Over the years a sizeable and diversified corps of supporters appeared throughout the Latin-American region. A recent study sums up the key elements of that support:

In these circumstances, Prebisch appealed to the Latin American nationalists by emphasizing inward-oriented growth. He attracted the modern liberals by emphasizing the state's responsibilities in the guidance of the economy. The intellectuals appreciated his theoretical skill and his appeals for bold, new ideas. Impotent governments supported his putting on the center countries the responsibility for international commodity agreements, extended financial and technical assistance; and other concessions. As for his advocacy of industrialization, it was appealing to all these groups, and also perhaps to the reactionary forces, because it could be construed, presumably, as a way to avoid difficult political and social reforms, particularly agrarian reform. Finally, both to Latin American and to the ECLA Secretariat's staff, Prebisch offered a coherent explanation of the reality to be transformed, a clear delineation of the means to be used to transform it, and the identity of the opposition to be tackled. Finally, in addition to personal charisma, Prebisch projected the image and the reality of professional competence as an economist. This was crucial in strengthening his authority and organizational loyalty.[2]

Few international officials have been as successful as Prebisch in achieving an impact on national attitudes. Several have similarly made efforts to give direction to, and win support for, their activities by basing them on broad unifying concepts or doctrine. John Boyd Orr, for example, while head of the FAO, sought for a doctrine of agricultural welfare based on the use and disposal of surpluses. In the WHO, Brock Chisholm attempted to use an extended concept of good mental health (a concept in the WHO constitution) as a basis for a programme to combat aggressiveness and violence. Gunnar Myrdal made a valiant effort in 1948–9 to bridge the East-West division in Europe through ideas of planning the use of common resources and trade on a continental basis. At one time in UNESCO Julian Huxley sought to formulate a philosophy of scientific humanism as a foundation for global programmes.[3] In the ILO David Morse built wide support for an expanded programme on the basis of a doctrine of economic development and social progress, and Wilfred Jenks formulated a conception of a common law of mankind, based on perceived mutual interests, as a foundation for economic and social rights.

Professor Ernst Haas of Berkeley has characterized these ideas as examples of 'organizational' ideologies which 'make possible the articulation of shared objectives' and can 'bind and fire the organization's staff'.[4] Lacking such ideologies, the organizations (in Haas' view) tend to 'opportunistic decision-making' and 'subgoal-dominated programming' that 'degenerate into survival policies'. They then do not undertake the programmatic innovation required to maintain sufficient support by the members (that is, by the various 'interest coalitions' of the members). With such ideologies they are better able to persuade clients and supporters that 'constantly revalued objectives linked to new demands and new expectations in the environment can be met only by strengthening the organization'.[5]

Whether or not one accepts the thesis that organizational ideologies are necessary, it is evident that just as facts become meaningful when they move into ideas, so ideas gather strength as they are linked together in a coherent interrelated pattern. In an international organization a coherent doctrine that combines various goals can attract diverse supporters, each group finding its own benefit in the totality. Under skilful leadership it can impart a sense of mission to staff and members alike. To be sure, this will not work unless the doctrine reflects or expresses the goals shared by members. Huxley's doctrine of 'scientific humanism' was rejected by the members who did not accept it as expressing their goals. Moreover, a viable doctrine must have a cutting-edge: that is, it requires sufficient specific content to influence decisions; a vague abstraction is no more than rhetoric. (Perhaps that vagueness was the weakness of Chisholm's doctrine of good mental health.) A third requirement is that the ideas should be validated in practical implementation. Mere slogans or catch-phrases may appeal to some and win applause, but their value is likely to be short-lived. In sum, it is not enough to describe the Promised Land. A way must be shown and it must be demonstrable in actuality, to be the right way.

While no one can be especially optimistic that intellectual initiatives by international officials will meet these exacting requirements, there are indications that opportunities for such initiatives may well increase in the next few years. A factor of some significance, in my view, is the growing recognition of the need for more comprehensive and better integrated approaches to problems previously dealt with in separated discrete segments. This has been evidenced particularly in two broad areas of current concern to the international organizations: one, development and modernization of the less developed countries; and the other, environmental deterioration. I might also add to this the question of the sea-bed and the regime of the oceans. In these fields, the emphasis has moved dramatically from specialized professional techniques to interrelationships and comprehensive planning. It has become more apparent than ever before that developmental and environmental goals must be sought on a global basis, global in the sense of both geography and intellectual discipline. A natural consequence is that the responsibility for preparing adequate strategies will fall increasingly on the staffs of the global institutions. National governments, of course, will share that responsibility, especially as they command the greater part of the resources required, but the global character of the problems and their interdependencies are strong reasons for turning to an international mechanism. That is not to say that the present international staffing is sufficient, only that there is a need and consequently an opportunity for the international secretariats to play a central role in the formulation of the required strategies. This has already been recognized in the extensive endeavour of the major organizations to appraise the lessons of the first development decade and to formulate a new world-wide strategy of development for the next decade. We have seen also the beginnings of a similar effort in response to the growing and widespread demands to stem the world-wide deterioration of the natural environment.[6]

From a broad intellectual perspective these developments may be seen as having a greater significance than opening up opportunities for international officials or even advancing the solution of the problems to which they are directed. They can be seen as revealing indicators of the penetration into the international consciousness of the importance of scientific inquiry and approach. (I do not, of course, mean here the natural sciences or engineering technologies but rather the outlook and methods that characterize the scientific approach in whatever area it may be applied.) When international groups of experts or for that matter of non-expert officials enter into a common effort to solve the problems of, say, underdevelopment or of environmental damage, they tend, more and more, to discuss their approach on the basis of a common set of concepts and methodologies of inquiry. There will of course still be statements of preferences for particular political ideologies or social systems but these are subordinated, as a rule, to analysis that relies on a frame of reference accepted by diverse political and ideological groupings. It may be said that this phenomenon is a natural consequence of a multi-partisan, 'multi-ideological' group trying to deal with a common problem. They have to be ecumenical if they are to proceed with the business in hand. That is probably true and not unimportant. It is also evidence that there has been a world-wide diffusion of the scientific approach and a realization that its rationality and objectivity are needed to produce reliable knowledge, the kind of knowledge that has predictive power and enables men to exert control over their environment. I cannot emphasize this point too heavily for it seems to me to be the solid rock on which the intellectual contribution of the international secretariat must rest.

That rock, though necessary, will not however be sufficient. An international administration cannot be effective in promulgating ideas or in carrying out operations without imaginative vision and a wise and courageous leadership. 'Imponderabilia' though these may be, without them the international staffs will consist largely of busy bureaucrats, intent on means rather than ends, and of ill-co-ordinated experts, each of whom (as Sir Isaiah Berlin once observed) 'sooner or later becomes oppressed and irritated by being unable to step out of his box and survey the relationship of his particular activity to the whole '.[7] To be sure, leadership cannot be simply placed on order. We have no ready formulas to produce officials with vision, directive wisdom, and courage; yet on occasion they have appeared (some will say almost by accident) at the head or in the higher echelons of the international civil service. There is no sure ground for believing that they will continue to appear, only a hope that the inadequacies of purely national efforts will drive home to governments the need for a vigorous and creative international public service.

5

EXCEEDING SMALL *

S. A. DE SMITH †

John McMahon was a loyal member of Hertford College, Oxford, and of the United Nations Secretariat. An international lawyer of great promise, he had produced some impressive work in New York, including the substantial paper mentioned at the beginning of my essay below. A convivial, unassuming, and courteous companion, host, and friend, he seemed to enjoy universal respect and affection. He had a ready sense of humour and relished the confusion when, after a party that he gave at Hertford in honour of Henry Moore, the sculptor, the departing guests bestowed profuse thanks upon his twin brother. That he had much to offer to legal scholarship and to a wide circle of friends was so obvious that all who knew him felt a poignant sense of bereavement in 1969.

I

DURING his period of service in the United Nations Secretariat, John McMahon wrote a comprehensive study paper on participation by small states and territories in the activities of the United Nations and its specialized organs and agencies. He concentrated particularly on those very small political entities which were not members of the United Nations Organization. This analysis of a bewilderingly complex set of rules and practices was timely.[1] The existence of multifarious diminutive territories has created a number of difficult problems, and the international community has hardly begun to grope towards solutions.

II

Independence and United Nations Membership

United Nations declarations, covenants, and resolutions have in effect proclaimed that all non-self-governing peoples have a natural and inalienable right to independence. The detailed implications of these affirmations need to be examined more closely. Here it is enough

---

* © S. A. de Smith. 1973.
† Downing Professor of the Laws of England in the University of Cambridge and Fellow of Fitzwilliam College, Cambridge.

to observe that the anti-colonialist movement, which has dominated the United Nations since 1960, has probably accelerated the emergence of diminutive independent states in the under-developed continents.

No application for United Nations membership has been rejected on the grounds that the applicant country, though independent, is too small or poor to support the burdens of membership. The Maldive Islands, an impoverished state with a population of about 100,000, were admitted to membership in 1965 without active opposition. It is unlikely that any future applicant will be turned down because of inadequate resources.

Nevertheless, the prevalent zeal for decolonization is not accompanied by a correspondingly widespread enthusiasm for universal membership of the United Nations. As the number of members extended beyond 120, and as the procession of the small and indigent lengthened, U Thant more than once urged the Organization to review the criteria for membership and to consider the possibility of evolving new categories of association with the United Nations falling short of full membership. It is indeed incongruous, for instance, that the Maldive Islands had to house their delegation in the first instance in a stamp shop on Manhattan, and that The Gambia has been unable to maintain a permanent mission in New York at all.[2] If a less onerous and costly form of association with UN activities had been made available, possibly some applications for membership would never have been submitted. And as the process of decolonization approaches an end, it is to be expected that most newly independent states will be weak in population, size, and resources. Can they be supplied with a sufficiently attractive disincentive?

There is, of course, no compulsion to seek membership. In Europe only four of the smallish independent states (Iceland, Luxembourg, Cyprus, and Malta) with populations of under 700,000 have applied for membership. Liechtenstein, Monaco, San Marino, and the Holy See[3] have not applied.[4] In the Pacific three newly independent small states—Western Samoa, Nauru, and Tonga—had not applied for membership by the end of 1972. But the pressure towards conformity is strong. All the African and nearly all the Asian independent states have applied for and been admitted to membership, although the cost of maintaining a mission in New York and payment of the minimum annual contribution (0·04 per cent. of the UN annual budget) impose a heavy strain on many of them.

Participation without Membership

Non-members of the United Nations are not relegated to outer darkness. States such as Liechtenstein and Monaco are parties to the

Statute of the International Court of Justice. Several non-member states are full members of certain specialized agencies (e.g. the World Health Organization); and some technical agencies admit to full membership, associate membership, or observer status territories which have not even achieved independence. Again, non-member states may be admitted to full membership, and non-self-governing territories to associate membership, of the four regional economic commissions established under United Nations auspices; thereby they become eligible for a share in the somewhat shallow pool of UN technical assistance funds.

It is also possible for a non-member state to maintain a permanent observer mission at UN headquarters. This is, in effect, ' distinguished visitor' status, importing rights to sit in the galleries, to receive most of the voluminous documentation, to use members' social facilities, but not to participate in the proceedings. At least an observer has the opportunity of making friends and influencing people. But his status is manifestly that of an outsider.

Finally, the Charter includes provisions for protecting non-member states from the threat or use of force, and for the examination, by the political organs of the United Nations, of disputes between members and non-members.

Improvements in Services for Non-Members

Nineteen of the states which acceded to membership of the United Nations between 1963 and 1972 had populations of under a million. Although the Organization is already bloated it may be able to accommodate a small number of new members without too much difficulty. But any mass incursion (e.g. if the British associated states in the Eastern Caribbean were all to opt for independence and apply for membership [5]) would present big practical problems. Suggestions for new approaches towards the mini-state problem have, on the whole, been prompted less by a solicitude for the international welfare of small states than by the need to protect the United Nations itself against the prospect of inundation.

Three preliminary points must be stressed. First, proposals involving amendments to the Charter are generally regarded as unrealistic. Formal constitutional amendment in a delicately balanced political society is often an imprudent exercise; at the United Nations it can be accomplished without acrimony only in highly exceptional circumstances. Secondly, there is little enthusiasm for hard work that yields negligible political dividends. Thirdly, schemes for accommodating independent mini-states *ought* to be distinct from (though in practice they tend to run into) ideas for facilitating the progress of small dependent territories towards international sovereignty.

Of the schemes hitherto published, only two merit serious consideration. The first originated in 1969. The United States representative on the Security Council proposed the establishment of a committee to consider the question of associate membership. The Security Council set up a committee of experts, consisting of *all* its members, to examine the problem. Between September 1969 and June 1970 it held eight meetings. On 15 June 1970 it issued a brief interim report [6] indicating merely that it was still considering the proposals already put to it and would submit a further report to the Security Council in due course.

Under the American proposal, an associate member would enjoy broadly the same rights as a full member other than the rights to vote and hold office, and would be exempt from the obligation to pay a financial assessment. Possible objections to this proposal are that it might (i) entail an amendment to the Charter and (ii) encourage rather than discourage the political appeal of the United Nations for mini-states. The United Kingdom's subsequent proposal for associate membership was rather more subtle. The associate member would initially apply for membership in accordance with Article 4 of the Charter, but at the same time it would voluntarily *renounce* its rights to vote and to be a candidate for election to offices. This proposal might meet objection (i) above, but would still be open to objection (ii) except in so far as the United Kingdom proposal envisaged that associate members would pay nominal financial contributions. A further objection to both proposals, in the eyes of members out of sympathy with the Western powers, might be that they would tend to diminish the prospective voting strength of the anti-colonial bloc. Such an objection would not be particularly cogent. There is already an overwhelming anti-colonial majority at the United Nations, and it is composed mainly of smallish and poor states.[7] Some of the candidates for independence who might be attracted by the idea of non-voting associate membership could well be countries heavily dependent on Western aid.

These proposals, however, failed to command sufficient support at the time; and in 1971 the United Nations acquired five new members —Bahrain, Qatar, Oman, Bhutan, and the United Arab Emirates— all with populations of under a million.

It is worth mentioning that Nauru, a wealthy phosphate island of 6,000 inhabitants in the Western Pacific, which became independent in January 1968, became a ' special member ' of the Commonwealth in November 1968 without opposition from the existing full members. Special membership, a new category devised *ad hoc*, entitled the member to full participation in Commonwealth affairs other than representation at Meetings of Heads of Government, the political forum of the Commonwealth. The relevance of this precedent is not that it is directly applicable to UN membership—the Commonwealth is the least rule-bound and most flexible of international organizations —but that a few countries may be willing to accept, in effect, limited membership of the United Nations because they have no strong desire to cut a dash on the international scene or to maintain a permanent mission in New York.

The second scheme, not necessarily incompatible with the proposals for associate membership of the United Nations, is for the establishment of a special unit within the UN Secretariat for the benefit of small non-member states.[8] It would be a clearing-house for factual information and possibly a channel for supplying specialized advice at the request of non-member states. In some aspects it would be comparable to the Commonwealth Secretariat. But if such a unit were to become a medium for affording significantly preferential treatment to its clients, the outcry from indigent and not so small member states would be formidable.

III

Decolonization: a Theological Text [9]

How far the activities of the United Nations since 1960 have accelerated decolonization is largely a matter for conjecture. One can point to a few unequivocal demonstrations of United Nations influence —Spain's grant of independence to Equatorial Guinea in 1968 is the most obvious example—and in other cases (e.g. Nauru, Tonga) the prevailing ethos at the United Nations must have been of some importance in directing local political leaders towards the goal of untrammelled independence.

Whatever may have been the direct practical effect of United Nations pressure towards decolonization, that pressure is a fact of life. Each year the General Assembly passes a number of resolutions asserting the inalienable rights of named dependent territories to self-determination and independence. In 1967, for example, there were special resolutions for Southern Rhodesia, territories under Portuguese rule, other dependent territories in Southern Africa, Oman (surely an independent state even at that time), Nauru (independent in 1968), New Guinea, Fiji (independent in 1970), Gibraltar (which was in effect designated for retrocession to Spain), Ifni (ceded to Morocco in 1969) and Spanish Sahara, Equatorial Guinea (independent in 1968), and French Somaliland. Finally, there was a general resolution covering American Samoa, Antigua, the Bahamas, Bermuda, the British Virgin Islands, the Cayman Islands, the Cocos (Keeling) Islands, Dominica, the Gilbert and Ellice Islands, Grenada, Guam,

Mauritius, Montserrat, the New Hebrides, Niue, Pitcairn, St. Helena, St. Kitts-Nevis-Anguilla, St. Lucia, St. Vincent, the Seychelles, the Solomon Islands, Swaziland, the Tokelau Islands, the Turks and Caicos Islands, and the United States Virgin Islands. Of the territories in this general list, only Mauritius and Swaziland had become independent by the end of 1972. Of the others, only the Bahamas was an obvious candidate for independence in the immediately foreseeable future. Pitcairn had fewer than 100 inhabitants, the Cocos (Keeling) Islands about 1,000; the Tokelau Islands barely 2,000; five others had fewer than 10,000; none had more than 160,000 inhabitants. And the list could well have been longer: various factors were responsible for some deliberate omissions. For instance, the British Indian Ocean Territory (under 1,000), created in 1965 for strategic purposes, was left out because the United Nations had refused to recognize its legitimate existence; the Falkland Islands, because sovereignty over them was in dispute between Britain and Argentina; the French overseas territories (other than French Somaliland), because for many years they had been treated as if they were integral parts of France.

The background to this elaborate exercise was General Assembly Resolution 1514 (XV), the ' Anti-Colonial Charter ', adopted in December 1960 after the massive influx of newly independent African states. This resolution, invoking references in the Charter to fundamental human rights and the principle of self-determination, proclaimed ' the necessity of bringing to a speedy and unconditional end colonialism in all its forms and manifestations ', and declared that the subjection of peoples to alien domination and exploitation was contrary to the Charter and an impediment to world peace, and that inadequacy of preparedness ' should never serve as a pretext for delaying independence '. The only form of freedom referred to in the Declaration was independence; the word independence appeared eight times. And the right to freedom was ' inalienable '.

The chosen instrument for securing the implementation of the Declaration was a special committee, known after 1962 as the Committee of Twenty-four. The committee has been composed of seven African members, five Asian members, four European Communist members, and eight other members including the United States, the United Kingdom, and Australia. It is not and seldom purports to be an impartial body; it is an inquisitor and a scourge, and its victims are the remaining ' colonial ' powers. (Australia withdrew from the committee in 1969 but rejoined in 1973. The United States and the United Kingdom have ceased to participate in the committee's proceedings.) Its disregard for unpalatable facts which happen to contradict the preconceptions of the majority of its members can be quite remarkable.[10] But it enjoys the acclaim of the Assembly.

The doctrinal exegesis of Resolution 1514 has been interesting. The Resolution enjoins respect for the territorial integrity of every country within its ambit. The 'self' to be determined is to be the existing political entity. Hence decolonization frowns on fragmentation, and the separatist ambitions of the Anguillans, the Barbudans, and the Banabans of Ocean Island in the Gilbert and Ellice group ought not to be encouraged. To this extent the Committee of Twenty-four, despite its absurd resolutions on Pitcairn and the Tokelau Islands, has tended to inhibit the proliferation of minuscule states. It has also expressed support for the idea of federal groupings in the West Indies. In some instances (e.g. Ifni, Gibraltar) decolonization is to be effected not by granting the colony independence as an entity, but by its integration, willy-nilly, with a contiguous independent state. The colonized cannot, of course, opt to remain under the yoke of 'colonialism', any more than a slave can consent to the perpetuation of his servitude.

Alternatives to Independence?

Apart from integration with a neighbouring independent state, accession to separate independence may appear to be the only acceptable form of decolonization. But in 1965 there was the special case of the Cook Islands, a New Zealand dependency in the South-West Pacific.

The case of the Cook Islands takes one back to General Assembly Resolution 1541 (XV), also passed in December 1960. In lineage and content it differed from Resolution 1514. Resolution 1541 was the last and most comprehensive attempt to identify the factors determining whether a territory had attained a 'full measure of self-government' so as to exempt the former administering authority from its obligations, under Article 73e of the UN Charter, to transmit to the Secretariat information in respect of a non-self-governing territory. A non-self-governing territory could be said to have achieved a full measure of self-government by one of three routes: emergence as a sovereign independent state; 'free association' with an independent state; and integration with an independent state. Integration had to be the result of a free choice and on a basis of complete equality; these conditions were not met by Portugal's overseas 'provinces'. Free association meant something less than full integration; the associated territory would retain its own individual characteristics and would be entitled not only to determine its own constitution but also to modify its own status by democratic processes. Freedom to associate implied freedom to dissociate.

In the 1950s the United Nations had accepted the following constitutional changes, falling short of separate independence, as conferring on dependent territories a ' full measure of self-government ': Greenland's integration with Denmark; the union, akin to a loose federal relationship, between the Dutch Antilles and Surinam, on the one hand, and the Netherlands, on the other; the accession of Hawaii and Alaska to statehood (full integration) within the United States of America; and attainment of ' Commonwealth status ' by Puerto Rico, an unincorporated territory of the United States.[11] Puerto Rico's unique relationship with the United States bore the closest resemblance to free association, but it might also be regarded as a case of imperfect integration entailing a large measure of internal self-government; the territory was not legally free to sever its relationship with the United States, nor was the legislative competence of the United States Congress or the executive competence of the President in relation to Puerto Rico relinquished or strictly circumscribed.

Given the climate of opinion formed by the changes in United Nations membership, the adoption of Resolution 1514 (XV), and the establishment of the Committee of Twenty-four, it is unlikely that the arrangements for the Kingdom of the Netherlands or the Commonwealth of Puerto Rico would have been approved by the General Assembly as authentic acts of decolonization after 1960. Indeed, Resolution 1541 (XV) seemed a sickly *enfant de vieux*, half-smothered in its cradle by its bouncing contemporary 1514. The Committee of Twenty-four hardly bothered to recognize its existence.

New Zealand, a minor ' colonial ' power, had taken the United Nations seriously. It had granted independence to its small trust territory, Western Samoa, in 1962; and it had not acted under duress. It remained saddled with three poor, minute dependencies—the Cook Islands (pop. 19,000), Niue (5,000), and the Tokelau Islands (2,000). With the Cook Islanders it took the initiative, offering them four optional destinations: independence, integration with New Zealand, membership of an as yet non-existent Polynesian Federation, or free association. The Islanders preferred free association, and a scheme was worked out whereby the Islands would have total self-government in internal affairs, with New Zealand retaining responsibility for their defence and external affairs but lacking effective authority to give effect to these responsibilities in the law of the Cook Islands in the absence of local concurrence. And the Cook Islands were empowered to end their relationship with New Zealand and proceed unilaterally to independence.

The New Zealand government was at pains to keep the United Nations informed of developments, and the elections in the Cook Islands preceding the introduction of associated statehood in 1965 were observed and reported on by a UN supervisor. It was clear that the Cook Islands had what they really wanted. But they had not chosen to take advantage of their ' inalienable ' right to independence. Some members of the Committee of Twenty-four were distinctly unhappy at this turn of events. The Committee passed a somewhat equivocal resolution. In the Fourth Committee of the General Assembly a more positive attitude was adopted, and it was accepted that the Cook Islands had freely determined their own future and attained a full measure of self-government; but the necessary resolution was passed only after a wrecking amendment had been rejected by 29:28 with 43 abstentions. The General Assembly approved the arrangements, noting that they were not inconsistent with Resolution 1514 (XV); the United Nations would be delighted to help propel the Cook Islands into sovereign independence one fine day.

The United Kingdom government had watched developments on the Cook Islands question, and saw free association as a sensible means of terminating colonial status for some of its small dependencies which could not realistically expect to support the burdens of independence but which were able to sustain a system of internal self-government. Late in 1965, after all hope of reconstructing a West Indies Federation had been shattered for the foreseeable future, it published a scheme for associated statehood arrangements for six small island colonies in the Eastern Caribbean—Antigua, Dominica, Grenada, St. Kitts-Nevis-Anguilla, St. Lucia, and St. Vincent.[12] After a series of constitutional conferences held in London in 1966, detailed agreements were reached with local political leaders. The West Indies Act 1967 was passed; constitutions were made in pursuance of it; associated statehood came into effect early in 1967 in the first five territories, and in 1969 in St. Vincent where there had been a confused political situation. There was ostensibly no serious controversy about the merits of the scheme. Even the Anguillan elected representative concurred.

From the United Nations Britain received little more than harsh rebukes for this exercise in decolonization. The United Nations had been faced with a fait accompli; no UN presence had been invited during the deliberative or penultimate stages before the introduction of associated statehood, and members of the Committee of Twenty-four were not satisfied—they are very hard to satisfy—that the territories really did not want independence. And, of course, there were extraneous issues—Rhodesia, the Middle East, Viet-Nam, and so on. It was in vain for the British delegates to invoke the Cook Islands and Resolution 1541. For the majority of members, fundamentalism and Resolution 1514 prevailed.

Anyone unfamiliar with the characteristics of debate at the United

Nations might be surprised that hardly any attention was paid to a rather important difference between the British Caribbean scheme and New Zealand's scheme for the Cook Islands. Under the West Indies Act 1967 the United Kingdom parliament and government retained paramount powers for giving effect to Britain's retained responsibilities for the defence and external affairs of the associated states. Only when these powers were exercised in an attempt to subdue the secessionist island of Anguilla, early in 1969, did attention focus on this aspect of the British scheme. The Committee of Twenty-four was comfortingly fortified in its conviction that associated statehood in the Caribbean was a bogus form of decolonization. This conviction hardened in 1971 when the British government, unable to curb separatist sentiment in Anguilla, in effect placed the island temporarily under colonial rule against the wishes of the government of the associated state of St. Kitts-Nevis-Anguilla.[13]

Assuming that future association schemes are treated by the United Nations strictly on their individual merits—and this is an optimistic assumption to make—it is reasonably clear that the former administering authority will have to discharge a heavy burden of proof before it can obtain its release from the 'UN hook'. Association, as an alternative to independence, tends to be unattractive to the majority of United Nations members for the very reason that makes it attractive to some administering powers: it keeps the territory within the general international orbit of the former 'colonial master'. And although the territory may still be entitled to proceed unilaterally to independence, the economic price that it will then have to pay for independence may be crippling for a very small state.

I V

The Curious Case of Micronesia

The political entity now called Micronesia is the Trust Territory of the Pacific Islands, under American administration.[14] Formerly the Japanese mandated territory, it covers a sea area of some three million square miles in the northwest Pacific. Its land area is barely seven hundred square miles. It includes about 2,100 islands, of which ninety-six are inhabited; the population is just under 100,000. Micronesia is one of the last two remaining trust territories—the other is Australian New Guinea—and it is unique in being a strategic trust territory. The administering authority is empowered by the UN Charter to use a strategic trust territory for defence purposes—the United States has interpreted this as justifying it in conducting nuclear tests and establishing an anti-missile missile station in Micronesia—and such a territory comes under the aegis of the Security Council, not the General

Assembly. The instrument of the Security Council for this purpose is the Trusteeship Council, which in 1972 was composed of the five permanent members of the Security Council (the United States, the United Kingdom, France, China, and the Soviet Union) and Australia, as an administering authority.

Few people know where Micronesia is; and fewer still are aware of what has been happening in Micronesia. Till the early 1960s the only well-known names in the territory were Bikini and Eniwetok, both in the Marshall Islands. The territory was administered first from Hawaii and then from Guam. The Mariana Islands other than Guam form part of the trust territory; [15] the seat of government was moved to Guam's neighbour, Saipan, an island within the trust territory, in 1961. Guam, itself a celebrated American naval and air force base, belongs to the United States; [16] it is an unincorporated territory, like American Samoa and the United States Virgin Islands. The Guamanians often claim, perhaps correctly, that they are the most patriotic Americans on the face of the earth. The Micronesians make no such claim. They are not American citizens and few of them wish to be; they do not aim to become part of the great American family. Anyone familiar with British colonial developments would regard Micronesia as in effect an American protectorate with a limited measure of internal self-government; whereas the unincorporated territories (and Puerto Rico) are analogous to colonial dependencies with a large measure of self-government. But American politicians and administrators will hotly deny that America has or has ever had colonies. Moreover, a great number of well-informed and intelligent Americans can hardly conceive that a territory and people enjoying the benefits of American rule could disdain the prospect of belonging fully to the American constitutional system. These are important clues to American thinking about the future status of Micronesia.

Again, American attitudes towards the destinations of its dependencies have persistently emphasized the need for ' political maturity ' and economic viability before constitutional advancement can be approved. To an outside observer all this may seem rather old-fashioned. But the fact is that America's first preference would be to persuade the Micronesians to become an unincorporated territory of the United States, like Guam. And this would, of course, offer the fullest safeguard to American strategic interests in the islands. Probably all members of the United Nations would disapprove of such an outcome; and many would be bitterly hostile. Up to the time of writing, every trust territory which has terminated its status has attained independence in its own right, or by integration with a neighbouring state, as an act of free will. Annexation by the trustee, under pressure and in the trustee's own interests, would be an almost unthinkable denouement.

Developments in Micronesia can be briefly outlined. For nearly twenty years after American occupation in 1945 the territory stagnated; the Japanese settlers, who had outnumbered the native Micronesians, were soon deported, and the thriving economy swiftly crumbled. Not until the Kennedy administration came to office was a serious effort made to rebuild the foundations; and appropriations by the United States Congress mounted till they reached the formidable figure of sixty million dollars in 1971. Still, the massive problems of distance, population dispersal, dearth of natural resources, and diminutive land areas militated against significant economic development outside the district centres.

Meanwhile, constitutional progress had begun. A wholly elected bicameral Congress of Micronesia was constituted in 1965. As in other American territories, it was set apart from the executive branch of government. Most of its members were youngish men, fluent in English, with secondary or higher education. In 1966 they were beginning to think about Micronesia's ultimate status. In 1967 the Congress of Micronesia set up a Future Political Status Commission. About the same time, the President of the United States submitted to Congress in Washington a proposal to set up a status commission to examine the issues with a view to enabling the people of Micronesia freely to express their wishes not later than mid-1972. The President's recommendation encountered some resistance in Congress and unfortunately proved abortive. The Micronesian Commission set to work, visited various island territories in the Pacific and the Caribbean, and in 1969 made a detailed final report suggesting two alternatives —free association with the United States, or independence.

One disadvantage of a free-association arrangement was that it might prove unacceptable to the United Nations. On the other hand, it made good sense for Micronesia. The territory would have full control over its internal affairs; the United States would remain responsible for its defence and external affairs; this arrangement might meet America's minimum requirements as well as relieving Micronesia of burdens it could not support and giving a reasonable assurance of continuing American financial and technical aid. It is undoubtedly true that for many Micronesians independence would be a preferable outcome. Yet the risks of opting for independence were enormous. The United States was providing well over 95 per cent of Micronesia's budget. It might lose interest in Micronesia and leave the territory to fend for itself, competing with other claimants for a dwindling pool of foreign aid. The short-term decline in local living standards would be catastrophic were America to stop its subsidies; it could not be expected to continue them at the existing level if its defence facilities were withdrawn or seriously jeopardized; and Micronesia could maintain itself as a going concern only if another power were to step into America's shoes—a contingency which the United States would hardly view with equanimity. Probably Micronesia needed America more than America—even if shorn of its Okinawan bases—would need Micronesia. Therein lay the weakness of the Micronesian bargaining position in negotiations with the United States.

Inconclusive discussions between a Micronesian delegation and representatives of the Federal government took place in Washington late in 1969; they were strictly confidential. When a visiting mission of the Trusteeship Council visited Micronesia early in 1970 the confidentiality of the negotiations on status was heavily underlined; the report of the mission, typically thorough on all other issues, must be regarded as a damp squib on this all-important matter, though the mission was sympathetic to Micronesian aspirations. The mission came and went, and then the Federal government got down to serious business. A high-level delegation of officials met the elected Micronesian delegation in May 1970. The outcome was disagreement and, for the time being, deadlock. The Federal government was willing to contemplate ' Commonwealth status ' for Micronesia along the lines of the relationship between the United States and Puerto Rico; this was at least an improvement on the idea of making Micronesia an unincorporated territory like Guam, lacking full internal self-government. But the Federal government rejected the concepts not only of Micronesian independence but also free association along the lines of the Cook Islands or Eastern Caribbean schemes, because that would have left Micronesia free to proceed to independence of its own volition. American strategic interests—presumably in denying access to Micronesia to potentially hostile powers—remained paramount.

For the Micronesians this was a bitter blow. Not only would their right of self-determination be circumscribed; they would be expected, under ' Commonwealth status ', to afford American businessmen free access to Micronesia and to acquiesce in the existing power of the Federal government to acquire land as it thought fit for military purposes.

The situation in mid-1970 was therefore profoundly unsatisfactory. In a spirit of realism the Micronesian Congressmen were prepared to sacrifice their emotional preference for independence. They were not prepared to see Micronesia integrated with the American constitutional system. However, the disparity in power between the Micronesians and the administering authority was enormous; and they were in danger of succumbing to subtle coercion combined with less than subtle financial inducements. Moreover, their own show of solidarity was constantly under stress because of internal dissensions. Insular separatism was and is a stronger force than Micronesian nationalism, and in the Mariana Islands district there was a particularly active movement in favour of union or association with Guam.[17] Nor was it clear how the Micronesians' bargaining position could be strengthened. The routine remonstrances of the Committee of Twenty-four [18] went unheeded by the administering authority; the voices of America's allies in the Pacific were muted; American public opinion was hardly a force to be reckoned with on the Micronesian issue. The Micronesians were obliged to pin their faint hopes on a re-appraisal of strategic needs by the Federal government—after all, America's vital interests called for little more than the denial of Micronesia's facilities to potentially hostile powers—and on the implications of the fact that in order to terminate the trusteeship agreement, the United States would need the approval of the Security Council, on which any of the permanent members would be able to cast its veto.

Deadlock continued till the latter part of 1971. But when the status negotiations were resumed in October 1971 in Hawaii, the United States delegation had shifted its position. No longer was there insistence on 'Commonwealth status' as the ultimate destination for Micronesia. Instead, relations between the United States and Micronesia could be regulated by a negotiated Compact of Association. The authority of the United States in relation to Micronesia would thereafter be confined essentially to defence and external affairs. The future constitution and laws of Micronesia would not have to conform to United States law, though they would have to be consistent with the Compact. Bases in Micronesia would be occupied by the United States, but any subsequent acquisition of land in Micronesia for strategic purposes would have to be on agreed terms. However, the Micronesian demand for a right to withdraw unilaterally from the Compact was rejected.

Further progress was made in April 1972 at discussions held in Palau in Micronesia. The American delegation conceded the principle of entitlement to unilateral withdrawal from the proposed Compact, subject to its having been in force for a period of fifteen years. The Micronesians were not satisfied with this limitation, and they also sought fuller assurances on financial matters; but the outlines of an acceptable free-association arrangement, under which the Micronesians would have full control over their internal affairs, had emerged. The proposed Compact would have to be approved by the Micronesian Congress and people as well as by the United States Congress. America's strategic presence in Micronesia would be guaranteed by a treaty which would not necessarily terminate if the free association arrangement were to be dissolved.

However, more difficulties lay ahead. The Congress of Micronesia refused to approve the draft Compact of Association, and began to make louder noises about independence. An important factor in the situation was the unexpected extent of America's new strategic demands in Micronesia. These included a large part of the land area of Palau district, as well as the restoration of an airfield on the small island of Tinian in the Marianas. It was from Tinian that a B29 had taken off on a mission bound for Hiroshima on 6 August 1945.

Early in 1973 the Americans were holding talks with their separatist admirers in the Marianas, negotiations with the Congress of Micronesia having reverted to a state of deadlock.

At the time of writing it was not clear how far (if at all) the United Nations would be associated with Micronesia's act of self-determination. Nor was it even clear that the climate of opinion at the United Nations had had any influence at all over the reshaping of American policy towards Micronesia; though one may reasonably surmise that the very fact that Micronesia was one of the two remaining UN trust territories was of some account. But the case of Micronesia epitomizes some of the problems besetting small and poor dependent territories and their rulers in the era of decolonization. The end of empire is not yet; colonialism may take an unconscionable time dying. Constructive initiatives emanating from the United Nations have been almost negligible. If the Organization is to play any useful role in resolving the dilemmas of Micronesia and other minute territories, its members will need to show a measure of realism and imagination that will confound their detractors.

A VIEW FROM WITHIN:
THE ROLE OF THE SMALL STATES
AND THE CYPRUS EXPERIENCE *

ANDREAS J. JACOVIDES †

*I met John McMahon at Cambridge as a fellow law student
soon after I went up in 1955. His keen sense of humour, his
generosity, his open-mindedness, and his other great human
qualities of heart and mind were only too apparent and we were
friends throughout the three years of undergraduate work, the
year of study for the LL.B. in international law, and later at
Harvard and in New York.*

*The present essay, which was prepared in draft form barely
two weeks before his death, was probably the last one that he
had the occasion to go through, at my request, for corrections
and suggestions. He returned it with a few minor observations
and an undue amount of praise. It is almost unbelievable that it
should now serve as a contribution to this memorial volume.*

I COME from a country which, from the beginning of its existence
as an independent state, has always attached cardinal importance
to its membership of the United Nations, has been dedicated by
word and deed to the Charter and its principles and proved by the
position it has taken on the variety of issues on which it has been
called upon to take a stand, whether in the Organization itself or in
the Non-aligned or the Commonwealth Conferences, that it is what
one might call ' United Nations-minded '. Being a very small country,
unencumbered by exclusive ties to either of the two major blocs in the
cold war and having no world-wide military, political, or economic
interests of its own to further, Cyprus found it possible to make the
United Nations and the principles of its Charter central to its foreign
policy,[1] particularly during the years 1960 to 1963 when it did not
labour under the strains of a political problem of its own. It never

* © Andreas J. Jacovides 1973. This essay is based on a paper for the
symposium 'Towards a More Effective UN: Prospects for Peacekeeping'
organized by the Iowa Soc. of Int. and Comparative Law for the Midwest
Regional Meeting of ASIL, Mar. 1969.

† Minister Plenipotentiary, Deputy Permanent Representative of Cyprus to
the United Nations. This essay presents the views of the author in his
personal capacity.

hesitated to take positions dictated primarily, if not solely, by its dedication to the furtherance of the aims of the United Nations. It so happened that this attitude, determined by its commitment to principle, coincided with the country's enlightened self-interest as a small and militarily weak state depending for its security on the collective security system of the United Nations and, as a developing country, standing to gain through multilateral technical assistance and know-how. Both in the political and the economic fields, the attitude of Cyprus as a small state was conditioned by its understanding of what was in the best interest of the United Nations consistently with what was in the best interest of Cyprus itself.

In saying this, I sincerely hope that I shall not be understood as wishing to portray the country of which I happen to be an official as being always on the side of the angels—indeed, some may hold a very different view—but because this attitude is illustrative of that which many small, newly independent, economically developing countries have towards the United Nations.

No doubt, dedication to the Organization is not limited to this category of states. However, while not wishing in any way to cast aspersions upon the major powers as regards their attitude towards the United Nations—and in fact their respective philosophies vary substantially—I cannot help but recall the picture of Dag Hammar-skjöld, who, sitting on the podium of the General Assembly Hall and holding his pencil in his typical way, in 1960, after hearing the then Premier of the Soviet Union denounce him from the very rostrum of the General Assembly, refused to resign and explained his position by stressing that ' It is not the Soviet Union or indeed any other big Powers which need the United Nations for their protection. It is all the others. In this sense, the Organization is first of all their Organiza-tion . . .' [2]

It is the nations of the Third World, which now constitute more than two-thirds of the total membership of the Organization, that are the main beneficiaries of the existence of the United Nations and its activities. At the same time their contribution should not be under-estimated. ' The new nations ', U Thant said in the course of his address at the University of Denver on 3 April 1964,

have brought new and refreshing perspectives to old controversies and issues. They have shown an independence and common sense which compares very favourably, for example, with the long, arid and vitu-perative debates of the worst years of the cold war. . . . In fact they have greatly contributed to a more balanced and realistic atmosphere by staying outside of the East-West ideological struggle. They have loyally supported the United Nations in its peace-keeping operations in sensitive parts of the world, and they have often produced useful and constructive initiatives in finding solutions to great political problems.[3]

COMMON ATTITUDES OF SMALL STATES TOWARDS
UNITED NATIONS PEACEKEEPING

While it would be a mistake to carry the generalization too far, it is correct, I believe, to state that there exist certain common characteristics in the attitude of smaller states towards the UN in general and towards peacekeeping in particular to warrant the use of the term ' role of the small states '. While this category is necessarily inexact and it is occasionally used to cover, in this context, the related and overlapping categories of the Third World, newly independent, and non-aligned states—some of which are far from small—the term, as used here, denotes those states manifesting certain common attitudes. In the first place they are the states which have a vital stake in the continuity and strengthening of the United Nations for their security and economic development, and are prepared to use their collective weight to prevent a confrontation of the major powers which might ruin the Organization or even destroy the world. In the second place, they are the states which, when confronted by a real emergency in which their security, independence and territorial integrity are threatened, are prepared to a less or greater extent to place reliance on the United Nations, in preference to other alternatives (such as a military alliance of which they are not parties or regional or quasi-regional arrangements [4]) to the extent of consenting to the limitations of sovereignty which the presence of a UN force necessarily implies. In the third place, these are the states upon which, as a rule, the Organization draws for contributing forces when the need for setting up a peacekeeping force arises. Moreover, it is primarily and perhaps in practice exclusively, in the territories of these states that the United Nations is likely to be called upon, and in fact permitted, to set up peacekeeping operations—as opposed to territories of states which are either major powers themselves or are considered by the major powers to fall under their exclusive sphere of influence, whether for strategic or ideological reasons, as indeed recent events in this hemisphere and in central Europe have reminded us.[5]

At the risk of being accused of flippancy, I would like to recall the saying that whenever a dispute is brought to the United Nations, something will inevitably disappear. If it is a dispute between two small powers, the dispute will disappear; if it is one between a large power and a small one, the small power will disappear; and if it is a dispute between two big powers, the United Nations will disappear. If one makes allowances for its cynicism, perhaps the picture is not too far removed from reality.

THE ORIGINAL CHARTER SCHEME FOR COLLECTIVE SECURITY AND THE PRESENT SITUATION

It was, no doubt, the express first purpose of the United Nations ' to maintain international peace and security' and it was stressed in Article 1 of the Charter that to that end it was ' to take effective collective measures for the prevention and removal of threats to the peace, and for the suppression of acts of aggression or other breaches of the peace.' Under Article 24, it was envisaged that the Security Council, upon which the Members of the Organization conferred primary responsibility for the maintenance of international peace and security, would take prompt and effective action in this respect, and, in Chapter VII, a detailed scheme was set out to regulate such action.

It would be belabouring the obvious to discuss at any length the circumstances under which the ostensibly watertight system of collective security—through the Security Council's being able to decide and act—was rendered impotent by the exercise of the veto which in turn was made inevitable through the advent of the cold war. ' Naturally ', stated Mr Gromyko in 1945, ' the very best and most perfect Charter in itself is not yet a guarantee that its provisions will be carried out and insure the preservation of peace. In order to achieve this important and noble task, it is also necessary, in addition to the existing Charter, to have the unity and co-ordination of members of the International Organization, and first of all the unity and co-ordination of actions between the most powerful military powers of the world.' [6] These essential preconditions were simply not present in the years immediately following the signing of the Charter, for reasons that we need not go into now, and there is no prospect of this situation changing in the immediate future. Whether in the next decade [7] or longer there will have taken place some fundamental realignment, particularly among the two super-powers, any valid expectation of change in this respect can only be a matter of speculation—although there have recently been indications to that effect—and for the purposes of the present essay, we should proceed on the assumption that the collective security system, as envisaged in the Charter,[8] will remain in a state of impotence.

In addition to the lack of unanimity among the great powers there has been another fundamental reason for the transition away from the collective security system as envisaged in 1945. Due to the radical changes brought about in the nature and effects of war through the development of atomic and hydrogen weapons of mass destruction by the great powers, it would be unreasonable to expect that military forces of these powers will be employed in practice, as contemplated by the Charter. The mutual balance of terror has precluded any thought of using the forces of great powers against each other—even if there were any possibility of circumventing the exercise of the veto—and, in cases where armed forces through the United Nations have been employed, the tendency has been in practice to rely upon the military resources of the smaller powers. This has had the distinct advantage of avoiding great power confrontation or entangling the United Nations too deeply in the antagonism of the cold war.

It is generally acknowledged that the one collective action undertaken under the aegis of the United Nations—in Korea—was made possible by highly exceptional circumstances. It raised many questions as to whether it was a genuine UN operation and it is not at all likely that anything in a similar form will recur in the future. It can only be a matter of speculation whether operations could be envisaged involving enforcement action within Chapter VII presupposing great-power unanimity. The 1966 decision of the Security Council authorizing Britain to use force in connection with Southern Rhodesia [9] is a possible example. The possibility of a Security Council decision under Chapter VII to take action, e.g. against South Africa in connection with the latter's refusal to implement United Nations decisions in connection with Namibia, cannot be excluded even though at present it does not appear to be a very realistic prospect. But, barring such exceptional cases, where the interests of the great powers and of their 'clients' may happen to coincide, the collective security system of Chapter VII, under present circumstances, does not have a bright future in front of it.

In the light of this situation what then is the prospect for United Nations peacekeeping?

PROPOSALS FOR A PERMANENT UNITED NATIONS PEACE FORCE

The proponents of a system of world government give their answer as the creation of a permanent United Nations peace force recruited by and for the United Nations with United Nations allegiance, organized, commanded, and financed by the United Nations.[10] Nor has this line of thought been limited to individuals. A number of states, including Cyprus, have not been shy in advocating the same objective. My own chief, the Chairman of the delegation of Cyprus, for example, had occasion to stress that 'Measures will have to be taken for the establishment and systematic development of a United Nations peace force, recruited by and for the United Nations, which would form the basis of an international security force. The primary allegiance of such a United Nations force would be directly to the United Nations, rendering this force truly international in the service of mankind.' [11] On another occasion, he remarked that 'loaned forces, owing allegiance to the States from which they come, cannot be fully relied upon for United Nations actions. They may, for one thing, be withdrawn at any time—as was the case in the Congo.' [12] And again, in connection with the financing of future peacekeeping operations, he said that 'there are many ways by which contributions could be obtained from the peoples of the world, as distinct from their Governments, for instance, through a very small special tax or a stamp duty.' [13]

There is no doubt that the idea of projecting the stability and orderliness of a well-governed state onto the plane of relations between states has a lot to commend it. It has long been a noble human aspiration, reflected in many a scheme from ancient times onwards to develop an international order regulated by a system of universal law and backed by an effective international force. The United Nations was seen by many at the time it was set up—and is still seen by some today—as that form of world government, whether with its present or with an improved or otherwise supplemented constitution. But I believe most will agree today that there is a great distance between the dream and the reality—the need and the fulfilment of the need. This ideal system presupposes an absence of fundamental conflict of interest and a willingness on the part of all states to surrender a very large measure of their sovereignty to a super-state or supranational authority. These essential preconditions simply do not exist at present and they are not likely to exist tomorrow. It will be a long process of evolution before we reach that stage if we ever do. On the opposite side of the spectrum we find the Soviet approach—and not the Soviet alone—to the United Nations as being simply an intergovernmental organization and an institutional form of multilateral co-operation between sovereign states. According to this view the competence and functions of such international institutions are determined by the states members, on the basis of their mutual consent.

U Thant in his address to the Harvard Alumni Association at Cambridge, Massachusetts, on 13 June 1963,[14] put the subject in its proper perspective, with his customary lucidity and with his admirable blending of realism and idealism: 'In my opinion', he said, 'a permanent United Nations force is not a practical proposition at the present time.' He doubted whether many governments in the world would yet be prepared to accept the political implications of such an institution and they would have serious difficulties in accepting the financial implications. 'Personally', he continued,

'I have no doubt that the world should eventually have an international police force which will be accepted as an integral and essential part of life in the same way as national police forces are accepted. Meanwhile, we must be sure that developments are in the right direction and that we can also meet critical situations as and when they occur. . . .

I believe that we need a number of parallel developments before we can evolve such an institution. We have to go further along the road of codification and acceptance of a workable body of international law. We have to develop a more sophisticated public opinion in the world, which can accept the transition from predominantly national thinking to international thinking. We shall have to develop a deeper faith in international institutions as such, and a greater confidence in the possibility of a United Nations Civil service whose international loyalty and objectivity are generally accepted and above suspicion. We shall have to improve the method of financing international organization. Until these conditions are met, a permanent United Nations force may not be a practical proposition.' [15]

DEVELOPMENT OF
AD HOC PEACEKEEPING OPERATIONS

These words were spoken in 1963. Ten years later, despite the goodwill, imagination and ingenuity shown by many ingenious and internationally minded men and women in many parts of the world,[16] we are not appreciably nearer to the goal of a permanent UN force. But there have been some encouraging developments which, in a practical and piecemeal fashion, have gone a long way towards fulfilling the role which member states permit the United Nations to play in the field of maintenance of peace and security. I am referring to the advent of peacekeeping operations.[17] They are pioneering, improvised, ad hoc, do not fit into any streamlined grand design nor do they fulfil a logician's dream. Not two of them are identical in kind and they present considerable disadvantages as compared to a standing United Nations force. Each is tailored to the particular situation. Yet in a pragmatic unspectacular way, to a greater or less extent, they served the purpose for which each was created. These forces are very different from those envisaged in Chapter VII and yet their existence is not inconsistent with the Charter. As U Thant described them they are ' essentially peace and not fighting forces and they operate with the consent of the parties directly concerned.' [18]

What kind of forces, then, does this category encompass? At the one end of the spectrum we have groups of a few observers keeping watch on a cease-fire line or overseeing the holding of a plebiscite. At the other end we have a sizeable military force of several thousand officers and men undertaking substantial functions in accordance with their respective mandates.

Observer forces and UNTEA

Under the former category [19] fall such operations as the United Nations Special Committee on the Balkans (UNSCOB), consisting of professional military officers and authorized by the General Assembly after a series of vetoes frustrated an earlier effort in the Security Council, to observe and otherwise assist in connection with the border situation of Greece with her northern neighbours; the United Nations Military Observer Group in India and Pakistan (UNMOGIP), set up by the Security Council in 1948–9 to watch over the Kashmir situation and which is still operational; the United Nations Truce Supervision Organization (UNTSO), which since 1949 has played a vital role in the context of keeping the peace in the Middle East and which was preceded by another group that had worked from July 1948 under the United Nations Mediator in supervising the first truce agreements in the Palestine war; the military observers team assisting the United Nations Commission for Indonesia (UNCI) in 1949 during the fighting which preceded Indonesia's independence from the Netherlands; the United Nations Observation Group in Lebanon (UNOGIL), set up by the Security Council in 1958 to ensure that no infiltration was occurring into Lebanon; the United Nations Yemen Observation Mission (UNYOM), created by the Security Council in 1963 to observe whether the UAR-Saudi Arabia disengagement agreement was being implemented; the United Nations India-Pakistan Observation Mission (UNIPOM), to patrol the border between India and Pakistan, created in 1965 by the Secretary-General as part of his action in discharge of the responsibility delegated to him by the Security Council after the outbreak of war between India and Pakistan.

This enumeration, which is not exhaustive, does not cover the unique case of the United Nations Temporary Executive Authority (UNTEA) created in 1962 by the General Assembly, charged with the interim administration of West Irian in implementation of the agreement between Indonesia and the Netherlands for the eventual transfer of administrative authority in 1963 to Indonesia with a plebiscite to take place in 1969 under United Nations supervision. It was a unique case: for the first time—following upon the relinquishing of Dutch sovereignty—control, together with security functions during the interim period, was being exercised by the United Nations as such. The operation was an outstanding success under the brilliant direction of Mr Rolz-Bennett.

Military forces—UNEF, ONUC, UNFICYP

I have not so far referred to the United Nations Emergency Force (UNEF), created by the General Assembly in 1956 after the concerted attack on Egypt by Israel, France and Great Britain, and which was given the task of patrolling within Egyptian territory, with the consent of the government of that country, along the Israeli borders in the Gaza strip and in Sinai.[20] These forces withdrew in May 1967, after a request to that effect by the government of the United Arab Republic, in circumstances which gave rise to some considerable controversy at the time but which, to my mind, did not provide any valid grounds for criticism of the Secretary-General for his willingness to accede to the request.[21] Nor did I cover the United Nations Operation in the Congo (ONUC),[22] authorized by the Security Council in 1960 to perform difficult functions in a volatile and complicated situation, an operation which put great strains upon the United Nations because of its size (at its peak it numbered over 20,000 personnel contributed by some 35 countries), its cost (over $400 million), and, more significantly, the political, constitutional, legal, and financial controversies which were raised in its wake and which still plague the Organization even though the operation was wound up in the summer of 1964.

These two operations together with the United Nations Force in Cyprus (UNFICYP),[23] fall within the second category to which I referred earlier. Because of their novelty and complexity, but also because of their potential significance, each of them was accompanied by a host of problems—as is indeed reflected in the abundance of writings upon them.[24] It would therefore seem advisable, bearing in mind the limitations of time and space, to concentrate upon the Cyprus operation, of which I have had some experience, and which is the major operation that is still in existence and for which it can rightly be claimed that it has been successful and useful.

BACKGROUND TO THE CREATION OF UNFICYP

A great deal has been said and even more has been written about the background [25] of the Cyprus crisis as well as about the legal [26] and political [27] factors that were involved, but this is not the place for a recapitulation. It was undoubtedly against a background of great complexity that the first shots were fired on the night of 20–21 December 1963 which marked the beginning of the crisis.

Following the aggravation of the crisis and the first manifestations of overt intervention by Turkey on Christmas day 1963, and after the failure of a number of efforts to arrange local cease-fires, the Cyprus government—from which, by then, the Turkish Cypriot members had withdrawn—had no alternative but to accept a British government offer that the British, Greek, and Turkish troops stationed in Cyprus under the 1960 arrangement be placed under British command to help restore order. In fact this ' tripartite ' force, which became operational on 27 December 1963, was essentially British and, irrespective of the motives which prompted its involvement, it was a factor in avoiding further exacerbation of the situation.

From the very beginning of the internationalization of the conflict the Cyprus government resorted to the United Nations. On 25 December 1963 it instructed its Permanent Representative in New York to lodge a complaint with the Security Council against Turkey's acts and threats of use of force in violation of its obligations under the Charter.[28] The Permanent Representative of Cyprus discussed the situation with the Secretary-General on 26 December 1963 and, on the next day, an emergency meeting of the Security Council was held at the urgent request of the Cyprus government.[29] The meeting was inconclusive and no decision was taken pending the clarification of the situation. Meanwhile in Nicosia, bowing to the pressure of events, the Cyprus government agreed to participate in a conference with the other signatories of the Nicosia Agreements, i.e. Great Britain, Greece, and Turkey, to be held in London in January 1964. Consequently the effort in New York was suspended, though not abandoned, while for most of January the effort was on in London. Nevertheless the Cyprus government was quick to accept the suggestion that the UN be further involved through the appointment by the Secretary-General on 16 January of a Personal Representative in the island.[30] After the failure of the London Conference, successive proposals of the British government and subsequently of the British and United States governments were put forward, in a rather pressing manner,[31] for a peacekeeping force drawn from NATO countries with inexact terms of reference and for a mediator drawn also from a NATO country. These proposals were firmly rejected by the Cypriot leadership which insisted that, should there be the need for a peacekeeping force in the island, it would have to be a United Nations force under the authority of the Security Council. Those of us in New York in that tense month heard other ideas—such as a Commonwealth or Nordic force—being mooted as alternatives. Quite apart from the other factors which may have dictated the clear preference for a United Nations peacekeeping force (such as the predictable attitude of the Afro-Asian members and of the Soviet Union, not to mention the fact that apart from the proponents of the scheme and one or two other willing NATO members, the idea of expanding the area of responsibilities of this alliance was not at all enthusiastically received by the other members), I suggest that this attitude is fully consistent with the overall philosophy of the foreign policy of Cyprus as a small non-aligned country, depending for its security on, and having confidence in, not military alliances such as NATO, of which it is not a member, but the United Nations. It neatly illustrates the problem of what alternatives there are to United Nations peacekeeping.

By the middle of February 1964 the idea had ripened that, having exhausted the possibilities available through direct negotiations or through the quasi-regional forum provided by the London Conference, the problem should be tackled squarely by the Security Council. A firm decision was taken in Nicosia to this effect and it was announced that the Minister for Foreign Affairs, Mr Kyprianou, and the President of the House of Representatives, Mr Clerides, were leaving for New York to present the case for Cyprus to the Council. At that particular moment the British Mission to the United Nations thought it advisable to steal a march by submitting its own request to the Council first, with the resultant advantage that it would not appear as having been ' dragged ' before the Council, and also of speaking first. This it did at 3 p.m. on 15 February and informed the Cyprus Mission a few minutes later. I will not recount the procedural moves and debates which followed, and the only reason why I have entered into this amount of detail is that an attempt was made to capitalize on the fact that it was Britain that wanted the Security Council to be seized of the subject [32]—a case of making virtue out of necessity.

In the long debates which followed, the various aspects of the Cyprus problem were fully set out and divergent points of view were expressed.[33] Obviously the priorities of the parties were not identical but it soon emerged that the result of the deliberations would be, on the one hand, an affirmation of the basic principle of the Charter in Article 2 (4) prohibiting the use of force by one state against another,[34] and on the other, the authorization of the setting-up of a UN force to be present in Cyprus for a fixed period. At the same time the Security Council recommended that the Secretary-General designate a mediator in an effort to promote a peaceful solution. I do not propose at present to examine which side gained more out of the Security Council resolution, but, to my mind, there is no room for doubt that the Cyprus government emerged far stronger as a result.[35]

The resolution, eventually adopted on 4 March 1964, was the result of hard bargaining and compromise at every point, and, as is customary in documents of this nature, certain intentional ambiguities were inserted for the sake of general acceptance. The relevant paragraphs for the present discussion are 4, 5, and 6.[36]

UNFICYP

Setting-up, composition, size, direction, and control by the Security Council

Under paragraph 4, the Security Council recommended the creation, with the consent of the government of Cyprus, of a United Nations peacekeeping force in Cyprus. The composition and size of the Force was to be established by the Secretary-General, in consultation with the governments of Cyprus, Greece, Turkey, and the United Kingdom. The commander of the Force was to be appointed by the Secretary-General and was to report to him. It was further provided that the Secretary-General, who was to keep the governments providing the Force fully informed, would report periodically to the Security Council on its operations.

Perhaps a few brief observations at this stage will be relevant. Consistently with the legal foundation of the resolution, it was expressly stated that the consent of the host country was essential. This consent was given promptly by the Cyprus government.[37] No provisions of the Charter, other than Article 2 (4), were expressly mentioned in the resolution—it is believed, intentionally—but it is beyond doubt that its constitutional basis is to be found within the general terms of Chapter VI of the Charter and is within the general framework of the principles originally enunciated by Mr Hammarskjöld in connection with UNEF.[38]

The wording used regarding the composition of UNFICYP was such as to leave the ultimate decision for the Secretary-General but the opinion of each of the four governments mentioned therein was also made relevant. In practice this has meant a composition reflecting the minimum common denominator of forces from countries to which none of the four governments objected.[39] Countries known to be leaning exclusively towards Turkey or Cyprus were also excluded. The question of finance was also pertinent and this may well explain the absence of African or other Third World participation.[40] On the other hand, it is noteworthy that, for the first time (as far as is known) it was made the practice for a UN Secretariat official from Eastern Europe to be included in the civilian side of UNFICYP.[41] In general, the result has been that UNFICYP has been composed of contingents contributed by Canada, Sweden, Finland, Denmark, Ireland, and the United Kingdom; and units of civilian police from Australia, New Zealand, and Austria together with an Austrian medical unit and field hospital.

The only unorthodoxy and an exception from the Hammarskjöld principles in so far as composition is concerned is the participation of the United Kingdom in that (a) it is a permanent member of the Security Council and (b) it has a special interest in the situation (as a signatory of the Treaty of Guarantee and as having the Sovereign Base Areas in the island). It is explained in terms of purely practical considerations, viz. the fact that UK forces were already present as part of the 'tripartite' force prior to the existence of the UNFICYP, the fact that the British sovereign bases in the island were the backbone of the logistical support for UNFICYP, etc. In practice, this matter has not given rise to difficulties and on the whole, British troops, wearing the blue berets of the United Nations, have demonstrated that, where the circumstances require it, the armed forces even of great powers under the proper command can and do behave in accordance with United Nations standards.

It is also significant that the enabling resolution expressly provided that the commander of the force would be appointed by the Secretary-General and would report to him. This is indicative of the wide margin left to the Secretary-General in this operation and evidence of the confidence that was in fact reposed in U Thant by all shades of opinion, especially bearing in mind the doctrinal positions of the Soviet Union and France in this respect. Although both of these powers abstained on a separate vote on this paragraph because of these very doctrinal differences of view, the fact that they voted for the resolution as a whole lends substance to the view that, irrespective of positions of principle, whenever the political conditions exist— as indeed they did in the case under examination—United Nations forces will be authorized by the Security Council and neither the USSR nor France will be unduly inhibited by their doctrinal positions (as indeed was the case with other situations, e.g. UNEF, UNTEA, UNIPOM).

The Secretary-General originally appointed his former Personal Representative, General Gyani, as commander of the force, and later General Thimayya, who had not only a fine record in the Indian army but also experience in Korea, then, after his unfortunate death in December 1965, General A. E. Martola, a distinguished Finnish military man whose experience included advising the former Secretary-General Dag Hammarskjöld in 1956 and 1957 on UNEF. The deputy commander and, subsequently, the chief of staff was originally a British officer and is now a Canadian. The system appears to work well and there have been no cases, as far as is known, either of insubordination of contingent commanders or other officers to the Force Commander, or of the Commander to instructions from UN Headquarters in New York.[42]

It is noteworthy that, unlike the Congo operation, this one has no institutional advisory committee to limit in any way the Secretary-General's freedom of action, but in the present operation the Secretary-General is required to keep the governments providing the Force fully informed. This the Secretary-General has done. He has likewise been careful to report on all significant developments to the Security Council, especially when potentially controversial matters arise, thus giving to the Council members the opportunity of airing, if they so wish, their views in the Council, which remains constantly seized of the subject. So far, however, no extraordinary Security Council meeting has been held as a result of an initiative by a Council member, though a number of meetings, emergency and other, have been convened at the request of interested parties.[43]

Mandate

Under paragraph 5 the Security Council recommended that the function of the Force should be, in the interest of preserving international peace and security, to use its best efforts to prevent a recurrence of fighting, and, as necessary, to contribute to the maintenance and restoration of law and order and a return to normal conditions.

It will be noted that, particularly in the complicated Cyprus situation, this formulation left something to be desired in terms of clarity and precision, but that is the price that had to be paid for a generally acceptable text. It is not therefore surprising that it was the object of diverse interpretations. The Secretary-General stated what he understood by the mandate in an aide-memoire issued on 11 April 1964 [44] and elaborated it further in his reports to the Security Council of June 1964 [45] and September 1964 [46] subsequently reaffirmed. The Cyprus government's view was expressed by the Minister of Foreign Affairs particularly in his statement before the Council in September 1964. All in all, the Secretary-General's interpretation has been one the Cyprus government has been content to live with and be satisfied with. Furthermore it was made clear, fairly early in 1964, that it was not the mandate of the force, nor was it equipped or willing,[47] to fight off an external invasion of the island but rather, through its very presence and calming effect, to discourage and take away the pretext for one.

The only subsequent occasion when there was a serious effort to enlarge UNFICYP's mandate was in September 1964, through the indirect device of saying that the Secretary-General would assume that renewal of the Force would imply enlargement of its mandate in the three specified areas stated therein (wider freedom of movement, creation of buffer zones, defortifications).[48] This effort foundered on the firm opposition of the Soviet Union and France against any enlargement of the mandate (the Cyprus Foreign Minister had expressed mixed views thereon) and was not further pursued. Since that time there has been no effort either to widen or narrow the terms of reference and those concerned have reconciled themselves to the original form, as interpreted by the Secretary-General and as applied in practice in the field. The emphasis has been a practical one for stability rather than for strict legalism. The fact is that there was no major need to alter the mandate and in any case it was most unlikely that any effort to do so would succeed without opening a Pandora's box in the process.[49]

Duration and financing

Finally, the Security Council recommended in paragraph 6 that the stationing of the Force should be for a period of three months, all costs pertaining to it being met in a manner to be agreed upon between them, by the governments providing the contingents and by the government of Cyprus. It was further stated that the Secretary-General might also accept voluntary contributions for that purpose.

As regards the time factor, the underlying thought in the Security Council was that in the three-month period, during which UNFICYP would ' hold the ring ', sufficient progress would have been made towards a political solution through the United Nations mediator [50] to warrant the termination of the Force. This, of course, proved to be a far too optimistic assumption and it became necessary again and again to renew the mandate of the Force.[51]

While, understandably, impatience has occasionally been expressed by the Secretary-General, as well as by Council members and by contributing countries, that this state of affairs cannot continue indefinitely, it is at the same time generally recognized that the alternative would be infinitely worse and renewal has on each occasion been forthcoming. Certain developments in 1968 raised hopes that the Force could soon be terminated; however, more recent events have once again made that hope appear unlikely to be realized for some time. In any case, in practice the size of the Force has been reduced from some 7,000 at its peak to nearly half that number.

The financial aspect of the Force is yet another story to which justice cannot be done here. As a reflection of political and constitutional differences, the financial aspect of peacekeeping operations has since 1956—beginning with UNEF—put the Organization into a state of near-bankruptcy and threatened its collapse politically. The confrontation over Article 19 of the Charter, which was but a reflection of fundamental constitutional [52] and political differences, frustrated the whole nineteenth session of the General Assembly, put serious strains upon the International Court of Justice in its effort to produce the requested advisory opinion on the *Expenses* Case,[53] was the subject of acute controversy not only among the great powers but also among such individuals as the Foreign Minister of Ireland, Mr F. Aiken, and the then Senator, Mr P. Trudeau of Canada, in the Twenty-first session of the Assembly, and is now in a state of semi-hibernation in the Special Committee of 33 with no immediate prospects for a solution.[54]

To return to the financing of UNFICYP, no similar ' mistake ' as that in the case of UNEF and ONUC was to be committed—in fact there would have been no UNFICYP if there had been such an effort—and, while most recognized the fragile and unsatisfactory nature of voluntary contributions, this was the line of least resistance and was adopted.

By the end of 1968, as it appears from the Secretary-General's report of December 1968,[55] the situation was as follows: the deficit was calculated to be approximately $8 million with an additional $8 million required to cover the period to 15 June 1969. However unsatisfactory this may appear to be, it is the general belief that, given all the factors involved, UNFICYP will not collapse through lack of financial support.

At the same time, the government of Cyprus met its responsibilities under Article 19 of the Status of the Force Agreement—even though, as one would expect from Ministries of Finance everywhere, not without some haggling—and has made sizeable contributions to the financing of the Force.

This then was the framework of UNFICYP: a peacekeeping force authorized by the Security Council, with the consent of the government of Cyprus, set up by the Secretary-General, operating under a commander appointed by and responsible to the Secretary-General, functioning on the basis of a vaguely worded mandate, composed of national contingents having international status, financed primarily through voluntary contributions under the overall direction of the Secretary-General who in turn has to report and is accountable to the Security Council.

Legal framework

As I have already remarked, the Security Council in its enabling resolution avoided reference to any particular provisions of the Charter, other than Article 2 (4) in the preamble. However, I am much afraid that this does not absolve me from the responsibility of at least touching upon this subject.[56]

It seems fairly clear that, in terms of Charter provisions, UNFICYP is a subsidiary organ of the Security Council within the meaning of Article 29.[57] In fact, the Security Council did not make a determination of the ' existence of any threat to the peace, breach of the peace or act of aggression ' within Article 39 and it is beyond doubt that the operation does not amount to enforcement action within Articles 41 and 42 of Chapter VII. The wording used in the resolution (' situation likely to threaten international peace and security ', the repeated use of the term ' recommends ' rather than ' decides ', the provision of ' mediation ' machinery, and the express requirement of the ' consent of the Government of Cyprus ') [58] points distinctly to Chapter VI and more particularly to Articles 33, 36, 37, and 38.

What is less clear is the applicability of Article 40. The argument might be put forward (on the analogy of that of Mr Schachter in his now celebrated article, under the name of E. M. Miller, on the 'Legal Aspects of the United Nations Action in the Congo')[59] that the wording 'call upon' all member-states in operative paragraph 1 of the resolution 'in conformity with their obligations under the Charter to refrain from any action', etc. may have been based on Article 40 and have constituted a 'provisional measure' within the meaning of that article.

Indeed, it might be said that operative paragraph 1, combined with the express reference in the preamble of the resolution to Article 2 (4), amounted to a call upon all member-states not to violate the express prohibition in Article 2 (4) against the use of force by one state against another, and, in practical terms, it could be interpreted as a call upon Turkey to refrain from taking forcible action against Cyprus. In any case, the invoking of Article 40 expressly does not prejudice the rights or position of the parties nor does it bring into play the enforcement provisions of Chapter VII; and consequently, it does not constitute an exception to Article 2 (7) of the Charter.[60]

In addition to the enabling resolution, three other legal documents had to be employed in order to complete the legal framework of the Force. The first was the Agreement on the Status of the Force,[61] concluded on 31 March 1964 by exchange of letters between the Secretary-General of the United Nations on the one hand and the Minister of Foreign Affairs of Cyprus on the other. It covered such diverse matters as respect for local law, jurisdiction, premises, uniforms, flags, arms, freedom of movement, use of roads, settlements of claims, etc. It followed closely the pattern of the equivalent ONUC and UNEF Agreements. The second was a model Participating State Agreement,[62] used, with appropriate variations, for each of the contributing states. The third was the Force Regulations.[63]

These problems had already been encountered and tackled in connection with the previous major peacekeeping operations and all they required was adaptation to the particular circumstances of UNFICYP.

Political basis

Perhaps I should also say a few words about the political basis for the March 1964 resolution. Once it became commonly accepted (given the delicate balance of power between the opposing sides, both inside and outside Cyprus, the potential danger to international peace that would be created by a possible conflict between Greece and Turkey, both NATO members, as well as the threat to world peace generally, given the proximity of the Soviet Union and its stand in support of an independent Cyprus) that an international peacekeeping force would have to be sent to the island, the question left was what force and drawn from where.

What were the options? A 'tripartite' force—of the United Kingdom, Greece, and Turkey—was not practicable in the circumstances (apart from other considerations); a British force, except as an immediate measure, was unpalatable to the Cypriots and would have been a heavy burden to the British; a NATO force was unacceptable to the Cyprus government (apart from other considerations). Consequently, a United Nations force was the obvious answer and one which the Cypriot side had preferred all along. Once the British and United States governments bowed to this necessity and the Secretary-General and his collaborators, with their usual dedication, appeared prepared to accept this additional burden, the problem remaining was primarily the constitutional–economic one which is familiar to those who know something of the previous peacekeeping operations— authorization, composition, command, financing. As we have seen above, all these were solved in a way reconciling doctrinal positions with practical political interests. Since the authorization was by the Security Council and the financing on a voluntary basis, the Soviet Union and France found it possible to accommodate their doctrinal position by simply abstaining on the operative paragraph dealing with the role of the Secretary-General. Neither wanted to demonstrate strongly any lack of confidence in U Thant, and the Russians in particular took into account—and said so publicly—the fact that the Cyprus government had indicated its willingness to receive the UN force. The alternative, possibly of a NATO force, may have been another factor in the Soviet Union's attitude, for by going along with the creation of UNFICYP, it retained a voice through its vote in the Council. Indeed, this is a case of 'when there is the will, there is the way'.

I now intend to touch very cursorily upon some of the aspects of the operation of UNFICYP.

Operation

As far as the military side is concerned, I have already alluded to the mandate and its application. By and large it has worked out well and it has been substantially assisted by the civilian police units which proved their value as, gradually and for most of the time, the situation has become one which calls less and less for a military approach. Ascertaining facts, reporting on incidents, calming down tense situations, calls for police methods and for diplomatic tact rather than military methods.

The civilian side of UNFICYP, which consists of the Secretary-General's Special Representative,[64] the Senior Legal and Political Adviser,[65] the UNFICYP Information Officer[66] and the Political Officer[67] and some financial, administrative and other officials, has done an excellent job in inspiring confidence and promoting the objectives of UNFICYP towards a return to normality and also in such diverse ways as offering their good offices, operating the Political Liaison Committee, and carrying out a variety of activities for a return to normal conditions with tact and impartiality. They deserve a great deal of credit for the success of the operation as also those high officials in the Secretariat [68] dealing with the operation for proving their dedication to the ideals of the Organization by their impartiality, competence, integrity, and sheer hard work in often critical and dramatic circumstances.

It would clearly be going beyond the scope of the present paper to examine in any detail the practical workings of UNFICYP. There have been surprisingly few major causes of friction or embarrassment. The latter did occur, only once but in a glaring way, when two UNFICYP Swedish armoured cars, commanded by officers, were apprehended and forcibly stopped by the Cyprus National Guard *in flagrante delicto*—smuggling large quantities of arms to the Turkish Cypriots. There were a few red faces in Stockholm and in New York and the two officers were tried (as provided for in the relevant regulations) by their national courts and sentenced to cashiering and imprisonment. Such incidents, however, perhaps unavoidable in the circumstances of Cyprus, have been rare and there have been no others of this magnitude, and such as have occurred are certainly not attributable to laxity on the part of UNFICYP authorities.

Another area in which there was some dispute, especially in the summer of 1964, related to the question of freedom of movement of UNFICYP as set out in Article 32 of the Status of the Force Agreement. As interpreted by the government, this meant what it said, viz. free and unimpeded movement along the roads of the Republic, not the right to go into buildings or customs-houses or docks and to inspect what was being loaded or unloaded. After some exchange of correspondence, the matter was amicably settled in a practical—as distinct from a strictly legal—way, by UNFICYP's agreeing to respect certain sensitive ' restricted areas ' (camps, fortifications, etc. of the National Guard), which only the Commander of UNFICYP might visit after consultation with the Commander of the National Guard. [69]

Another difference of interpretation of a legal provision occurred with regard to Article 19 of the Status of the Force Agreement, dealing with the financial obligations of the government in respect of UNFICYP. This, again, was settled amicably in a non-legalistic way by the government's making an ex gratia payment and UNFICYP's writing-off a part of what is claimed was owed to it.

The same approach was followed with regard to claims for compensation by private individuals against UNFICYP. Instead of setting up the cumbersome machinery of the claims commission as provided in Article 38 of the Status of the Force Agreement such claims were settled by a claims officer of UNFICYP in an equitable and expeditious way.

Assessment of UNFICYP

To sum up, UNFICYP furnishes an excellent illustration of a successful and effective United Nations peacekeeping operation in its proper role of insulating a crisis and filling a power vacuum while the processes of peacemaking are under way with the ultimate aim of making its presence no longer necessary. In the case of Cyprus all the political, constitutional, and financial obstacles were overcome and the necessary conditions were present for the setting up and successful operation of a United Nations peacekeeping operation.[70]

GENERAL CONCLUSIONS IN THE LIGHT OF
RECENT DEVELOPMENTS

From this often superficial examination what general conclusions can we draw and what are the prospects and the pointers for the future?

As U Thant said in his address to the Joint Meeting of both Houses of the Canadian Parliament on 26 May 1964,[71] the Organization is facing a basic dilemma as regards its role in the problem of peace-keeping. On the one hand governments and peoples by and large accept the need for the United Nations and its central role as the keeper of the peace. The Organization is entrusted, especially in times of crisis, with great problems of incalculable importance and danger. On the other hand, the stage has not yet been reached when the necessary material and political support is forthcoming, as a matter of course, to enable the United Nations to meet these problems with the adequacy with which an effective national government meets similar responsibilities on the national level. This results in a con- siderable strain upon the Organization and exposes it on occasion to serious criticism and hostility. The political, economic, constitutional, and even psychological conditions cannot be changed overnight—and they can only be changed gradually as a result of a conscious effort by all to put to good use the lessons of the past and of the present with a view to strengthening the Organization and making it better equipped effectively to meet the challenge in the future.

Barring for the foreseeable future the ideal solution of permanent United Nations forces, there are still several marginal steps that can be taken to this end within the framework of existing political and constitutional realities.

By far the most significant of these is the practice of earmarking stand-by national contingents by individual governments for future use by the United Nations as and when required. Even though the original proposal can be traced to the Uniting for Peace resolution, in 1950,[72] it has in fact developed on a different basis, especially since 1963, and today the United Nations can count on substantial forces in this respect.

Canada [73] deserves a good deal of credit for taking practical steps in this direction as early as 1957, and it was followed closely by Sweden,[74] Norway,[75] Denmark,[76] Finland,[77] the Netherlands,[78] and Austria.[79] Iran has made an offer to earmark forces, and others may do likewise. The United Kingdom [80] offered formally to provide, subject to certain conditions, logistical support of a substantial nature. Several other countries are regular contributors to United Nations operations, for example India, Yugoslavia, Brazil, Ireland, Ethiopia— even though, for a variety of reasons, they have not taken the formal step of earmarking. The United States has been a major contributor of logistical support.[81] The various aspects of administration, logistics, training, operational techniques, composition, recruitment, standardization of weapons, equality of pay, etc. involved have been the object of extensive consultation between governments and interested individuals [82] even though the United Nations as such could participate only through an observer (in fact General Rikhye, the Secretary-General's Military Adviser), it being precluded by political considerations from appearing as directly involved. But the Secretary-General has referred with obvious approval e.g. to Mr Pearson's constructive suggestions for the further development and co-ordination of such stand-by forces and expressed the belief that consultation and co-operation among interested governments can be of much value in contributing to the improvement of the peacekeeping effectiveness of the United Nations.[83]

Earmarking, while not involving the obligation of automatically acceding to a potential request by the Secretary-General,[84] enables the Secretary-General to know in advance what he can rely on. It also has the merit of permitting some advance planning of how to mesh these potentially available forces into one force and facilitates the provision of likely equipment (communications, etc.), the creation of uniform operating procedures and so on.[85] It has likewise had the beneficial effect of making possible the use of United Nations indoctrination material in national military training. All in all, it has constituted an encouraging and significant step in the right direction.

Other such steps that have been suggested are the creation of field manuals and standard operating procedures and the strengthening of the staff of the senior Secretariat officials dealing with peacekeeping.

The former has already been done and it is doubtful whether the latter represents an urgent need in present circumstances. Although these officials can be counted on the fingers of one or, at the most, two hands, they have never the less shown an admirable capacity to respond to challenges in time of pressure; and when multiple crises do not occur simultaneously, they are adequate to cover the field, even though no one can accuse them of being underworked at any time.

An important factor in the same direction is the creation of conditions whereby East European forces could be employed, in the same way as forces from Western countries, under United Nations command to participate in peacekeeping operations. If this proves feasible it might well be the turning point in the direction of creating confidence among that important section of United Nations membership. For instance, if it proved possible for the UNFICYP Commander to rely upon his deputy who was a British officer why should not, in appropriate circumstances, a commander of a future UN force rely, say, upon a Czech or a Pole as his second-in-command? I have already referred to the creditable participation in UNFICYP of East European Secretariat officials. Indeed, Yugoslavia has participated with distinction in past peacekeeping operations. At present the East European attitude on the surface remains one of strict adherence to the original Charter scheme and is reflected in the Soviet Union's memoranda of 10 July 1964 and 16 March 1967,[86] as well as such documents as the letter of the Permanent Representative of Czechoslovakia addressed to the President of the Security Council offering to conclude an agreement in accordance with the forms of Article 43 for action under Chapter VII of the Charter.[87] However, there are indications that, assuming Security Council authorization of the operation, this attitude might well prove more flexible in specific cases where political considerations so dictated.

There might be the possibility, which should be seriously borne in mind, that—especially if the next few years witness a significant degree of rapprochement between the two super-powers—two other measures might be taken which, though falling short of the scheme envisaged by the Charter, would nevertheless constitute gestures in that direction. The one is to make agreements under Article 43 (i.e. between individual states and the Security Council) not for enforcement action—such would be unrealistic, as we have seen—but for peacekeeping by consent. The other is to utilize the Military Staff Committee, perhaps with an enlarged membership, for purposes of the planning, co-ordination, etc. of peacekeeping operations. This in turn might open the door to other possibilities, but, in the long term, it all depends on political developments.

Another suggestion which is frequently put forward is the strengthening of the office of the Military Adviser of the Secretary-General. While different views may be taken regarding the advisability of such a step, the fact is that the Secretary-General dispensed with the office altogether (after the retirement of General Rikhye) although undoubtedly, he could, whenever the need arises draw upon the available talent. Such functions as require military advice are being performed in the Secretary-General's office by Colonel Koho, whose title is that of military liaison officer.

It is sometimes suggested that the United Nations should also engage upon advance contingency planning for possible future peace-keeping operations in different parts of the world. However harmless and innocuous this may appear on the surface, I am not convinced that the existing political climate can bear such an activity; in fact, a premature leak of such action taken by the Secretariat, apart from raising a political storm, might well ruin in advance the likelihood of any particular peacekeeping operation materializing in the future. However, these considerations would not preclude the Secretary-General's office from being apprized, through the various offices of the United Nations around the globe and otherwise, of such developments on the international scene and such straws in the wind as might be relevant and significant in this context, but the utmost discretion and tact would be essential.

What then is a realistic assessment of the operations by reference to the present position, and the foreseeable outlook for peacekeeping operations by the United Nations?

These operations are a hopeful and significant factor in the effort to keep the peace in various parts of the world, particularly in areas where the process of decolonization or other circumstances have left a power vacuum. Subject to what has already been said as to the direction in which institutional improvement should be aimed and to the continuing effort at educating world public opinion,[88] which is perhaps the most significant area of potential improvement, the margin for more to be done at present is necessarily narrow. It is clear that, ultimately, all suggestions will be considered to have merit only to the extent that they reflect a realistic assessment of what states —and especially the great powers—are at a given time prepared to accept.

The main effort should be to exploit the ad hoc approach to the limit of the available political consensus in each case, particularly in so far as the vital interests of the super-powers are concerned, so as not to risk ruining the Organization by stretching things too far and being conscious of the fact that for better or worse the Organization is based on the sovereign equality of all its members (Article 2 (1)). The know-how, military and administrative, exists and the legal wrappings can easily be adapted from existing precedents.

The direction in which things have been going recently points steadily to accepting that in practice future peacekeeping operations, as a rule, will be authorized by the Security Council, that executive responsibility will rest with the Secretary-General, subject to stricter or looser control by the Council, and that they will be financed on a consensual basis (whether by the interested parties or through voluntary contributions or a combination of arrangements). This is not as pessimistic an outlook as it might appear at first sight and in fact the experience of the past few years leaves some room for optimism. This may fall far short of the dreams and expectations of those wedded to the idea of the United Nations as a form of world government, but it goes a good deal beyond the image of the United Nations as an impotent debating society or a static conference machinery. Politics, after all, is the art of the possible, and, short of the collective security system envisaged in 1945 or of a permanent United Nations peacekeeping force—both of which are at present unattainable—the picture suggested by the present peacekeeping potential of the United Nations is by no means bleak. In a troubled world beset by conflict and the far too frequent use of armed force, United Nations peacekeeping, even within these limits, presents an acceptable alternative and is likely to lead to a more peaceful world.

It would clearly go beyond the scope of this paper to talk of the necessary corollary of peacekeeping which is peacemaking. But, as the experience of Cyprus [89] as well as of so many other situations has demonstrated, it is only when the one is supplemented by the other that the circle is completed, a solution to problems is reached, and the United Nations has, *pro tanto*, discharged its responsibilities and fulfilled, even to that modest limited extent, the expectations of the majority of mankind as an instrument of peace in the world.

INTERNATIONAL CONTROL OF MARINE POLLUTION *

MICHAEL HARDY †

*John McMahon came to New York in October 1966 in order to do
some research on United Nations materials, and between August
1967 and January 1969 served as a Legal Officer in the Office of
Legal Affairs of the United Nations Secretariat. After returning
to Oxford he continued to act as a Consultant to the Legal Office,
and was in New York on a brief visit in that capacity at the
time of his death in April 1969. In the Secretariat, as elsewhere.
he quickly made many friends, and it was during this period of
his life that I got to know him. The particular milieu of the
United Nations, with its blending of international and national
styles and the interplay of personalities, diplomacy and political
issues, appealed to him. He certainly worked hard. While in the
Legal Office he dealt with problems in a number of areas: the
practice of United Nations organs, the problems of ' mini-states',
issues relating to the Middle East, and, in particular, legal aspects
of the future regime for the sea-bed beyond national jurisdiction.
It therefore seemed appropriate to choose a marine topic for the
collection of essays in his memory.*

WHEN people speak of the law they usually mean the law already
existing, and they think of the lawyer's function as being to advise
on the law in force. This is, of course, the lawyer's most habitual and
primary task. But the matter is not always so simple and clear cut,
and the question of what the law should be often follows hard on
the heels of a statement of what the law is. Thus in international as
in municipal affairs, the standards and procedures applicable to
particular activities may have to be examined from time to time and
decisions taken as to what modifications should be made. This happens
most obviously when a development takes place in technology—the
civil application of atomic energy and outer space activities are cases
in point—but may also occur, usually with greater difficulty, when

---

* © Michael Hardy 1973. Prepared in Mar. 1970 and published, by permission
  of the Royal Institute of International Affairs, in essentially the same form,
  in the *Natural Resources Journal* (Albuquerque, NM), 11/2 (1971).
† Senior Legal Officer, Office of Legal Affairs, United Nations. The views
  expressed are put forward in a personal capacity.

a series of different factors converge in such a way as to require that a fresh look be taken at the basic approach underlying existing law, and an assessment made of the extent of the need to change that assumption, together with its accompanying procedures and institutions (or the lack of them). Whatever the precise blend of old and new which may be arrived at, the process of determining what kind of amendment to make is more protracted and uncertain in the international setting than within a national framework; the means of collecting information, relating it to current interests and to current law, and then deciding whether or not to take action are less developed and operate under distinctly greater handicaps in the loosely organized society of sovereign states than they do within a given country with an established division of functions. In consequence the international lawyer is more likely than his municipal colleague to be drawn into the task of considering what new arrangements should be made, and, in order to do so, to be required to assess, or at least to understand, the factual and extra-legal elements which form the basis on which the existing law should—or might—be modified. By reason of the nature of the situation, this task may well proceed even while the establishment of the extra-legal data is continuing, as part of the total process by which policy and future law are determined. Accordingly, this essay deals, if only briefly, with non-legal considerations (in a narrow sense), even though not all the scientific information required for a conclusive evaluation of the problem of marine pollution is yet available.[1] By the same token, although it would be possible to deal at greater length with any of the main forms of pollution considered below, the present stage is one at which an effort has to be made— if only on a preliminary basis—to distinguish the principal dangers and sources, and, beyond that, to consider whether (or to what extent) the problem requires to be looked at as a whole, both in order to understand its nature and to provide a series of effective solutions. The purpose of the present essay is not therefore to give a detailed analysis of every possible legal contingency, but to provide essentially an overall survey, in which the various elements are examined and shown in relation to their general setting, so as to indicate the boundaries of such arrangements as may be adopted for the future.

The past ten to twenty years have seen a revolution in scientific knowledge of the sea-bed and of its formation;[2] not only is the geological nature of the area now understood, in fundamentals if not in detail, there has also been a rapid increase in technical command over the use of the sea and its resources. This has taken place in virtually every marine activity: the construction of giant oil tankers and other carriers, a stupendous growth in the fishing industry,[3] the development of submarines and submersibles able to descend to the abyssal depths, and an increasing ability to extract minerals from the sea-bed and sub-soil. This redoubling of the means of using the seas has been accompanied—as cause and effect—by a rise in world population (largely concentrated in coastal areas) and a demand for higher living standards, as well as by an increase in the scale and sources of marine pollution.

The task of establishing suitable means for the prevention and control of marine pollution may be regarded as part of the wider problem of balancing two general objectives: the need on the one hand to keep the oceans relatively unsullied, as a valuable part of the environment, both for our own and for future generations, and, on the other, to permit more intensive and diversified use to be made of the sea and its resources as soon as possible. Even regarded purely as a scientific and technical problem, without regard for political, economic or legal considerations, the task of isolating the extent and consequences of marine pollution is one of considerable difficulty and complexity. The seas are immensely vast, covering 70 per cent of the world's surface and having an average depth of more than 2 miles; the greatest depth is 35,000 feet or approximately 7 miles. The bottom of the sea-bed is the part of the world which is still the least explored, and the deep oceans are the least known part of the seas. Because they occupy the hollows of the earth, the seas have, by a divine arrangement of geography, always received the waste disposed of by the land, not merely the waste produced by human activity, but also the silt and water volume carried down by rivers and streams and material transported by wind and rain. Sea water itself contains, in solution, all naturally occurring chemical compounds and a wide range of more complex carbon compounds, and suspended in it are particulate organic material, insoluble organic compounds, and living organisms. The fact that it is the result of a continuous series of different chemical reactions has rendered sea water itself relatively immune from permanent changes of composition. The ceaseless mixing of sea water, moreover, caused by tides, currents and the effect of the wind, further increases the seas' capacity to assimilate foreign material. As regards objects living in the seas, the marine flora and fauna, it is agreed that these, generally speaking, lack the security consciousness and the capacity for change shown by organisms living on land—the comfort and relative constancy of the seas, not for nothing regarded as one of the great feminine symbols, have protected them. Furthermore the various parts of the marine ecosystem are closely interlocked, no constituent being able to continue without the support of the others: the cycle is complete, from floating plants (phytoplankton) which nourish planktonic animals which in turn sustain larger fish, which on death are decomposed by bacteria into the nutrients required (together with carbon dioxide and sunlight) by the plants. Harm to one link affects the rest of the chain.

These basic facts regarding the environment (or part of the environment), indicate why it is difficult to specify from the outset, simply and categorically, what constitutes pollution; the task involves the alignment of a complex series of natural phenomena with different acts of human intervention (deliberate or accidental, with consequences variously foreseeable or unforeseeable), and legal, political, and economic considerations. The need that all these factors be taken into account can be seen by examining the most authoritative definition of marine pollution so far put forward, namely that adopted by the Intergovernmental Oceanographic Commission (IOC) for the purpose of its Long-Term and Expanded Programme of Oceanographic Research, and accepted by the Joint IMCO/FAO/UNESCO/WMO/ WHO/IAEA Group of Experts on the Scientific Aspects of Marine Pollution (GESAMP). This definition specifies marine pollution as being the

Introduction by man, directly or indirectly, of substances or energy into the marine environment (including estuaries) resulting in such deleterious effects as harm to living resources, hazard to human health, hindrance to marine activities including fishing, impairment of quality for use of sea water and reduction of amenities.[4]

Although these organizations had an obvious need to provide guidelines and a common basis for their deliberations, it is evident that the definition chosen is in fact no more purely ' scientific ' than it is ' legal '. Pollution may take physical, chemical, or biological forms but there is no physical, chemical, or biological process of ' pollution ' as such, in the sense that there is, say, of nuclear fission or of the formation of acids under specified conditions, or of photosynthesis by plants. Nor, of course, does the definition have any immediate legal value. While it would be possible to conclude a general multilateral convention with this definition as its kernel and making it an obligation for states not to commit acts falling under the definition, this is not the position at the present time. The possible use of the definition, for legal purposes, depends on the choice of interests to be protected and the means of control to be used, which leads directly to one of the main issues and difficulties from the standpoint of existing law. Traditionally the interests which international law has sought to protect have been state interests, by and through the mechanism of states. This has meant that a state has normally been able to claim against another only if it or its nationals have suffered damage within its boundaries, or to the person and property of its nationals elsewhere. This, and the liberty left to individual states to decide whether or not to pursue claims, has entailed that the general interest (including the maintenance of common facilities, such as the sea and air) has normally gone unprotected and unregarded. The rules of international public policy have, in this sense, been little developed and there has been no public right of action on behalf of the community as such, in striking contrast to the situation within states.[5] Nor, of course, on this basis has anticipatory international regulation been possible, designed to prevent accidents occurring.[6] Examination of the topic of marine pollution leads to the realization that the possibility of 'tort action' on the part of individual states after the event provides a very inadequate means for protecting the condition of the marine environment. If, for reasons of accepted social necessity, the oceans are to be used for maximum—or even merely for greater—gains for the general benefit, a more systematic and uniform means of control will accordingly have to be developed to replace the previous freedom of *laissez aller* allowed to states, and suffered by the seas. The changes are unlikely to take the form, from the outset, of a totally comprehensive and unified set of procedures, but a greater degree of co-ordination between national and international forms of control, within an overall pattern, however loosely defined, may be regarded as already a prerequisite to further pursuit of the agreed goal of providing increased benefits for all states in their use of the seas.

In the next section of this essay a classification is made of the major causes and forms of marine pollution, based on consideration of the scientific and technical aspects and the human activities involved. The main categories distinguished are then examined in turn against the background of existing legal and administrative controls, the problems which present themselves, and the various proposals which have been, or may be, made, in order to prevent or control pollution. Following a summary of the recent activities of the main international organizations concerned with this topic, the essay concludes with a review—part diagnosis, part forecast—of needs and possible solutions in this sphere.

I. CLASSIFICATION OF THE MAIN FORMS OF MARINE POLLUTION

Before considering further the hybrid notion of pollution—sometimes presented as an objective, scientifically determined phenomenon and at others as a matter principally of economic or legal concern—it is necessary to draw a distinction between the functioning of the environment, as a system operating independently of man, and the effects upon the environment of human activities. The condition of the seas is maintained by a host of factors, chief amongst them, for present purposes, being the interaction with the atmosphere [7] and the disposal in the seas of the water and other debris carried down by rivers and streams, as well as ' run off ' from the land. The seas are capable— or such is the assumption—of absorbing foreign matter introduced in this way without significant or lasting effects, in the same way that they suffer, without major damage, instances of natural pollution. Oil seepages from the sea-bed occur in certain parts of the world (for example, as many people promptly pointed out, in the Santa Barbara area) even without drilling; marine flora and fauna may be affected by diseases or blights from causes independent of man; and toxic metals may be present in sea water as well as being transported by rivers from deposits deep in the earth. The question which is now posed, at its most general, is to determine the effect upon this intricate and balanced environment of the introduction, through human inter- vention, of foreign materials on a scale which threatens, if not the operation of the marine environment as a whole, then at least the operation of parts of that environment in a way that is detrimental to man's interests.

Since it is common ground that the problem of marine pollution is caused by human activities—this is the keynote of the IOC-GESAMP definition previously cited—the means of regulating the problem have also to be presented, in the last resort, in terms of specific activities. Whilst this is so from an administrative and regulatory standpoint, it is not, however, possible to conduct scientific and technical inquiries simply on the basis of the origin of marine pollution in given human occupations; particular instances of pollution may be caused by a whole variety (or combination) of activities, or may indeed be brought about by natural forces.[8] Scientific investigations have therefore pro- ceeded according to the chemical and physical characteristics of particular pollutants and not exclusively on the basis of the kind of activity responsible for producing given pollutants. Nevertheless, such is the nature of the problem that those concerned with the scientific aspects have turned, in the course of their broader inquiries, to sur- veying human activities in order to provide themselves with orientation and some indication of the boundaries of the situation,[9] and those concerned with potential direct regulatory systems have sought more scientific information before proceeding.[10] The task of providing an adequate classification of the main types of pollution is not easy there- fore, and any system proposed may vary in emphasis according to whether the question is approached from a scientific or regulatory standpoint, although the essence of the matter, judged overall, is, of course, to bring these two into the correct relationship.

Looked at historically, regulation of the disposal of material into the sea has depended either on the evident nature of the pollution— the production of oil slicks, for example, or the dumping of rubbish in rich fishing areas—or on the degree of possible danger (the disposal of radio-active wastes being the best instance in this category). For the rest, apart from national sewage and inland and coastal water legislation, the matter has been largely unregulated. Nor, until the recent steep rise in the quantities involved, were legislative intervention and scientific inquiries required on a wide scale. A beginning has now been made as regards the conduct of scientific investigations, however, and on the basis of the evidence so far available, expert scientific and technical bodies [11] have distinguished the following main groups of pollutants: halogenated hydrocarbons, petroleum hydrocarbons, organic and inorganic chemicals, nutrient chemicals, suspended solids and turbidity, radioactive materials, and the release of thermal energy.[12] The direct disposal of radioactive materials or of petroleum hydrocarbons into the seas are relatively familiar and distinct cases, which have already received a measure of international attention. What has so far been little considered is the dispersal of petroleum hydrocarbons in other ways—not only through sea-bed seepages or through the decomposition of marine plants, but as a result of the use of fossil fuels on land. The 1970 Study of Critical Environmental Problems contains some striking, if approximate, calculations on the matter. Direct losses of petroleum origin into the oceans, amounting to just over two million metric tons in 1969, were subdivided as follows: normal ship operations were responsible for the release of just over 1 million metric tons (49·4 per cent),[13] rivers carrying industrial automobile wastes 450,000 metric tons (21·6 per cent), refineries 300,000 metric tons (14·4 per cent), accidental spills 200,000 metric tons (9·6 per cent), and offshore production of minerals 100,000 metric tons (4·8 per cent.). To these direct losses must be added a fallout of airborne petroleum hydrocarbons. ' If 10 per cent of the hydrocarbons emitted to the atmosphere eventually find their way to the sea surface, the total hydrocarbon contamination of the ocean would be about five times the direct influx from ships and land sources.' [14] Although airborne petroleum hydrocarbons are easier for the seas to absorb and decompose, nevertheless, given a situation in which the amounts disposed of, in the case of all pollutants, are growing rapidly [15] it would appear that consideration will have to be given to deciding at some stage what action should be taken with respect to this particular source of pollution.

As regards the other pollutants listed above, the main sources of thermal energy released into the seas are power stations placed at the water's edge. Although the amount of thermal waste is expected to rise, this is, at present, a local problem and not yet one of major proportions. Since the responsible activity can be pinpointed fairly easily, the introduction of controls at source should be relatively easy. Pollution caused by suspended solids or associated turbidity is chiefly produced, so far as human activities are concerned, by dredging,[16] dumping, or other operations involving the movement of large quantities of materials. Although this may do damage to the marine ecosystem, here too the problems raised, so far as the evidence goes, do not extend beyond local effects. There is the further consideration —although scientific opinion shows some variation—that human-produced turbidity is, in any case, far less than that which may be produced by environmental forces and to which the seas have long been accustomed.

The remaining pollutants distinguished above—halogenated hydrocarbons,[17] inorganic [18] and organic [19] chemicals, and nutrient chemicals [20]—produce a wide range of effects on marine flora and fauna, and are themselves the result of a diverse array of human activities. Out of the complex picture which emerges from scientific investigation,[21] the following principles provide the elements for some degree of preliminary systematisation. First, these pollutants are largely the results of land-based as opposed to sea-based activities. Secondly, in certain instances appreciable quantities of these pollutants are carried to the seas by interaction with the atmosphere—first picked up as fumes or particles and then deposited by rain or dry fallout; the most significant examples at the present time are pesticides, and, to a less but still important degree, heavy metals such as lead and mercury, which are highly toxic. Thirdly, these pollutants are, except for the case of pesticides used in agriculture or to control diseases, produced during industrial, and, to a less extent, domestic [22] processes and disposed of as domestic and industrial waste. Control of these pollutants thus forms part of the general problem of the disposal of the ever-growing volume of the waste products of modern society.

To turn from this summary account of technical findings to the legal aspects—one of the principal issues so far as the law (and society as a whole) is concerned may be put very shortly: on whom should the consequences of pollution fall? The question invites the ready answer—on him who caused the pollution—but this reaction provides at best a rough guide to positive action. Not only does it lead away from the prior question of what is to be done to prevent pollution in the first place (and who is to pay for that), but the person who caused the pollution may not have known (and, in many cases at present, could not have known) of the full consequences of his acts. What if the pollution is the result of a cumulation of separate activities and it is impossible to determine the actual degrees of responsibility of numerous human agencies? What, more centrally, are the other beneficial uses of the sea which may be affected, and which will be more costly, to interfere with them or to control particular forms of pollution? What if it proves to be far more expensive to make stretches of coastal waters free from pollution than the economic value of the fish which might be nourished there—as is almost certainly the case in many areas? If those waters are used for recreation, how much is to be paid for the holidaymakers' and yachtsmen's pleasure? It will be clear from what has been said above that the various users of the sea—those who use it for recreation, for catching fish (which they and others eat), for transporting goods and for navigation, for communication, for exploiting minerals, and for disposing of coastal and industrial wastes—may all suffer consequences to their interests if pollution occurs and have a legitimate concern in the nature of any control measures introduced.

The balancing of those interests within a state—let alone amongst states—is an intricate task which has so far proceeded in a loose and unsystematic way. Certain measures of legal regulation do, however, exist with respect to marine pollution having its origin in human activities, and it is these which are referred to below, in order to show how these interests are reconciled at present, and, from that, to project what further adjustments may need to be made.

II. THE EXISTING LEGAL FRAMEWORK

The existing legal framework includes both national and international provisions. Although it is usual to regard these as distinct and mutually exclusive methods of control, such an approach is plainly inappropriate with regard to marine pollution; the very nature of the sea renders controls which stop one side of a notional boundary inadequate. In so far as existing controls have been based on a division between national and international areas, the national legislation concerned is generally more developed and particularized, it suffers from the fact that it is only of certain application in waters under national control, or, in the waters beyond, to ships and citizens of the state in question. The international arrangements, by contrast, are cast for the most part in broad terms and lack adequate means of enforcement; only in one case have detailed treaty provisions been made, and even here, only in respect of one specific pollution hazard, the discharge of oil from ships. The legal position differs, however, to a greater or less degree, with respect to the human activity and the kind of pollutant concerned.

1. *Marine pollution caused via the atmosphere by land-based activities*

Apart from the general case of the disposal of domestic and industrial wastes, and the other, more particular, activities considered below, there is evidence that a considerable (if undefined) proportion of marine pollution is caused by activities which take place on land and which result in material being carried as gas or particles by the atmosphere into the seas.[23] Although the number of individual pollutants which may be released in this way is large and the variety of human activities almost equally great, in terms of relative danger and quantity prevailing scientific opinion [24] indicates that three areas [25] are of particular concern: the use of various synthetic chemicals (particularly chlorinated hydrocarbons) [26] for agricultural purposes; the release of heavy metals,[27] especially lead and mercury, in industrial and other processes; and the passage into the atmosphere of petroleum hydrocarbons from the use of petroleum to provide energy.

As regards existing controls applicable with respect to these dangers, nationally many states have laws relating to air pollution, or to the protection of workers who may be directly exposed to harm during manufacture, and although such legislation is designed (and may be expected to continue to be designed) primarily for the benefit of the country concerned, it may also operate to prevent the infliction of harm upon others.[28] Efforts are now under way in many countries to strengthen the body of legal and administrative controls which may be invoked. The measures to be taken vary, however, according to the way in which the pollutant is produced. In the case of lead, attention has been concentrated on banning the addition of this metal to petrol, in order to stop the pollution at source; in this instance the problem posed as regards the nature of the control is determined by the impossibility of recapturing the lead once it has been released into the air. The same applies with respect to pesticides which, once dispersed over crops, cannot be caught and recycled. The use of DDT (and its associated compounds) as a pesticide is now being phased out in a number of states [29] and GESAMP has recommended that restrictive or preventive measures be taken.[30] Since DDT is used both to raise agricultural production and to prevent malaria, a direct ban is unlikely to be acceptable to states, mostly developing countries, which consider these objectives have a higher value than the prevention of marine pollution or of harm to certain species of birds. The World Health Organization, in its most recent statement on the subject,[31] has declared that the withdrawal of DDT from malaria operations would be fraught with great danger and is unjustifiable in the light of present knowledge. Nevertheless the Organization recommends that the use of DDT in outdoor locations should be reduced to the minimum, and that research on substitute insecticides and methods should be pursued. Assuming, however, that DDT was confined primarily to disease control, and that its future use for agricultural purposes was not indiscriminate (which would require, *inter alia*, that the volume now produced by the developed countries was not simply 'dumped' on the developing countries, as some have feared might happen), the amount finding its way into water, both inland and the high seas, would be held to a level which, if not ideal, would at least prevent pesticide contamination of large parts of the marine ecosystem from reaching major proportions. The steps necessary to reach agreement on these measures—in effect, a choice by the community as to the priority of uses to which this particular chemical should be put, and an acceptance of degrees of world-wide limitation —have only just begun, and it is difficult at this juncture to forecast precisely how informal and consensual the arrangements may be, and how information will be obtained. There would not appear to be any inherent need, however, for permanent or complex organizational machinery if general consensus can be reached on the main lines of communal policy.

Internationally, apart from the attention directed towards DDT pesticides, some tentative beginnings have been made on a regional basis towards the limitation of the use of particular chemicals affecting atmospheric or indeed environmental conditions in general. Such efforts have so far been very largely confined to Europe [32] and North America. Apart from treaty or administrative arrangements made on a regional basis (which are, in any case, generally few), the level of control exercised over the activities of states, and their means of recourse in the event of a dispute arising, are regulated by the application of the general principles of international law.[33] In this respect the position is the same as that in the case of harm caused by the disposal of domestic and industrial wastes, which is considered below.

2. Disposal of domestic and industrial wastes
(including ocean dumping)

In terms of bulk, domestic and industrial wastes [34] form, together with the discharge of polluted river waters, the largest source of marine pollution at the present time. River discharge—in effect the use of rivers as part of the national sewage system—is, according to recent reports,[35] becoming indeed the main cause of marine pollution, thus making improvement of estuaries and coastal waters dependent, in many cases, on prior cleansing of the rivers themselves. Most countries have a system regulating the disposal of domestic and industrial wastes (which may indeed overlap with those on air and inland water pollution), often in the form of detailed ordinances prepared with particular regard to the safeguarding of public health. The multiplicity of local and central authorities who may be involved and the absence hitherto of possible international consequences appear to be responsible for the lack of any detailed comparative study of such regulations.[36] The wastes concerned may be released into the sea in various ways, either by river, or by pipeline, or by dumping in the sea, and may or may not first be processed in order to remove constituents which are commercially valuable or particularly dangerous, or placed in containers, according to the nature of the substance concerned and the stringency of national regulations. As regards the actual area of disposal, there appear to be considerable variations; however, it is probable that the majority of states dispose of considerable quantities of waste in areas beyond their territorial sea.[37] The self-interest of the state concerned in disposing of its garbage safely and the capacity of the sea to absorb it,[38] has so far prevented any serious international complication from arising. No international dispute appears to have yet arisen between two states (although charges have been exchanged) [39] with regard to damage caused by marine pollution as a result of the disposal of coastal wastes. If such a dispute were to occur, the matter (apart from whatever action the offending state might agree to take for reasons of comity or out of good neighbourliness) would thus fall to be decided according to the general principles of international law. These principles, in relation to the situation indicated, are indeed very general: the principles of the freedom of the seas, of reasonable regard to the rights of others, of non-abuse of rights, and the invocation of the maxim *sic utere tuo ut alienam non laedas*. Article 2 of the 1958 Convention on the High Seas does not include the right to dispose of waste materials amongst the freedoms of the high seas there specified, but having regard to the non-exhaustive character of the definition given and the universal character of the practice it is highly improbable that an international tribunal (assuming that the matter was placed before it) would sustain the argument that the disposal of domestic and industrial wastes in the high seas is *ipso facto* prohibited. By way of clarification, it should be stressed that this is not to say that pollution is itself a permitted use of the seas, but that waste disposal is.[40] The issue in practice would be likely to turn, not on the basic question of the legality or illegality of waste disposal *per se*, but on the extent of knowledge, the foreseeability of the harm, and the standard of proof required— all matters of which international tribunals (by comparison with national courts) have relatively little experience or case law to guide them.[41] The matter might be somewhat differently presented, moreover, according to the nature of the complainant state's interest and of its resulting claim—for example, whether the injury occurred within its territorial sea or was in respect of expenses incurred in anticipation of such injury, or whether damage was done to actual or potential mining interests on its continental shelf, or to fish stocks in the high seas.[42] The number of variables prevents any simple answer to the question of what ruling an international tribunal might give: as a generalization, the greater the degree of knowledge the defendant state had, or ought to have had, of the consequences of its action, the more likely it is that it will be held to be liable and be required to make reparation to the injured state.[43]

The possibilities of complaints between nearby states with regard to the disposal of coastal wastes are undoubtedly growing. The volume of such wastes is increasing enormously [44]—by far the largest volume of any of the sources under discussion—and almost of necessity the tendency is to dispose of the waste further out to sea as inland and estuarine waters become polluted.[45] In order to avoid the contamination of more distant waters (which might have the effect of increasing the damage already done, or threatened, to coastal and estuarine areas) there have been increasing calls to extend national powers over ocean dumping,[46] possibly in conjunction with some form of international reporting system. Whilst stronger unilateral controls over the dumping in adjacent waters by nationals [47] of the state concerned are to be expected (and are indeed already being formulated), the need is growing for joint or co-ordinated action between government authorities in this regard. The problem of the disposal of domestic and industrial wastes is one which affects coastal areas, not the deep oceans, and internationally the position is likely to become critical first in the case of shallow enclosed, or semi-enclosed, seas, such as the Baltic and the Mediterranean, or even the North Sea, all of which are near crowded industrialized areas. Scientific observers and official bodies have collected evidence regarding the pollution, from coastal and other sources, of these seas,[48] and it would appear only a matter of time before regional or sub-regional arrangements are entered into.[49] The form and scope of such arrangements might raise some nice questions in so far as they diverged from the accepted division between areas subject to national control (internal waters, territorial sea, contiguous zones) and the high seas, particularly as regards the legal position of third states. However the basic change would lie in acceptance by the states concerned of the principle of prior agreed regulation, rather than reliance on *post hoc* complaints by individual states. Assuming such arrangements were limited to the surrounding coastal states, these might find that they had sufficient mutual interest to accept a degree of self-regulation, to standardize their methods of control and measurement, to inform one another of the quantities and character of wastes dumped, and of the safety measures taken, and to decide, on a basis of available information, what further controls might be introduced. If it were discovered that, in a particular sea, or in limited areas of it, concentrations of a certain pollutant (for example, heavy metals or paper and pulp waste) were approaching a dangerous level, it might then be agreed by all the states concerned that further quantities of the substance in question should be disposed of elsewhere or in other ways. The work done by international panels, such as GESAMP, might be of assistance in this regard, in determining categories of dangerous pollutants and ways of measuring their effects. It would be a practical prerequisite of any common measures adopted to curb pollution that, so far as possible, none of the states parties should be placed at a competitive disadvantage. The economic impact of pollution measures may indeed be considerable; [50] the fact that the states round semi-enclosed, intra-continental seas tend to be similar in economic and social standards may, however, be of assistance in this connection. It is not possible at this stage to say whether co-operative arrangements such as those indicated would inevitably need to include the exercise of enforcement and regulatory powers on the part of a specially established regional body, or whether they might proceed on the basis of regular meetings of national officials and mutual restraint. States are unlikely to move directly to the former without having tried the latter; the more loosely organized ' consultative ' approach is more probable, at least in the interim.[51]

A point of general interest is that, in either event, the states concerned would have moved, as regards this specific aspect at least, towards acceptance of one of the central principles (the *Kohärenzprinzip*) of international river law, whereby the waters of a given drainage basin are regarded as an integrated whole and not as a series of separate entities wherein each state may proceed as it wishes.[52] While this principle may often appear more of an aspiration than a reality, the increased demands for integrated development of river basins, in which a number of countries may be involved, together with the difficulty of separating the problem of pollution of inland and river waters from that of pollution of coastal waters, suggest that the law relating to international rivers and the law of the sea may be about to show, in this respect, a converging pattern of development.

3. *Radioactive pollution*

Apart from such radioactivity as may be introduced into the seas naturally, either from the earth's crust or from rain carrying the products of the action of cosmic rays on the upper atmosphere, radioactive materials may also be present as a result of various human activities: after the testing or installation of nuclear weapons; from civil applications, such as the use of nuclear energy to provide power for engineering or monitoring devices or for ship propulsion; from the possible release of radioactive materials which are being transported by sea; and from the dumping of radioactive wastes. This diversity and the difficulty of controlling radioactive materials once present in the marine environment, cause the problem of adopting suitable methods of prevention and control to be, in a number of respects, more difficult than in the case of coastal and industrial wastes, and future control schemes may need to distinguish between, on the one hand, measurement of existing levels of radioactivity, irrespective of source, and, on the other, the introduction of particular forms of control with respect to specific nuclear activities.

As regards nuclear weapon tests, the International Atomic Energy Agency (IAEA) has stated that these form by far the largest cause of radioactivity in the seas.[53] The 1963 Nuclear Test Ban Treaty [54] placed a general prohibition on the testing of nuclear weapons. However, as is well known, not all nuclear states are parties to this agreement and the non-party nuclear states have continued to conduct nuclear tests in the atmosphere. In addition the Treaty makes no provision (nor is it easy to say what provision could have been made) regarding the radioactivity already released into the atmosphere. Lastly, the ban contained in the Treaty contains an exception with respect to testing conducted beneath the sea-bed, if this can be accomplished without effects on the superjacent floor or water.[55] These facts together indicate that the control of radioactivity from this source, although it has advanced, is not complete. The problems posed—other than those of a scientific nature—concern the issue of disarmament, and indeed the state of international relations in general, and are hardly to be tackled within the scope of the present essay. The matter is, however, noted here for its importance from the standpoint of monitoring and other forms of technical surveillance. The same considerations apply with respect to the possible installation of nuclear weapons in the sea or on the sea-bed.[56] The successful conclusion of the Treaty on the Prohibition of the Emplacement of Nuclear Weapons and Other Weapons of Mass Destruction on the Sea-Bed and the Ocean Floor and in the Subsoil Thereof, which was signed on 11 February 1971, should, in the words of the USSR representative to the United Nations, *inter alia*, ' help to diminish the threat of pollution of the marine environment '.[57]

The use of nuclear means either to propel ships and submarines or to provide a source of power for various forms of machinery or instrumentation is, as yet, not very extensive. Apart from nuclear submarines (all of which are military), there are less than half a dozen nuclear powered ships in the world. A convention was drawn up in 1962 on the liability of nuclear ship operators, largely, it would appear, to provide a basis for insurance arrangements and to help secure acceptance of the idea of nuclear shipping.[58] The high cost of operating nuclear ships has been the main reason why they have not been employed more widely, and this situation is likely to continue for some time to come. The use of radioactive sources of power for marine instruments (for example, ocean buoys) or for larger-scale machinery is relatively in its infancy, but an extensive development may occur in the near future.[59] Even if the more ambitious schemes for placing nuclear power plants on the sea-bed to provide electricity for underwater cities are some way from realization, nuclear power sources may be the most suitable for oil drilling and pumping on the sea-bed, and are being actively considered.[60] Apart from national controls, which were not primarily drafted with such applications in mind, the body of law to govern the use of nuclear energy for these purposes has yet to be written. The actual maritime transport of radioactive materials, on the other hand, with the resulting need to obtain insurance coverage, has resulted in consideration of the legal questions involved by IAEA, the European Nuclear Energy Agency (ENEA), and IMCO, in collaboration with the Comité Maritime International: the solution presently envisaged is that a new convention on maritime liability should be prepared, reconciling existing maritime liability provisions with the regimes established by the Paris and Vienna Conventions on civil liability for nuclear damage, whereby liability is borne solely by the nuclear operator.[61]

The last source of possible radioactivity pollution, the dumping of spent radioactive materials, is the one which has received the most attention, perhaps, it may be added, because it seemed the one which would be easiest to tackle. The fact that these materials were known from the outset to be dangerous to public health, to be in many instances extremely long lasting,[62] and to be capable of entering the marine ecosystem has meant that their disposal in the oceans has been conducted with extreme care. As the Intergovernmental Oceanographic Commission (IOC) Working Group on Marine Pollution noted, ' no case is known of adverse effects ' having occurred as a result of such disposal.[63]

The method of disposal has been either through a pipeline or by the sinking of containers in selected deep areas far out at sea; the main danger (apart from the possibility of an accident—for example, if a fishing vessel or a mining venture were to break some containers in the course of operations, or if there were an earthquake) lies in the risk of accumulations of radioactivity if dumping were to be continued indiscriminately and in increasing amounts. States engaged in such activities on any appreciable scale have exercised control within the framework of national legislation relating to nuclear materials. Attempts have, however, also been made to arrive at an international system of controls or, at the least, of common observation of international standards. Article 25 of the 1958 Convention on the High Seas provides:

1. Every State shall take measures to prevent pollution of the seas from the dumping of radioactive waste, taking into account any standards and regulations which may be formulated by the competent international organizations.

2. All States shall co-operate with the competent international organizations in taking measures for the prevention of pollution of the seas or air space above, resulting from any activities with radioactive materials or other harmful agents.

Besides this degree of regulation with respect to the activities of states, the 1958 Conference on the Law of the Sea adopted a resolution recommending that IAEA should assist states by promulgating standards and drawing up internationally acceptable regulations relating to the discharge of radioactive materials into the sea. Pursuant to this resolution, IAEA established a panel of experts to study the technical and scientific problems involved.[64] The panel submitted a report in 1960 in which it put forward a series of recommendations, the principal of which were as follows: that waste disposal sites should be designated by a responsible national or international authority which should provide for the necessary monitoring of the area; that all authorities setting up disposal sites should provide to a suitable international authority information necessary to maintain an adequate register of radioactive waste disposal into the sea; and that IAEA should maintain this register and should receive (a) notice of the licensing requirements of all sea-disposal areas; (b) annual reports on the state of such sites; and (c) the monitoring programme and all relevant scientific findings.[65] It has not, however, as yet proved possible to establish the proposed international register. Although IAEA has conducted various inquiries and sponsored a number of meetings [66] on the subject of radioactive waste disposal, the proposal for a centralized method of collating information (and so evaluating the degree of danger from a general standpoint, thereby forestalling possible cumulative effects) has remained unrealized. The reason for this may be attributed to several causes, including not only such political considerations as may be involved, but also the technical difficulty of determining with accuracy the effects of radioactivity on the individual resources of the ocean and of distinguishing radioactivity in the marine environment due to different sources.[67] However, in the light of technical advances, a further panel meeting was held in November 1970, which resulted in further progress being made towards a set of recommendations which would be generally acceptable.[68] State practice with respect to the disposal of radioactive wastes has continued on a basis of national regulation and limited international co-operation on regional lines.[69] If an accident were to occur the principles of international law which might be cited in argument would be much the same as those referred to above in the case of a dispute concerning pollution due to the disposal of domestic and industrial wastes, together with reference to the provisions of the 1958 High Seas Convention. In this instance, however, it may be regarded as very much more likely that, having regard to the pattern followed in the international conventions relating to liability for nuclear accidents in other spheres, the standard of strict or absolute liability (and not that of proof of negligence) would be applied in determining responsibility.[70]

4. *Disposal of military materials*

The disposal of military wastes in the oceans may be regarded as, in part, an aspect of the use of the seas for military purposes, already touched on as regards radioactivity hazards, and also as merely a particular form of ocean dumping.[71] It does, however, have its particular characteristics. Because of the military aspect, information as to the exact character and quantity disposed of is usually classified, or only made partially available after the event. From the nature of the case, however, the materials in question are likely to include many substances which are highly toxic.[72] As regards the legitimacy *per se* of the disposal of unwanted weapons into the seas, if ocean dumping itself is not illegal it would not become so because of the military purposes for which the goods were manufactured. Nevertheless, there is a matter of psychological sentiment—or a choice of values if you will—in the attitude often taken towards military dumping which requires mention. In the case of domestic and industrial waste, there is a realization that the substances in question were produced, directly or indirectly, in the course of processes which most people would regard as normal and beneficial for everyday purposes. There is a reluctance to make the same assumption with respect to the production and disposal of war *matériel*; in this instance there is accordingly a tendency to require the producer state to beat his surplus sword and poison gas into a ploughshare in his own backyard, and not in the public oceans. The enormous toxicity of the weapons which may be produced has undoubtedly raised fears in this respect, and increased the pressure that the disposer state shall not expose others to harm.

As regards current law, as has already been indicated, the matter stands regulated by general principles, in the same way as other acts of ocean dumping. The question, however, received some degree of international attention as a result of the disposal by the United States of a quantity of nerve gas in the Atlantic during August 1970, and it may be that the law in this area may be developed towards some measure of agreed controls. It is, perhaps, of interest to note the various steps taken by different parties. There was, first, a series of actions brought by individual citizens before local courts, designed to halt the United States authorities. The resultant publicity prompted international complaints (or requests for information) by various states, either bilaterally through diplomatic channels or before United Nations bodies. The United Nations Sea-Bed Committee, which was meeting at the time in Geneva, issued a unanimous statement expressing its concern ' at the practice of dumping toxic, radio-active and other noxious materials ' on the sea-bed, and appealed to all governments to refrain from using the sea-bed as a dumping ground for materials which might cause serious harm to the marine environment. The Committee noted the assurances given by the United States delegation that effective precautions had been taken ' and that such action will not be taken again '.[73]

The conclusion suggested by the above is that the disposal into the oceans of highly dangerous military materials is no longer a matter at the discretion of the individual state, but is one where nascent ' community ' or ' general ' interest is beginning to make itself felt in explicit terms. While states disposing of substances which have such a high degree of toxicity may be expected to be even more careful in future than they have been so far, the question of what further measures may be instituted is difficult to answer at this juncture. If an international sea-bed authority were to be set up with jurisdiction over the area, it might be entitled to control and supervise such actions; it is hard to say whether this would be acceptable to all the major states involved, although, since they must all have to deal with the problem, perhaps they might manage to agree to such a proposal; it is encouraging in this regard that the United States proposal concerning an international sea-bed regime was put in terms which would encompass such powers. In the absence of an international sea-bed authority with wide enough authority, the alternative which suggests itself is a system of registration, possibly as part of a general system of registering acts of ocean dumping. The questions to be answered would then be, how specific would the information have to be, and what form of surveillance, if any, would exist? What form of protection (other than forewarning) would be given to a state which wished to prevent a particular act of dumping which it felt might endanger its interests? These would, in effect, be the questions raised with respect to any system of control of ocean activities via registration.

5. Ship-borne pollutants

States, of course, have long regulated the conditions under which ships flying their flag may carry harmful or noxious cargoes. Since such regulations have not been uniformly adopted or enforced, however, there have been limits to their effectiveness as a means of preventing the deliberate discharge of such cargoes or of enabling states to deal with the problem of accidental spillages. In the case of the most frequent ship-borne pollutant, oil, recourse has therefore been had to international measures.[74] Besides the requirement in Article 24 of the 1958 Convention on the High Seas that states ' . . . shall draw up regulations to prevent pollution of the seas by the discharge of oil from ships . . . taking account of existing treaty provisions on the subject ', a series of multilateral conventions have been adopted, designed to regulate oil pollution caused either in the course of a ship's operations (e.g. a release of oil or oily water from a tanker in ballast), or as a result of a major accident (a massive oil spill).[75]

The International Convention for the Prevention of Pollution of the Sea by Oil, which was concluded in 1954 and amended, under the auspices of IMCO, in 1962 and 1969,[76] is the only existing international convention dealing solely with the prevention of a major potential source of marine pollution prior to its commission. Under the 1954 and 1962 versions of the Convention, the discharge of oil or of oily mixture was prohibited within specified zones; [77] the 1969 amendments do away with the system of prohibited zones and in principle prohibit oil discharge, except under specified conditions, more stringent than those previously applicable. By way of enforcement each tanker or ship using oil fuel covered by the Convention is required to maintain an oil record book, specifying the ship's operations involving the receiving or discharge of oil or oily mixture. Any state party is authorized to inspect any ship covered by the Convention while in its ports, as well as the ship's oil record book. The effectiveness of the Convention, as a means of preventing oil pollution, has been somewhat limited in practice. The size of the prohibited zone may make detection difficult, and even when ships are caught in the act of violating the provisions of the Convention, the penalties which may be imposed are those of the flag state, which may be minimal or even non-existent.[78]

The 1954 Convention provides in any case little or no help in dealing with the problem of an accidental massive oil spill, a possibility which the increasing use of bulk tankers has rendered more likely. There is a number of technical measures which can be adopted to reduce the possibility of these accidents, such as improved methods of construction and equipment, ' load on top ' procedures [79] and the use of oil-water separators, the elaboration of traffic routing rules, better training of officers and crew, and the development of better means for removing oil and other pollutants from the sea. Besides preventive steps of this character, which are currently under study by IMCO,[80] as well as by other international bodies and national authorities, consideration has also been given to the possibility of direct action by a coastal state to prevent or limit pollution when an accident occurs or threatens.

Under general principles of international law, jurisdiction over ships on the high seas has been limited to the flag state; accordingly, in the absence of treaty arrangements, a coastal state would lack clear authority to intervene in order to take protective action. In order to fill this gap, as regards oil tankers at least, a multilateral Convention was concluded in November 1969 under the auspices of IMCO, defining the conditions under which the coastal state may intervene. This Convention, the International Convention Relating to Intervention on the High Seas in Cases of Oil Pollution Casualties, was complemented by a second, the International Convention on Civil Liability for Oil Pollution Damage, which regulates the system of financial liability in respect of major oil spillages.[81] Both these Conventions, it should be stressed, are only secondary or indirect means of preventing oil pollution; they come into operation after accidents have occurred or are immediately imminent. Their effect, as a means of forestalling pollution (as opposed to controlling or limiting pollution once it has taken place) largely depends therefore on such factors as the conditions which those who may be called upon to pay in the event of an accident (chiefly the marine insurers) may choose to impose on shipowners and operators in return for providing financial coverage. Such indirect, though important, means of accident prevention thus complement the steps which states may take directly.[82] This division of functions, together with the existence of the earlier instrument, the 1954 International Convention for the Prevention of Pollution of the Sea by Oil, indicates, however, some of the difficulties of providing outright an effective and unified system of international regulation in spheres where many states and large economic interests are involved: to draw a not too far-fetched municipal analogy, it is as though the police had power to remove cars which caused accidents but it was the insurers who were normally responsible for seeing that cars had effective brakes and steering in the first place.

The International Convention relating to Intervention on the High Seas in Cases of Oil Pollution Casualties (the so-called ' Public Law ' Convention) provides that states parties

. . . may take such measures on the high seas as may be necessary to prevent, mitigate or eliminate grave and imminent danger to their coastline or related interests from pollution or threat of pollution of the sea by oil, following upon a maritime casualty or acts related to such a casualty, which may reasonably be expected to result in major harmful consequences.[83]

Before taking any steps, the coastal state is required to consult with the flag state and to notify those whose interests may be affected (normally the owners of the ship and cargo). The state may also consult independent experts drawn from a list maintained by IMCO.

In cases of extreme urgency the coastal state may take action without prior notification or consultation. The measures taken, which are to be notified, *inter alia*, to IMCO, are to be proportionate to the danger, and may not go beyond what is reasonably necessary or unnecessarily interfere with the rights and interests of the flag state, third states, or any persons concerned [84]; compensation is payable in the event that damage is caused by measures taken beyond those reasonably necessary. Disputes between states parties as to whether particular measures were justified or as regards the payment of compensation in respect of any measures taken, are to be submitted to a conciliation commission and, failing that, to arbitration, according to detailed procedures set out in an annex to the Convention.

The second treaty, the so-called ' Private Law ' Convention, provides that, except in the case of certain limited exceptions,[85] the owner of the ship [86] is to be liable for any pollution damage caused within the territorial boundaries of a contracting state, including liability for the costs of any preventive measures taken.[87] As is customary in international instruments providing for strict liability, a ceiling is placed on the amount of compensation payable in respect of any one incident; in the present instance the upper figure is set at 2,000 gold francs per ton or 210 million gold francs in aggregate (approximately $14 million). In order to claim the benefits of this limitation, the ship-owner is required to deposit the relevant sum, or a guarantee in lieu, with the court or competent authority in the event that an action is brought against him under the Convention. The fund thus provided is to be distributed proportionately amongst the claimants.[88] The owner of a ship registered in a contracting state and carrying more than 2,000 tons of oil as bulk cargo is required in any event to maintain insurance or other financial security ' such as the guarantee of a bank or a certificate delivered by an international compensation fund ',[89] up to the limits of liability prescribed by the Convention. A certificate attesting that this insurance or financial security is in force is to be carried on board the ship; contracting states are required to ensure that ships, wherever registered, actually carrying 2,000 tons or more of oil as bulk cargo, possess the required amount of insurance or other financial security when entering or leaving their ports or terminals.[90] If pollution damage does occur, actions for compensation may be brought, within stated periods,[91] in the courts of a contracting state in whose territory (including territorial sea) pollution damage has occurred or which has taken preventive measures.[92]

The Brussels Conference at which the Conventions were concluded also adopted two resolutions. The first of these recommended that, pending the entry into force of an international instrument or the extension of the 'Public Law' Convention to cover pollution by agents other than oil, IMCO should intensify its work with respect to such agents and that states 'which become involved in a case of pollution danger by agents other than oil co-operate as appropriate in applying wholly or partially the provisions of the Convention'.[93] The IMCO Legal Committee decided in January 1970 that further technical information was required before consideration could be given to specific proposals.[94] GESAMP has since examined the pollution potentialities of a list of substances carried as cargo, selected from the General Index to the International Maritime Dangerous Goods Code.[95]

The second resolution dealt with a proposal made during the Conference that a supplementary scheme, such as an international fund, should be established to ensure that adequate compensation would be available for all victims following an accident, even where there was no liability on the shipowner under the 'Private Law' Convention, or where the compensation due from the shipowner under the Convention was insufficient to repair the damage inflicted.[96] The resolution, noting that the Convention 'does not afford full protection for victims in all cases', recognized that a 'supplementary scheme in the nature of an international fund is necessary to ensure that adequate compensation will be available for victims . . .'. IMCO was requested to elaborate a draft of a compensation scheme, based on the principles of providing full and adequate compensation for victims under a system of strict liability, and, secondly, of relieving the shipowner of the additional financial burden imposed by the Convention. IMCO, which has set up a working group to examine the matter,[97] was asked to convene, not later than 1971, an international conference to consider the adoption of such a compensation scheme, which, if brought into operation, would thus complement or extend the security afforded by the 1969 'Private Law' Convention.

For one state at least, the provisions of the 1969 Conventions provided, in her view, inadequate protection for her needs. Canada has objected to the two draft Conventions principally on the following grounds: that they failed to give a sufficient measure of prior control to enable the coastal state to ensure that accidents would not occur; that, in the case of the 'Private Law' Convention, liability was not placed on the cargo owner (and thus directly on the oil industry) as well as the shipowner; and because financial reparation under that Convention extends only to damage inflicted within territorial limits and does not include pollution damage caused on the high seas to fishing vessels and to fishing interests in zones contiguous to the territorial sea.[98] For these reasons, and because oil and other forms of pollution present special dangers to the ecological balance that now exists in the Arctic—and also, it may be said, to emphasize Canadian sovereignty over the Northwest passage—the Canadian government has prepared two acts, one [99] extending the limit of Canada's territorial sea from three to twelve miles and enabling fishery conservation zones to be established in areas beyond, and the other to prevent pollution of Arctic waters.[100] Under the Arctic Waters Pollution Prevention Act, commercially owned ships intending to enter Arctic waters designated by the Canadian government as shipping safety control zones will be required to meet Canadian hull, construction, and navigation safety standards and to comply with ice-breaker escort regulations. The shipping safety control zones may extend up to 100 nautical miles from the Canadian coastline north of 60° latitude. The owners of ships and cargoes are required to provide evidence of financial responsibility, in the form of insurance, or an indemnity bond, in an amount determined by the Canadian authorities. The deposit of waste is prohibited and penalties may be imposed, ranging from $5,000 to $100,000 a day, for any violations. Civil liability for any harm caused, though subject to a maximum ceiling figure, is absolute. Provision is made for the application of similar protective measures, including prior review of proposed activities, with respect to the exploration and exploitation of the natural resources of the land or submarine area adjacent to Arctic waters.

Canada's special position in the area and the distinctive character of the region place the Arctic, and the impending legislation, in a somewhat particular category, and it is difficult to determine at this juncture whether the steps which Canada proposes will remain a solitary example, the unilateral creation of a unique ' regime ' acquiesced in by other states, or the forerunner of similar acts on the part of other states.[101] So far as the general question of protecting and regulating marine interests outside existing territorial limits is concerned, a distinction may be drawn between the special interests put forward by individual states (most notably as regards fishing), and the common interest, shared by all, in preserving the entire marine environment, and, beyond that, in the continued orderly conduct of marine affairs. In so far as there may be a danger of a gradual deterioration in the ecology of the sea, caused by rising levels of pollution in different areas and by different activities, it would seem clear that this cannot be dealt with by one state alone but only by agreement on measures of international surveillance and regulation. As regards the protection of special interests, Canada's position vis-à-vis the Arctic does not easily find parallels elsewhere,[102] and fishing states, tempted though they may be to follow the Canadian example, may in fact hesitate to do so unless it appears the only course open to them. The difficulties in maintaining a continuous

patrol over large areas of open sea, the varieties of sources of pollution, the need to allow exploration and exploitation of mineral resources to continue, and the technical problems of gauging ocean
pollution may all incline fishing states towards participation in an
international solution, if one acceptable to them, as well as to states
with other interests, can be agreed upon. Resolution of the issues raised
will entail difficult negotiations and a general willingness to accept
innovations, with the alternative to the introduction of stronger
measures of international control being a move on the part of a number
of governments towards unilateral measures, designed to safeguard
their immediate concerns. Whatever the exact modalities which may
be arrived at, a greater regulation and protection of marine interests
(both particular and general), and a considerable change in the existing law of the sea and its institutions look likely to result.

6. *Pollution as a result of mineral exploitation*

The exploration and exploitation of the mineral resources [103] of the
sea-bed and subsoil may take place either in areas subject to national
control or in the area beyond, since it is now agreed that there *is* an
international area beyond that of national jurisdiction,[104] even if its
precise delimitation and legal regime have yet to be determined. The
legal setting for otherwise identical activities may thus vary considerably, even though, from the point of view of a potential operator, the
operational standards imposed may prove to have many common
features.

Taking the two sectors in turn, in the case of mineral exploitation
in areas subject to national jurisdiction, the only multilateral obligations laid down by treaty are those contained in the 1958 Convention
on the Continental Shelf. These provide that ' The exploration of the
continental shelf and the exploitation of its natural resources must not
result in any unjustifiable interference with navigation, fishing or the
conservation of the living resources of the sea . . .',[105] and that, in the
safety zones established around installations, the coastal state is obliged
to take ' all appropriate measures for the protection of the living
resources of the sea from harmful agents '.[106]

The extent of the appropriate measures is not further defined. The
intrinsic risk of sea-bed operations and the coastal state's need to
ensure that its coasts and local fisheries are not polluted have caused
states engaged in exploiting the mineral resources of their continental
shelf to regulate the activities with some care.[107] In a United Nations
study dealing with the common denominators of states' practice with
respect to the development of mineral resources on the continental
shelf, it was noted that ' in every case reviewed, the countries concerned
refer to the relevant stipulations of the Geneva Convention on the

Continental Shelf '.[108] The requirement that ' all appropriate measures ' be taken to protect the living resources of the sea appears in practice to have been largely interpreted as requiring operators to observe the provisions of ' good oil industry practice ' and to provide the requisite equipment to stop the flow of petroleum if a blow-out occurs, or if there is a break in the well casing or pipeline. Whilst operators are generally liable for damage caused to third parties, provisions relating specifically to the prevention of harmful effects are relatively scanty and only in some of the most recent legislation (most notably in the United States Federal Regulations introduced on 18 August 1969, following the Santa Barbara incident) are specific requirements included designed to afford protection against pollution. The policy followed by the United States is of special interest in view of that country's extensive experience with marine exploration and its dangers. That the full costs of repairing the damage have been placed squarely with the oil-exploiting companies [109] and that responsibility has been cast by statute in terms of absolute liability,[110] are features which other countries may need to consider (the main inhibiting factor being, of course, the heavy cost of insurance, with a consequential slowing-down of sea-bed exploitation, unless the state agrees to underwrite any damage caused).

As regards the exploration and exploitation of the mineral resources of the area beyond the limits of national jurisdiction,[111] agreement has not yet been reached as to the nature of the regime which should govern such activities. In the course of discussions in the United Nations Sea-Bed Committee, the question of pollution has, however, been raised and it is possible to discern, in outline at least, the various possible solutions to the issues posed. The Declaration of Principles, adopted on 17 December 1970, states in paragraph 11 that:

With respect to activities in the area and acting in conformity with the international régime to be established, States shall take appropriate measures for and shall co-operate in the adoption and implementation of international rules, standards and procedures for, *inter alia*:

(a) Prevention of pollution and contamination, and other hazards to the marine environment, including the coastline, and of interference with the ecological balance of the marine environment;

(b) Protection and conservation of the natural resources of the area and prevention of damage to the flora and fauna of the marine environment.[112]

The Declaration is necessarily couched in general language and constitutes a politically agreed indication of intent rather than a legally precise text. The issues to which further attention will have to be given may, with some compression, be reduced basically to two: (i) whether the operational standards and regulations to be imposed are to be set and enforced nationally or internationally; and (ii) what is to be the substantive content of the rules and procedures to be adopted in order to prevent pollution and to govern liability for damage if pollution should occur. The first issue is closely tied to the fundamental question of the character of future arrangements to be established for the sea-bed: thus an international body with wide powers might well be given regulatory authority, including authority to adopt and apply measures with respect to the control of pollution; [113] if, on the other hand, activities are to be authorized by states (which will bear international responsibility), then the adoption and application of appropriate measures might be a matter for individual governments.[114] Perhaps a 'mixed' system may also be envisaged: a 'two-tiered' arrangement, such as has been suggested,[115] whereby concessions are given to states which in turn authorize other entities to carry out the actual operations, might be compatible with the application of provisions of national law,[116] within the guidelines laid down internationally. According to the basic approach adopted, international standards might be stated in general terms in the agreement establishing the international regime and supplemented by more detailed regulations developed by the administering authority; alternatively, fairly explicit rules could be embodied in the fundamental agreement itself.[117] The complexity of the subject matter may also have a bearing on the division of national and international functions; as the United States representative pointed out,[118] whereas the United States Outer Continental Shelf Lands Act is relatively short, the implementary regulations are many pages in length and are supplemented by regional directives, as well as being frequently revised. Adoption of international measures on a comparable scale would thus be a considerable undertaking and require a high degree of knowledge and expertise in a number of disciplines.

The actual process of adopting regulations and of establishing operating conditions on an international basis may itself perform a useful function, however, not only as a valuable act of multinational co-operation with respect to the major part of the world's surface, but also in so far as it may give states with special interests (most notably those whose chief concern is with fishing) a chance to safeguard their interests other than by recourse to liability procedures after pollution has occurred or, possibly, by prior resort to unilateral action. Iceland, with its natural preoccupation over this issue, has sought to argue that coastal states should be entitled to exercise some measure of control over activities in adjacent waters, including power to approve or disapprove of plans for exploration and exploitation,[119] and the Canadian legislation on Arctic waters specifically embodies such a power, together with other regulatory measures. It will be one of the many questions to be determined whether states will wish to concede such a unilateral right to particular coastal states (beyond at least quite narrow territorial limits), or whether protection of fishing interests (including representation of states such as Iceland) cannot more effectively be incorporated in the international regulation process—if one is adopted.

As regards the actual content of the rules and principles to be adopted, the Legal Sub-Committee of the United Nations Sea-Bed Committee has so far chiefly confined itself to discussion, in general terms, of the question of liability.[120] On this issue it is possible to argue that liability should be made dependent on fault (such as acting without appropriate operational safeguards or without having obtained authorization), or, alternatively, that it should be imposed irrespective of whether there is proof of negligence or wrong doing.[121] In favour of the easier requirement would be the arguments that, since the operator would be working at a greater distance from the coast, the danger of pollution of beaches, and perhaps of harm to marine life also, would be lessened (although the risk to the safety of those actually working on the installation would increase as the depth and distance from the shore increased),[122] and, secondly, if liability is made too stringent, operators may be reluctant to attempt to exploit the area. On the other side weighty arguments may be advanced, pointing to the standard of municipal regulations and the danger to other interests, notably fishing, if areas of the sea and sea-bed were to be polluted. Resolution of the issue requires consideration, too, of the scope and nature of the resource concerned and of the technical means of its exploitation. In the case of surficial deposits, such as manganese nodules, although there may be some risk of pollution from the chemicals used during beneficiation, and turbulence caused by the release of debris, these are both dangers which can (provided appropriate regulations exist) be brought under control fairly easily.[123] The position with respect to the drilling of petroleum deposits is more complicated. The cost of marine drilling increases with the depth of water and, in order to provide economies of scale which will make the venture profitable, the offshore deposits which are exploited tend, on average, to be larger than those exploited on land, and may need to be larger still to justify exploitation at greater depths than is now undertaken.[124] Since at the present time it would be hard to deny that marine drilling techniques are in advance of means for restraining or removing oil pollution if a blow-out or other incident occurs, the conclusion is reached, in the words of the United States delegation, that ' the chance for accidents of massive proportions in this environment is a very real one '.[125] In the case of marine exploitation of oil, states may accordingly need to give careful consideration to the adequacy of operational procedures (including the process by which the adequacy of such procedures is to be determined—which goes back to the fundamental question of the nature of the institutional arrangements to be made for the sea-bed) and to the adoption of suitable provisions with respect to liability. In keeping with the risk that accidents may occur which result in large-scale damage, the suggestion has been made that insurance or financial security should be required to cover such eventualities and that the activities of would-be operators should be made dependent on their participation in an insurance fund.[126] (The suggestion thus neatly parallels the arrangements proposed with respect to accidents on a similar scale involving oil tankers.) Others have proposed that states should be responsible for the national activities they authorize.[127] The two approaches could be combined, as in the 1969 'Private Law' Convention with respect to tankers; it could be made a condition of the international arrangements to be agreed upon for the sea-bed that individual operators should have adequate insurance coverage or a financial security in lieu, either from a private, governmental, or international source (or from all or several of these, in the event of a multinational venture).

As regards the particular interests to be protected, the danger to the nearest coast would be reduced as the distance from the shore increased. In principle, however, coastal states would be entitled to recover for such damages as they might suffer within their boundaries by reason of accidents occurring in the international zone. Navigation would be relatively little affected.[128] The main economic interests which would need protection are those of other mineral exploiters, who might be forced to suspend their operations,[129] and, of course, those of persons or states engaged in fishing. If the latter could demonstrate a decline in the size of their catch due to oil pollution, or a drop in sales, it would be difficult to deny a claim for recompense. Besides these considerations relating to specific interests, there is, also, the question of overall environmental protection. Even if the chances of a catastrophic accident are set aside, there may be a need to guard against a gradual deterioration in the marine environment, brought about by activities continued over a period of years.[130] As in the case of the other pollutants, the establishment of international means to observe and report on the state of the seas would help to prevent such an eventuality, independently of the position (essentially the security of reparation and participation in the regulatory process) granted to particular economic interests.

III. INTERNATIONAL PROPOSALS AND DISCUSSIONS

This section is intended as a brief summary of the proposals which have been made or discussed by international bodies during recent years with respect to the problem of marine pollution.

In 1969 the Intergovernmental Oceanographic Commission (IOC) completed the preparation of its proposed long-term and expanded programme of oceanographic research,[131] which includes a series of projects relating to marine pollution. Having noted that ' the levels achieved by some pollutants in some parts of the ocean are already a matter of deep public and scientific concern, and dangerously high levels may be imminent with respect to others ', the Commission emphasized that ' Losses or impairment of use through contamination may only be prevented by rational policies based on research and monitoring '. For this to be effective all pollutants, whatever their source, would need to be monitored, and, eventually, so far as possible, controlled; at the same time detailed investigations should be made of the complex effects of each type of pollutant. The Commission therefore proposed a number of scientific projects, including the establishment of a world-wide system of monitoring of the constituents of marine pollution,[132] designed to lead (together with the other inquiries conducted) to the preparation of periodic, comprehensive reports on the health of the oceans. These reports ' would review the state of the ocean and its marine resources as regards pollution, and forecast long-term trends to assist governments individually and collectively to take the steps required to counteract its effect '. No specific proposals are made with regard to the means by which the suggested world-wide system of monitoring might be conducted. Elsewhere in the IOC programme, however, a description is given of the Integrated Global Ocean Station System, which is being developed in conjunction with World Weather Watch (operated by the World Meteorological Organization (WMO)), to provide oceanographical and meteorological information and to facilitate understanding of the interaction between the oceans and the atmosphere. The Integrated Global Ocean Station System is arranged on a basis of voluntary participation whereby states provide facilities and staff to operate fixed and mobile observing stations, the necessary co-ordination being supplied by IOC in collaboration with WMO. At a more advanced level of co-ordinated inquiry, IOC has also proposed the adoption of a convention which would establish uniform rules for the deployment of ocean data acquisition systems (ODAS), which would make available further information about the characteristics of the environment of the oceans.[133]

IOC does not itself have funds and institutional means instantly at its disposal to carry out the projects described; the long-term and expanded programme represents an agreed list of desirable items, drawn up by experts in order to show what is required scientifically, in the hope that governments and others will then provide the financial and material support to enable the requisite knowledge to be obtained. One of these means, so far as marine pollution is concerned, is to be found in the Joint IMCO/FAO/UNESCO/WMO/WHO/IAEA Group of Experts on the Scientific Aspects of Marine Pollution, which was established in 1969. At its first session in March 1969,[134] the Group agreed to identify certain main categories of pollutants and to establish research priorities with respect to them. The Group pointed out, *inter alia*, that, if the effects of pollutants are to be measured effectively, a norm must be established by which changes in the environment itself can be measured, and for this a high degree of monitoring will be required. In the case of the dumping of various materials, particularly radioactive substances, petrochemical, and other chemical wastes and pesticides, the Group noted the view expressed by an earlier IOC working group, that a measure of international control should be introduced by means of the registration of the activities in question, and suggested that further efforts should be made to establish the exact categories of pollutants to be brought under international control by such means. With respect to the information system relating to marine pollution, the Group distinguished two problems, besides that of the registration of deliberate or accidental discharges or spillages: the collection of pertinent environmental data (the essential need here being to ensure that all relevant data are deposited in, or known to, the World Data Centres for Oceanography and, as appropriate, specialized data centres such as those maintained by the International Council for the Exploration of the Sea and by FAO); and information about scientific documentation (the priority need under this heading being for a good reference retrieval system—marine pollution is already covered, at least in part, in at least nine English-language abstracting and bibliographic periodicals, and by some in other languages).

Since GESAMP's first session in March 1969, the problems relating to ocean monitoring have been further examined, both by GESAMP itself [135] and by an expert group advising IOC on its long-term and expanded programme of oceanic research.[136] The more extensive consideration of the matter which has been undertaken has served to evidence the very considerable scientific and technical difficulties in the way of simply instituting a system (or series of systems) of ocean surveillance. Although the task can be carried out, it cannot be done easily; a large amount of preliminary work will have to be done first. This was brought out by the 1970 Study of Critical Environmental Problems [137] and at the Technical Conference on Marine Pollution and its Effects on Living Resources and Fishing, held by the Food and Agriculture Organization (FAO) in December 1970. This Conference, and the Seminar which preceded it, resulted in the most comprehensive examination so far made of the scientific aspects of pollution as it affects the flora and fauna living in the seas, and of the problems involved in attempting to measure both the existing state of the seas ('base line studies') and changes in that state.

Whereas the activities of IOC and FAO concern the scientific investigatory aspects or the effects upon living resources respectively, the work of IMCO has been concerned primarily with the prevention and control of ship-borne pollution. In addition to the 1962 and 1969 amendments to the 1954 Convention, and the two 1969 Conventions, drawn up within the framework of IMCO, an international conference will be convened by IMCO in 1973 'for the purpose of preparing a suitable international agreement for placing restraints on the contamination of the sea, land and air by ships, vessels and other equipment operating in the marine environment'.[138] The subjects under consideration for the Conference are: deliberate dumping by ships and barges; operational discharge from ships; accidental release from ships and submarine pipelines; and exploitation of sea-bed mineral resources.[139]

The United Nations itself has been concerned with the problem of marine pollution from various standpoints, including that of providing co-ordination of the activities of all United Nations agencies concerned with marine affairs. The Administrative Committee on Co-ordination established a subcommittee on marine science which, in 1966, sent a questionnaire to member states on the subject of marine pollution. The replies received were incorporated in a comprehensive survey of activities in marine science and technology, prepared by the Secretary-General,[140] in accordance with the terms of General Assembly resolution 2172 (XXI) of 6 December 1966. Having considered this report at its twenty-third session held in 1968, the General Assembly endorsed the concept of a co-ordinated long-term programme of oceanographic research, which IOC has since prepared, and invited member states and organizations, especially IMCO and IAEA, 'to promote the adoption of effective international agreements on the prevention and control of marine pollution as may be necessary'.[141] At the same session the General Assembly adopted resolution 2467 (XXIII) relating to the international area of the sea-bed, part B of which dealt with possible marine pollution.[142] In operative paragraph 1 of resolution 2467 B (XXIII) the General Assembly welcomed 'the adoption by States of appropriate safeguards' against the dangers of pollution and other hazards which might arise from the exploration and exploitation of sea-bed resources beyond the limits of national jurisdiction, 'notably in the form of concrete measures of international co-operation'. In operative paragraph 4 of the same resolution the Secretary-General was requested to undertake a study 'with a view to clarifying all aspects of protection of the living and other resources of the sea-bed and ocean floor, the superjacent waters and the adjacent coasts against the consequences of pollution and other hazardous and harmful effects ' arising from the exploration and exploitation of resources beyond the limits of national jurisdiction.[143]

In addition to these specific proposals, at its twenty-third session the General Assembly also adopted resolution 2398 (XXIII) of 3 December 1968, providing for the convening, in 1972, of a United Nations Conference on the Human Environment. In 1969 the General Assembly, having referred to this Conference and those proposed by IMCO and FAO, and IOC's expanded programme of oceanographic research, requested the Secretary-General:

. . . in co-operation with the specialized agencies and intergovernmental organizations concerned, to complement reports and studies under preparation, with special reference to the forthcoming United Nations Conference on the Human Environment, by :

(a) A review of harmful chemical substances, radio-active materials and other noxious agents and waste which may dangerously affect man's health and his economic and cultural activities in the marine environment and coastal areas;

(b) A review of national activities and activities of specialized agencies of the United Nations and intergovernmental organizations dealing with prevention and control of marine pollution including suggestions for more comprehensive action and improved co-ordination in this field;

(c) Seeking the views of Member States on the desirability and feasibility of an international treaty or treaties on the subject.[144]

In the course of preparations for the Conference on the Human Environment, further reference was made to the possibility of international monitoring of environmental conditions. In his initial report [145] the Secretary-General pointed out that, while several existing or planned international research programmes (in particular World Weather Watch [146] and the International Hydrological Decade) provide an institutional basis for monitoring, there is as yet little international agreement on the methodology to be used. In meetings held during March 1970 of the Preparatory Committee for the United Nations Conference on the Human Environment, attention was drawn to the way in which national and regional monitoring systems might participate in international monitoring arrangements and, also, to an aspect which has as yet been relatively little considered in relation to marine pollution, namely the effect, in economic terms, of the introduction of pollution controls on different countries, in particular the possibility that such controls might place developing countries at a further disadvantage in their efforts at industrialization. In the course of subsequent meetings of the Preparatory Committee further consideration has been given to the methodological problems involved in instituting monitoring or other regulatory systems within an agreed overall framework. Having regard to the number of organizations concerned, directly or indirectly, with international aspects of marine pollution, and the decision of the General Assembly to call a conference on the law of the sea in 1973, which will deal both with the establishment of an international regime (including machinery) for the international area of the sea-bed and with ' a broad range of related issues ' including the prevention of pollution,[147] it is apparent that attention will also have to be given to ensuring that the objectives and functions of the various bodies are effectively co-ordinated. Of the three international Conferences which have been announced, that on the Human Environment in 1972, on the Law of the Sea in 1973, and the third to be called by IMCO, also in 1973, the division of responsibilities in this area may be broadly expressed as follows: whereas the 1972 Stockholm Conference may be expected to lead to the adoption of a Declaration on the Human Environment and to provide the political consensus and guidelines for action in specific areas,[148] it will in all probability devolve on other bodies to work out the full array of legal texts (including adjustments of existing law) which technological advances and the need to adopt a more conscious approach towards environmental management will require. The 1973 Conference on the Law of the Sea and the IMCO Conference may be expected to help in this respect—the former dealing with the fundamental issues to be resolved with regard to the law of the sea (in particular the question of the limits of areas of national and extra-national jurisdiction and the form of regime to be applied to the latter area), and the IMCO Conference assisting in providing the more technical body of legal regulation which will be needed as regards pollution from ships.

IV. A PATTERN OF NEEDS AND OF POSSIBLE SOLUTIONS

There is general agreement that some degree of international action is now required with respect to marine pollution: [149] the matter has to be assessed, on an international basis, and a decision, or decisions, reached on what is to be done. Thus the difficulty is to devise a series of measures of prevention and control which will be both adequate to the task and acceptable to the community of states. While the difficulty appears, when put in those terms, a truism scarcely worth recording, it serves to focus attention on the fact that much will depend on the way in which states now perceive and evaluate the problem. If it is decided to treat marine pollution as part of a wider concern for the maintenance of the environment as a whole, then comprehensive steps are more likely to be envisaged and, in general, a more radical approach adopted as regards existing procedures. If, on the other hand, marine pollution is regarded as a marginal issue which has not yet crossed the threshold of serious danger, attention is likely to be focused on protection of immediate economic interests, and marine pollution will be treated (as it has been so far) as a series of particular hazards and receive a series of specialized solutions. This division between an 'overall' and 'sectional' approach to marine pollution can be overdrawn; a golden compromise can, and perhaps will, be arrived at. Nevertheless it presents itself very near the outset as a fundamental issue to which states will have to address themselves; the importance in this context of scientific evidence and of the need for strong scientific reasons to justify any major innovations does not require comment. In order to place the issue in its full setting, attention should be drawn to the fact that a similar choice is presented, or is about to be presented, in a number of sectors of the law of the sea: the future status and regime of the international area of the sea-bed, the development of mineral resources, the rapid increase in fishing, and the impending changes in means of marine transport will all require major reassessment to be made of existing maritime law within the relatively near future. The question which presents itself is, at what stage should this be done and what institutional changes should be made? If, by reason of the factors just indicated, or because of their sheer accumulation, it was decided to make some change on a fairly large scale in the law of the sea and its institutions, then almost certainly the case would be strongly presented for an overall approach to be adopted with respect to pollution and for the devising of a single system of pollution surveillance and control.

In the meanwhile, it is necessary to continue to regard marine pollution as a separate issue, with its place in the total scheme of future marine affairs still to be determined. The problems involved can be grouped under three broadly distinct, though related, headings: the need for scientific study, on a regular basis, of the state of the oceans, as part of the environment, and of the exact effects of pollution; the establishment of various technical and regulatory means for the prevention and control of different forms of pollution having their origin in separate human activities; and, lastly, the problem of liability if the pollution due to specific activities causes damage to others.

In respect of the first function, it would appear unassailable that means must be devised to increase knowledge of the seas and of the consequences of the release, accidental or deliberate, of foreign substances into the seas. The oceans form so large and important a part of the world that surveillance of the environment (with all that that

implies with respect to weather control and forecasting, the understanding of physical laws, and the preservation of human existence)
can only be conducted on a basis which includes the marine zones.
Furthermore, only by conducting inquiries which encompass the
entire environment, including the oceans, will it be possible to distinguish between the effect on the one hand of human activities which
may lead to marine pollution and, on the other, that of the operation
of natural phenomena which may produce a deterioration in marine
conditions. Lastly, only a comprehensive scheme will enable accurate
determination to be made of the consequences of particular pollutants.
The work of IOC in seeking the establishment of the Integrated Global
Ocean Station System, together with World Weather Watch, and
other suggestions which have been made [150] relating to various institutional means of monitoring the environment, are all founded on
the need, scientifically speaking, to establish the ' natural ' parameters
of the environment, in order to measure the scale of such changes as
man may wish to impose, and to guard against the possibility of a
gradual (as well as of a sudden) deterioration in existing conditions.
All of these projects have as their characteristic that, to operate
effectively, they must eventually be global in scope and scientifically
inclusive in the range of their inquiries. The division between national
and international mechanism required to operate such systems has
yet to be determined. To some extent the means at our disposal, such
as space satellites,[151] reduce the need for scientists on the ground
or in the water, but national co-operation, through the assistance of
scientists in different countries, the compilation of information on
national practices (for example, waste disposal statistics) and the
reporting of accidental or deliberate discharges and so on, may be
regarded as an essential component of any monitoring and information
system likely to be adopted.

The operation of an ocean surveillance system (however organized
in its details) will be of importance to, though functionally distinct
from, the adoption of technical and regulatory means for the prevention and control of pollution caused by specific human activities.
The information provided by the surveillance system will indicate the
degree of urgency (or otherwise) with which action may need to be
undertaken, as well as of the exact impact of particular pollutants on
the marine environment (a matter affecting the question of liability
also). Nevertheless enough is already known for there to be a number
of areas in which technical measures can be taken, and where a start
has already been made. In the case of waste disposal (whether of
normal coastal wastes or of radioactive materials) the matters to be
considered range from the siting of industrial plants and the incor-
poration of waste disposal and anti-pollution devices at source, to the

means of disposal to be used and local conditions in the disposal area. The possibility of ship-borne pollutants and of pollution as a result of mining activities raises technical questions of a different character, concerning methods of ship construction, the training of personnel, the method of loading cargoes or of operating drilling or dredging machinery, the establishment of navigational rules and procedures, and the reporting to the appropriate authorities of accidental or deliberate discharges of oil. Each of these concerns is at the present time receiving attention from various specialized bodies, whether national, international, or industrial, and it may be presumed that such efforts will continue (as well as inquiries into ways of combating pollution once it has occurred), whatever institutional changes may be made.

Technical measures of this nature may be distinguished from more direct regulatory arrangements. In the case of pesticides and various other substances which result in atmospheric pollution or in marine pollution via the atmosphere, there may be limitations on the nature of the controls which can be introduced. Where, as in the case of pesticides spread on the ground or lead added to petrol, the pollutant cannot be recaptured, the choice is either to find an effective substitute or to discontinue the use of the substance—or, as an intermediate step, to reduce the quantities involved by determining which, amongst a number of purposes, the international community regards as the most valuable. Regulatory systems, other than on a ' prohibitory ' or ' reduction ' basis, may be introduced in other areas, however, besides actual technical means of preventing pollution. Ocean dumping, for example, could be controlled or supervised in a number of ways including, as has been suggested, a system of registration. Conditions in particular areas, notably shallow enclosed or semi-enclosed seas, may well lead to the adoption of regional arrangements on the part of neighbouring states more stringent than those which may be advocated on a world-wide basis.

Arrangements of this nature would apply with respect to deliberate acts of waste disposal (including disposal of radioactive wastes) coming from the land. The discharge of oil in the course of routine ship operations has already received a measure of regulation by international agreement, and the remaining question here would be whether any further enforcement measures may prove necessary. As regards mining operations, it may be presumed that national safeguards will continue to apply with respect to operations in areas under national jurisdiction; the adoption of pollution controls on a national or international (or mixed) basis as regards mining activities in the international area will depend to a large extent on the form of machinery which is established to regulate such activities, an issue which will be determined on a wider basis than that of pollution alone, and it is only when this question has been settled that the pattern and substantive content of the regulations concerned will finally emerge.

While a system of international, as well as national, registration may be applied with respect to the disposal of radioactive wastes (a separate matter, it may be pointed out, from the monitoring of the seas for radioactivity), in this instance the possibility exists (however remote) of the occurrence of a catastrophe, namely the sudden infliction of harm on a wide scale. In this respect the situation is distinguishable from those instances where a deterioration in marine conditions is likely to come about more gradually, after ' routine ' acts, such as the dumping of coastal wastes. The position as regards the dumping of radioactive wastes thus has some features in common with that in respect of bulk carriers or mining operations, which also involve the possibility of large-scale accidents. In these instances the question of liability has therefore to be considered, if only as an eventuality, as well as that of the day-to-day regulation of the activity itself. The solution adopted with respect to accidents involving oil tankers has been described in the text. A solution along similar lines with respect to other dangerous bulk cargoes appears probable, and a ' financial guarantee ' or ' insurance fund ' requirement may well form part of future arrangements for the international area of the sea-bed. In general, however, the question of liability, important though it is (and will surely always remain), will be only one, and not necessarily the most significant, amongst the means whereby marine pollution is controlled. The problem of the adoption of suitable forms of control of marine pollution proves on examination to be extremely complicated, with a host of scientific, technical, economic, and legal ramifications. While the international community is unlikely to adopt overnight the principles of a managed universe, the issue of liability may tend to shrink in importance by comparison with an emerging body of regulatory law, and be determined, in practice, by information derived from scientific inquiries and a monitoring system operating on an international basis.

In summary, therefore, it is suggested that the problem of marine pollution should be regarded from a triple standpoint:

(i) As part of the need for the protection and observation of the environment as a whole—a need which requires the eventual adoption of measures on a world-wide basis, within the framework of agreed scientific programmes of inquiry.

(ii) The adoption of (a) technical, and (b) regulatory, means of control with respect to various human activities which may give rise to major instances of marine pollution—a range of means extending from operational procedures, on which many different agencies are working, according to the nature of the subject-matter, to the adoption of various institutional arrangements, whether on a universal or a regional basis, and including in all probability a large degree of national activity and co-operation within the mechanism of a number of international agreements.

(iii) Recourse to agreed principles of liability and reparation to cover specific items of damage established, at least in part, by the scientific means referred to above, and subject to the conditions (such as channelling of responsibility to a single party and ceilings on the amount of maximum financial liability) laid down by treaty.

NOTES

CHAPTER 1

1 The European Coal and Steel Community Treaty, Art. 31. The European Economic Community Treaty, Art. 164. The Euratom Community Treaty, Art. 134.

2 However, under Art. 96 (1) of the Charter, the General Assembly or Security Council may request the International Court to give an advisory opinion ' on any legal question '. Many important advisory opinions, too well known to require enumeration here, have been given by the Court, interpreting the Charter, under this provision. It will also be recalled that the PCIJ gave a number of important judgments concerning the Covenant of the League of Nations and the ILO.

　　See also Res. 171 (II) of 14 Nov. 1947, *GAOR* (II), plenary meetings, vol. 2, p. 1559 (A/459): '. . . considering that it is of paramount importance that the interpretation of the Charter . . . and the Constitutions of the Specialized Agencies should be based on recognized principles of international law . . . recommends as a general rule that States should submit their legal disputes to the International Court of Justice '. See generally L. Kopelmanas, *L'Organisation des Nations Unies* (1947), pp. 252–311; ' Pollux ', ' The Interpretation of the Charter ', 23 *BYBIL* (1946) 54.

3 ILO Treaty, Art. 37 (1); WHO Treaty, Art. 75; IMCO Treaty, Art. 55; FAO Treaty, Art. 16 (1); UNESCO Treaty, Art. 14 (2). See generally C. W. Jenks, ' The Status of International Organizations in relation to the International Court of Justice ', 32 *Transactions of the Grotius Society* (1947) 1–41.

4 IMF, Art. 18 (*a*).

5 Ibid. (*b*).

6 ICAO, Art. 84.

7 WHO, Art. 75.

8 WMO, Art. 29.

9 FAO, Art. 16 (1).

10 J. E. S. Fawcett, ' The Place of Law in an International Organization ', 26 *BYBIL* (1949) 328: ' Three conclusions may be drawn from this discussion . . . the first is that the concept of judicial control is incompatible with the design of the Fund, and that even the indirect control which may be had through advisory opinions of the International Court will not work in an organization which has for technical reasons been made the interpreter of its own constitution.' See also E. P. Hexner, ' Interpretation by International Organizations of their Basic Instruments ', 53 *AJIL* (1959) 341; J. Gold, ' The Interpretation by the IMF of its Articles of Agreement ', *ICLQ*, 1954, p. 256.

11 UN Conference on International Organization, *Report of Rapporteur*, IV/2, Doc. 933, IV/2/42(2), pp. 7–8. L. M. Goodrich and E. Hambro, *Charter of the UN* (1949), pp. 547–51.

12 *SCOR*, 2nd year, 68, p. 1711: ' It is now jurisprudence in the Security Council . . . and the interpretation accepted for a long time . . . that an abstention is not considered a veto.'

13 F. A. Vallat, ' The Competence of the UN General Assembly ', 97 (Hague) *Recueil des cours*, II (1959) 203; S. Engel, ' The Changing Charter of the UN ', *The Yearbook of World Affairs*, 1953, pp. 71–101.

14 *International Status of South West Africa, ICJ Rep. 1950*, p. 136; *Competence of the General Assembly regarding Admission to the UN*, ibid. p. 9; *Competence of the International Labour Organization*, PCIJ, 1922, Series B, 2, p. 41.

15 H. Lauterpacht, *The Development of International Law by the International Court* (1958), p. 170.

16 43 *Annuaire de l'Institut de Droit International* (1950) 420.
17 H. Lauterpacht, 'Restrictive Interpretation and the Principle of Effectiveness in the Interpretation of Treaties', 26 *BYBIL* (1949) 76.
18 H. Kelsen, *The Law of the UN* (1950), p. xv.
19 G. Fitzmaurice, 'The Law and Procedure of the International Court of Justice 1951–4', 33 *BYBIL* (1957) 203–38. See also 27 *AJIL* (1937), Suppl., 937–77; J. Stone, 'Fictional Elements in Treaty Interpretation—a Study in the International Judicial Process', 1 *Sydney Law Review* (1953–4), 344–68.
20 Lauterpacht, 26 *BYBIL* (1949) 53.
21 A. M. Donner, 'The Court of Justice of the European Communities', *ICLQ*, Suppl. 1, 1961, p. 68.
22 The judgments of the Court are published in the *Recueil de la Jurisprudence de la Cour*, hereafter referred to as *Recueil*. The two appeals mentioned earlier in this sentence are: *Eva von Lachmüller, Bernard Peuvrier, Roger Ehrhardt c. Commission de la CEE*, 6/2 *Recueil* (1960), p. 933; *Rudolf Pieter Marie Fiddlelaar c. Commission de la CEE*, 6 *Recueil* (1960) 1077.
23 Above, p. 1.
24 D. G. Valentine, *Court of Justice of the European Coal and Steel Community* (1955), p. 56: 'It is not clear whether the words "shall ensure the rule of law" are to be taken as meaning that the Court is to be guided by the general principles of international law, and is to subordinate the interpretation and application of the Treaty to these principles; or whether the phrase has a more restricted sense and merely implies that in the interpretation of the Treaty, the Court is to be bound by recognized rules of interpretation and that the application of the Treaty shall be subordinate to the law as set out in the Treaty thus interpreted.'
25 ECSC Treaty, Art. 33, para. 1: 'The Court is competent to pronounce upon appeals for annulment for incompetence, violation of a substantial procedural requirement, violation of the Treaty or of any rule of law concerning its application or for *détournement de pouvoir* brought against the decisions and recommendations of the High Authority by one of the member States or by the Council.' EEC Treaty, Art. 173, para. 1; Euratom Treaty, Art. 146, para. 1: 'The Court of Justice shall determine upon the legality of the acts of the Council and of the Commission other than recommendations and opinions. To this effect, it is competent to pronounce upon appeals for incompetence, violation of substantial procedural requirements, violation of the present Treaty or of any rule of law concerning its application, or for *détournement de pouvoir* brought by a member State, the Council or the Commission.'
26 ECSC Treaty, Art. 33, para. 2: 'Enterprises or associations referred to in Article 48 may, under the same conditions, bring an appeal against individual decisions and recommendations concerning them or against general decisions and recommendations which they believe vitiated by a *détournement de pouvoir* with respect to them.' EEC Treaty, Art. 173, para. 2; Euratom Treaty, Art. 146, para. 2: 'Any natural or legal person may bring, under the same conditions, an appeal against decisions of which he is the recipient and against decisions which, although taken under the appearance of a regulation or of a decision addressed to another person, concern him directly and individually.'
27 ECSC Treaty, Art. 33, para. 2.
28 See D. G. Valentine, 'The Jurisdiction of the Court of Justice of the European Communities to Annul Executive Actions', 36 *BYBIL* (1960) 174.
29 ECSC Treaty, Art. 12. Twenty-three out of the hundred articles in the ECSC Treaty make some reference to the Court.
30 Ibid. Art. 10.
31 Ibid. Arts 36 and 66, para. 6.
32 Ibid. Art. 95.
33 Ibid. Arts 40, 42, 43.
34 This power is strictly limited by Art. 33 of the ECSC Treaty. However, that article provides for certain exceptions; see also Arts 36; 66, paras 5 and 6; 95; and 88.

[35] ECSC Treaty, Art. 89; EEC Treaty, Art. 182; Euratom Treaty, Art. 170.

[36] See G. Bebr, 'The Development of a Community Law by the Court of the European Coal and Steel Community', 42 *Minnesota Law Review* (1957–8) 845. The author wishes to acknowledge that he is much indebted here (and in his article 'The Court of the European Communities' in the *Journal of Common Market Studies*, 1/1, 1962) to the above most valuable article by Mr Bebr.

[37] See M. Gaudet, 'The Common Market and the Law', *Community Topics*, 4.

[38] ECSC Treaty, Arts 6, para. 3; 43, para. 2; 51, para. 1; 52, paras 1 and 2; 59, para. 3; 67, paras 1, 2 and 3; 68, paras 1, 2 and 3; 69, paras 1 and 4; 70, paras 2, 3, 4 and 5; 71, para. 1; 72; 73; 74, para. 3; 75, paras 1 and 2; 86; 90; 96.

[39] Gaudet, 'The Legal Framework of the Community', *ICLQ*, 1961, Suppl. 1, p. 15.

[40] *Friedrich Stork et Cie* c. *Haute Autorité*, 5 *Recueil* (1958–9) 63.

[41] *Comptoirs de vente du charbon de la Ruhr 'Präsident', 'Geitling', 'Mausegatt' et Entreprise I, Nold KG* c. *Haute Autorité de la CECA*, 6/2 *Recueil* (1960) 890.

[42] EEC Treaty, Arts 100 and 101. See Bebr, 'The Relation of the European Coal and Steel Community Law to the Law of the Member States: a Peculiar Legal Symbiosis', 58 *Columbia Law Review* (1958) 767.

[43] D. Thompson, 'The Project for a Commercial Company of European Type', *ICLQ*, 1961, p. 851.

[44] *Mannesmann AG et autres* c. *Haute Autorité*, 6/1 *Recueil* (1960) 322: 'Nous croyons toutefois ne pas devoir entrer jusque dans les détails de cette question de droit international privé ... Il suffit donc, à notre avis, de constater si l'appréciation des faits en cause nous conduirait aux mêmes résultats dans les deux droits. Il semble que ce soit le cas.'

[45] See Gaudet, 'The Common Market and the Law', *Community Topics*, 4.

[46] Art. 38.

[47] P. Reuter, *La Communauté européenne du charbon et de l'acier* (1953), p. 89. See generally, P. Mathijsen, *Le Droit de la communauté européenne du charbon et de l'acier* (1958), p. 4.

[48] *Fédération charbonnière de Belgique* c. *Haute Autorité*, 2 *Recueil* (1955–6) 264: 'Il faut donc se livrer à une exégèse pour combler cette lacune. Bien que le Code Napoléon ne soit pas applicable ici, nous ne pouvons pas ne pas rappeler son Article 4, aux termes duquel 'le juge qui refusera de juger', sous prétexte du silence, de l'obscurité ou de l'insuffisance de la loi, pourra être poursuivi comme coupable de déni de justice.'

[49] This will include the annexes and protocols referred to by the treaties.

[50] *De Gezamenlijke Steenkolenmijnen in Limburg* c. *Haute Autorité*, 5 *Recueil* (1958–9) 36.

[51] *Friedrich Stork et Cie* c. *Haute Autorité*, ibid. p. 83.

[52] *Associazione Industrie Siderurgiche Italiane (ASSIDER)* c. *Haute Autorité*, 1 *Recueil* (1954–5) 149.

[53] Ibid. p. 291. See also *Chambre syndicale de la sidérurgie de l'est de la France et autres* c. *Haute Autorité*, 6/2 *Recueil* (1960) 652: 'Nous estimons que si cette théorie est de mise en droit des gens, elle n'est pas valable pour le droit de la Communauté, donc pour une communauté qui se distingue fondamentalement des unions habituelles du droit des gens.'

[54] *Fédération charbonnière de Belgique* c. *Haute Autorité*, 2 *Recueil* (1955–6) 263.

[55] *Hamborner Bergbau Ab Friedrich Thyssen Bergbau AG* c. *Haute Autorité*, 6 *Recueil* (1960) 1049.

[56] *Barbara Erzbergbau AG et autres* c. *Haute Autorité*, 6/1 *Recueil* (1960) 386.

[57] Donner, cited in n. 21 above, p. 68.

[58] *Eva von Lachmüller, Bernard Peuvrier, Roger Ehrhardt* c. *Commission de la Communauté Economique Européenne*, 6/2 *Recueil* (1960) 967.

[59] See M. Lagrange, 'L'Ordre juridique de la CECA vu à travers la Jurisprudence de sa Cour de Justice', 74 *Revue de droit public* (1958) 862–3.

[60] Robert Schuman, Préface to Reuter's *La Communauté européenne du charbon et de l'acier* (1953), p. 7.

[61] Congrès international d'études sur la Communauté européenne du charbon et de l'acier, *Rapport de Paul de Visscher*, 2 *Actes officiels* (1957), pp. 38–9.

[62] ECSC Treaty, Art. 89; EEC Treaty, Art. 182; Euratom Treaty, Art. 170.

[63] *Rapport de Paul de Visscher*, op. cit., p. 36.

[64] See the ratification debates concerning the ECSC Treaty. Coste-Floret, Rapporteur of the Foreign Affairs Commission, *Assemblée Nationale, Official Reports* (1951), p. 8855, col. 1. 'If I wished to define this new organ in a single word, I would say that it is a Conseil d'État.'

[65] *Fédération charbonnière de Belgique* c. *Haute Autorité*, 2 *Recueil* (1955–6) 263.

[66] *Gouvernement du royaume des Pays-Bas* c. *Haute Autorité*, 1 *Recueil* (1955), 232.

[67] Bebr, 42 *Minnesota Law Review* (1957–8) 849.

[68] *Fédération charbonnière de Belgique* c. *Haute Autorité*, 2 *Recueil* (1955–6) 264.

[69] Ibid. p. 263.

[70] Ibid. p. 264.

[71] *Groupement des industries sidérurgiques luxembourgeoises* c. *Haute Autorité*, ibid. p. 77.

[72] *Associazione Industrie Siderurgiche Italiane (ASSIDER)* c. *Haute Autorité*, ibid. p. 172.

[73] *Société des fonderies de Pont-à-Mousson* c. *Haute Autorité*, 5 *Recueil* (1958–9) 470, 471, 492.

[74] See *Gouvernement de la république fédérale d'Allemagne* c. *Haute Autorité*, 6/1 *Recueil* (1960) 128, 130, 146; *Barbara Erzbergbau AG et autres* c. *Haute Autorité*, ibid. pp. 403, 407, 430, 434, 441.

[75] *Fédération charbonnière de Belgique* c. *Haute Autorité*, 2 *Recueil* (1955–6) 264: '. . . la volonté commune . . . est le plus souvent difficile à établir avec certitude pour des actes tels que les conventions internationales qui sont habituellement le résultat de compromis plus ou moins laborieux et où l'obscurité ou le manque de précision de la rédaction ne font souvent que dissimuler des désaccords de base.'

[76] Ibid. p. 263. See also ibid.: 'Nous avons l'impression qu'il n'y a pas en réalité deux doctrines différentes pour interpréter les textes internes et les textes internationaux, mais qu'en fait, les juridictions internationales ont une tendance à être plus timides pour s'écarter de l'application littérale que les tribunaux nationaux, ce qui s'explique aisément.'

[77] Argued by one of the parties in the *International Labour Organization and the Conditions of Agricultural Labour*, PCIJ, 1922, Series C, no. 1, p. 174: 'It is a fundamental principle that States, justly jealous of their sovereign prerogatives, do not abandon them willingly and that all limitations of their sovereignty must be formally embodied in the text. One of the great principles of civil law is that in cases of doubt, liberty cannot be presumed to have been restricted; a fortiori, when important legal personalities such as States are concerned, it is a principle that, in cases of doubt, their special attributes, which include not merely liberty but sovereignty, cannot be considered as having been in any way restricted.'

[78] *Algera et autres* c. *Assemblée Commune*, 3 *Recueil* (1956–7) 159–60.

[79] See ECSC Treaty, Art. 6: 'The Community shall be represented by its institutions, each one of them acting within the framework of its own powers and responsibilities.'

[80] *Fédération charbonnière de Belgique* c. *Haute Autorité*, 2 *Recueil* (1955–6) 267.

[81] *Gouvernement du royaume des Pays-Bas* c. *Haute Autorité*, 1 *Recueil* (1954–5) 201.

[82] Ibid. p. 232.

[83] Ibid.

[84] F.-C. Jeantet, 'Les Intérêts privés devant la Cour de justice de la Communauté européenne du charbon et de l'acier', 70 *Revue du droit public* (1954), 702.

[85] See H. Lauterpacht, *The Development of International Law by the International Court* (1958), pp. 116–41.

[86] *Competence of the General Assembly for Admission of a State to the UN*, *ICJ Rep. 1950*, p. 23: '. . . it is well known that (according to those who are in favour of using them) the value of *travaux préparatoires* is based, for purposes of interpretation, on the voluntas legislatoris, to which no great importance is attached to-day.'

[87] Ibid. p. 18.

[88] EEC Treaty, Art. 240.

[89] *Fédération charbonnière de Belgique* c. *Haute Autorité*, 2 *Recueil* (1955–6) 252.

[90] *Gabriel Simon* c. *Cour de justice des Communautés Européennes*, 7 *Recueil* (1961) 244.

[91] Ibid. p. 256: 'D'après les principes d'interprétation généralement admis, il faut faire preuve de la plus grande prudence dans l'usage de travaux préparatoires inédits.'

[92] Ibid. p. 244: '. . . attendu qu'à défaut de travaux préparatoires exprimant clairement l'intention des auteurs de la disposition, la Cour ne peut se baser que sur la portée du texte tel qu'il a été établi et lui donner le sens qui ressort de son interprétation littérale et logique.'

[93] *Procédure de revision au titre de l'article 95, alinéas 3 et 4 du traité CECA* (Avis 1–60), 6/1 *Recueil* (1960) 103.

[94] *Gouvernement du royaume des Pays-Bas* c. *Haute Autorité*, 1 *Recueil* (1954–5) 247.

[95] *Associazione Industrie Siderurgiche Italiane* (*ASSIDER*) c. *Haute Autorité*, ibid. p. 172.

[96] *Gouvernement du royaume des Pays-Bas* c. *Haute Autorité*, ibid. p. 232: '. . . il fait appel au droit des différents États membres dont il faut tenir compte dans une mesure décisive pour l'interprétation de notre droit communautaire.'

[97] *Société nouvelle des usines de Pontlieue-Aciéries du Temple* (*SNUPAT*) c. *Haute Autorité*, 5 *Recueil* (1958–9) 300.

[98] *Phoenix-Rheinrohr AG* c. *Haute Autorité*, ibid. pp. 172–7.

[99] *Firme I. Nold KG* c. *Haute Autorité*, ibid. p. 143.

[100] *Jean-E. Humblet* c. *État belge*, 6/2 *Recueil* (1960) 1158.

[101] *Barbara Erzbergbau AG et autres* c. *Haute Autorité*, 6/1 *Recueil* (1960) 427.

[102] *Felten und Guilleaume Carlswerk Eisen- und Stahl AG Walzwerke AG* c. *Haute Autorité*, 5 *Recueil* (1958–9) 221–2.

[103] *Mannesmann AG et autres* c. *Haute Autorité*, 6/1 *Recueil* (1960) 273. See also *Firme I. Nold KG* c. *Haute Autorité*, 5 *Recueil* (1958–9) 160: 'La Cour n'a compétence pour examiner les actes juridiques qu'à l'aide du droit de la Communauté, mais qu'elle n'est pas obligée de constater les infractions au droit interne. Cela n'exclut pas qu'éventuellement, dans le cadre de l'examen du détournement de pouvoir, il faille aussi respecter des principes élémentaires de droit qui trouvent également leur expression dans des dispositions des constitutions nationales.'

[104] *Friedrich Stork et Cie* c. *Haute Autorité*, 5 *Recueil* (1958–9) 83.

[105] *De Gezamenlijke Steenkolenmijnen in Limburg* c. *Haute Autorité*, ibid. p. 36: 'A titre d'analogie dans les droits nationaux, nous citerons deux arrêts du Conseil d'État français: *Merveilleux*, 26 mai 1944, *Rec.* p. 155, et *Cerciat*, 27 avril 1953, *Rec.* p. 195.'

[106] *Acciaieria Ferriera di Roma* (*FERAM*) c. *Haute Autorité*, 5 *Recueil* (1958–9) 527.

[107] *Acciaieria e Tubificio di Brescia* c. *Haute Autorité*, 6/1 *Recueil* (1960) 186.

[108] *Gouvernement du royaume des Pays-Bas* c. *Haute Autorité*, 1 *Recueil* (1954–5) 288: 'En droit interne, dans les pays de la Communauté, le

recours en interprétation n'est connu comme tel qu'en France et en Belgique. . . .'

[109] *Groupement des industries sidérurgiques luxembourgeoises* c. *Haute Autorité*, 2 *Recueil* (1955–6) 120: 'Il est incontestable que la structure technique du recours en annulation a été empruntée à la procédure contentieuse administrative française.'

[110] Possibly under Arts. 84 (4) and 42 of the ECSC Treaty.

[111] *Associazione Industrie Siderurgiche Italiane (ASSIDER)* c. *Haute Autorité*, 1 *Recueil* (1954–5) 148.

[112] *Friedrich Stork et Cie* c. *Haute Autorité*, 5 *Recueil* (1958–9) 63.

[113] *Firme I. Nold KG* c. *Haute Autorité*, ibid. p. 160.

[114] Ibid. p. 132: 'Il est donc possible de dire que la procédure de la Communauté renvoie au droit national pour savoir à quelles conditions personelles les avocats peuvent faire valablement des actes de procédure.' Ibid. p. 133: 'C'est là une question de capacité juridique et, en l'absence de dispositions particulières du droit de la Communauté, il faut l'apprécier selon les règles du droit national, donc du droit allemand, puisqu'il s'agit d'une société allemande. Les dispositions du code de commerce allemand, de la jurisprudence et de la doctrine allemandes permettent de faire les constatations suivantes . . .'.

[115] *Associazione Industries Siderurgiche Italiane (ASSIDER)* c. *Haute Autorité*, 1 *Recueil* (1954–5) 172.

[116] *Chambre syndicale de la sidérurgie française* c. *Haute Autorité*, 4 *Recueil* (1958) 386.

[117] *Meroni et Cie, Industrie Metallurgiche Società Accomandita Semplice* c. *Haute Autorité*, ibid. p. 101.

[118] *Miranda Mirossevich* c. *Haute Autorité*, 2 *Recueil* (1955–6) 415.

[119] *Dineke Algera, M. Giacomo Cicconardi, Mme Simone Couturaud, M. Ignazio Genuardi, Mme Félicie Steicher* c. *Haute Autorité*, 3 *Recueil* (1956–7) 115.

[120] *Acciaieria e Tubificio di Brescia* c. *Haute Autorité*, 6/1 *Recueil* (1960) 192–4.

[121] *Società Industriale Metallurgica di Napoli (SIMET), Meroni et Cie, Industrie Metallurgiche à Erba, Meroni et Cie, Industrie Metallurgiche à Milan, Fer. Ro. (Ferriere Rossi) et Acciaieriea San Michele* c. *Haute Autorité*, 5 *Recueil* (1958–9) 343: '. . . les recours introductifs d'instance ont été postés le 19, ce qui est suffisant, car, selon le droit des six États membres, l'acte est réputé notifié par la simple remise à la poste.'

[122] H. Lauterpacht, *Private Law Sources and Analogies of International Law* (1927).

[123] G. Fitzmaurice, 'Law and Procedure of the International Court of Justice', 28 *BYBIL* (1951) 8.

[124] See Advisory Opinion concerning the *International State of South West Africa, ICJ Rep. 1950*, p. 128; *Reparation for Injuries suffered in the Service of the UN, ICJ Rep. 1949*, p. 185.

[125] *Constitution of the Maritime Safety Committee of the Inter-Governmental Maritime Consultative Organization, ICJ Rep. 1960*, pp. 170–1.

[126] *Gouvernement de la république française* c. *Haute Autorité*, 1 *Recueil* (1954–5) 23.

[127] P. Reuter, 'Le Droit de la Communauté européenne du Charbon et de l'Acier', 80 *Journal du droit international* (1953) 18.

[128] *Gouvernement du royaume des Pays-Bas* c. *Haute Autorité*, 1 *Recueil* (1954–5) 232.

[129] Bebr, 42 *Minnesota Law Review* (1957–8) 861–7.

[130] *Gouvernement de la république française* c. *Haute Autorité*, 1 *Recueil* (1954–5) 53–5.

[131] *Groupement des hautes fourneaux et aciéries belges* c. *Haute Autorité*, 4 *Recueil* (1958) 242. See also ibid. pp. 384, 419, 456, 493, 513.

[132] *Chambre syndicale de la sidérurgie française* c. *Haute Autorité*, ibid. p. 279.

[133] See ibid. pp. 383, 417, 454, 491.

[134] See ibid. Many cases in this particular volume refer to the application of the general articles.

[135] However, as the Court will seldom admit, by name, that it is following a particular principle of interpretation, it may frequently reach a particular finding by means of a teleological approach without expressly acknowledging it.

[136] *Groupement des industries sidérurgiques luxembourgeoises* c. *Haute Autorité*, 2 *Recueil* (1955–6) 53 ff.

[137] See Congrès international d'études sur la Communauté Européenne du charbon et de l'acier, 2 *Actes officiels* (1957), pp. 218–19.

[138] See *International Labour Organization and the Conditions of Agricultural Labour*, PCIJ, 1922, Series B, no. 2, p. 215; *International Labour Organization and the Personal Work of the Employer*, PCIJ, 1926, Series B, no. 13, p. 18: 'It results from the consideration of the provisions of the Treaty that the High Contracting Parties clearly intended to give to the International Labour Organization a very broad power of co-operating with them in respect of measures to be taken in order to assess humane conditions of labour and the protection of workers. It is not conceivable that they intended to prevent the organization from drawing up and proposing measures essential to the accomplishment of that end.'

[139] See J. E. S. Fawcett, 'The Place of Law in an International Organization', 36 *BYBIL* (1960) 333.

[140] *Reparation for Injuries suffered in the Service of the UN*, ICJ Rep. 1949, p. 182.

[141] *Effects of Awards of Compensation made by the UN Administrative Tribunal*, ICJ Rep. 1954, p. 57.

[142] *Reparation of Injuries*, &c., ICJ Rep. 1949, p. 198.

[143] *Fédération charbonnière de Belgique* c. *Haute Autorité*, 2 *Recueil* (1955–6) 302.

[144] Ibid.

[145] Ibid. p. 303: 'Si les prix du charbon belge étaient livrés au jeu de l'offre et de la demande sur le marché, leur abaissement ne serait pas assuré.'

[146] Ibid. p. 303.

[147] Ibid. p. 304.

[148] Ibid.

[149] *Fédération charbonnière de Belgique* c. *Haute Autorité*, 2 *Recueil* (1955–6) 304–5: 'La requérante a soutenu, au cours de la procédure orale, que l'absence dans le Traité d'une attribution expresse du pouvoir de fixer d'autorité les prix s'oppose à la reconnaissance d'un tel pouvoir au moyen d'une interprétation qu'elle estime extensive et inadmissible en droit. La Cour n'est pas de cet avis en tant qu'il s'agit dans l'espèce d'un pouvoir sans lequel, comme elle vient de le constater, la péréquation ne peut fonctionner au vœu du paragraphe 26 de la Convention, c'est-à-dire sur la base d'un abaissement des prix immédiat et assuré.'

[150] Ibid. p. 305.

[151] Ibid.: 'Il en résulte que l'accomplissement de sa mission postule, dans l'espèce, pour la Haute Autorité le pouvoir de fixer les prix. Il faut reconnaître, cependant, que l'étendue de ce pouvoir est limitée au seul objectif d'assurer à l'ensemble des consommateurs du charbon belge une baisse de prix de ce charbon, dès le début de la période de transition, et dans la mesure prescrite par la Convention dans son paragraphe 26'.

[152] *Gouvernement de la république italienne* c. *Haute Autorité*, 62 *Recueil* (1960) 688: 'qu'en effet la doctrine et la jurisprudence sont d'accord pour admettre que les règles établies par un traité impliquent les normes sans lesquelles ces règles ne peuvent être appliquées utilement ou raisonnablement'; *Gouvernement du royaume des Pays-Bas* c. *Haute Autorité*, ibid. p. 757.

[153] See *International Labour Organization and the Conditions of Agricultural Labour*, PCIJ, 1922, Series B, no. 2, p. 215; *Reparation for Injuries Suffered in the Service of the United Nations*, ICJ Rep. 1949, p. 179; H. Lauterpacht,

The Development of International Law by the International Court (1958), pp. 267–81.

[154] *Lotus* Case, PCIJ, 1927, Series A, no. 10, p. 8: 'International law governs relations between independent States. The rules of law binding upon States therefore emanate from their own free will. . . . Restrictions upon the sovereignty of States cannot therefore be presumed.' However, see Lauterpacht, ' Restrictive Interpretation and the Principle of Effectiveness in the Interpretation of Treaties ', 26 *BYBIL* (1949) 84 : ' In so far as there is a case—and there is some case—for eliminating unnecessary and cumbersome rules of interpretation, that relating to restrictive interpretation of treaty obligations ought to be considered as first on the list of priorities.'

[155] Bebr, 42 *Minnesota Law Review* (1957–8) 867–75.

[156] *Groupement des industries sidérurgiques . . . c. Haute Autorité*, 2 *Recueil* (1955–6) 86.

[157] *Société des fonderies de Pont-à-Mousson c. Haute Autorité*, 5 *Recueil* (1958–9) 445.

[158] *Fédération charbonnière de Belgique c. Haute Autorité*, 2 *Recueil* (1955–6) 224.

[159] Ibid. p. 226. See Bebr, as cited in n. 155 above, p. 870.

[160] *Société nouvelle des usines de Pontlieue—Aciéries du Temple (SNUPAT) c. Haute Autorité*, 5 *Recueil* (1958–9) 298: '. . . attendu que, dès lors, sous peine de priver les entreprises de la protection dont l'article 33 du traité CECA leur a reconnu le bénéfice, il faut admettre que les décisions prises par la CPFI en vertu de l'article 12, paragraphe 2, de la décision 2–57 valent décision de la Haute Autorité et sont, de ce fait, susceptible de recours en annulation dans les conditions prévues par l'article 33.'

[161] *Meroni et Cie, Industrie Metallurgiche, SPA c. Haute Autorité*, 4 *Recueil* (1958) 9.

[162] See *Gouvernement de la république italienne c. Haute Autorité*, 1 *Recueil* (1954–5) 97: ' Il n'appartient pas à la Cour de s'exprimer sur l'opportunité du système imposé par le Traité ni de suggérer une révision du Traité, mais elle est tenue, selon l'article 31, d'assurer le respect du droit dans l'interprétation et l'application du Traité tel qu'il est établi.'

[163] Ibid. p. 96.

[164] Ibid. p. 97.

[165] *Meroni et Cie, Industrie Metallurgiche, SPA c. Haute Autorité*, 4 *Recueil* (1958) 20.

[166] Ibid. p. 44: ' . . . pareilles délégations ne peuvent porter que sur des pouvoirs d'exécution, exactement définis, et entièrement contrôlés, dans l'usage qui en est fait, par la Haute Autorité.'

[167] *Gouvernement du royaume des Pays-Bas c. Haute Autorité*, 6/2 *Recueil* (1960) 723.

[168] Ibid. p. 761: ' Attendu que l'article 88 ouvre des voies d'exécution et constitue l'*ultima ratio* permettant de faire prévaloir les intérêts communautaires consacrés par le traité contre l'inertie et contre la résistance des États membres, qu'il s'agit là d'une procédure dépassant de loin les règles jusqu'à présent admises en droit international classique pour assurer l'exécution des obligations des États . . . , pourtant, l'article 88 est de stricte interprétation.'

[169] *Groupement des industries sidérurgiques luxembourgeoises c. Haute Autorité*, 2 *Recueil* (1955–6) 77.

[170] *Jean-E. Humblet c. État belge*, 6 *Recueil* (1960) 1154, 1156; *De Gezamenlijke Steenkolenmijnen in Limburg c. Haute Autorité*, 7 *Recueil* (1961) 13, 24, 28, 31: ' L'article 92 du traité instituant la Communauté économique européenne confirme cette interprétation de l'article 4 (*c*) du Traité instituant la Communauté européenne du charbon et de l'acier.'

[171] *Interpretation of the Convention of 1919 concerning the Employment of Women during the Night*, PCIJ, 1932, Series A, 13, no. 50, p. 381: ' If in the Eight Hour Day Convention, after a prohibition applicable to " persons ", it was necessary to make an exception in respect of persons holding positions of supervision or management, it was equally necessary to make

a corresponding exception in respect of women in the Convention on night work of women, if it was intended that women holding positions of supervision or management should be excluded from the operation of the Convention.'

[172] *Società Industriale Metallurgica di Napoli (SIMET), Meroni et Cie, Industrie Metallurgiche à Erba, Meroni et Cie, Industrie Metallurgiche à Milan, Fer. Ro. (Ferrière Rossi) et Acciaierie San Michele* c. *Haute Autorité, 5 Recueil* (1958–9) 345–6: 'Les récents traités instituant la Communauté Économique Européenne et l'Euratom devraient suggérer à la Cour d'interpréter libéralement la protection juridictionnelle des entreprises de la CECA. . . .'

[173] *Alberto Campolongo* c. *Haute Autorité, 6/2 Recueil* (1960) 845–9: 'Si, actuellement, il n'est certes pas possible de parler d'une unité juridique des trois Communautés européennes, on ne peut cependant écarter la constatation que les liens juridiques des trois Communautés qui existent déjà et leur unité spirituelle constituent une réalité qui appelle une unification juridique plus poussée.'

[174] *Firme I. Nold KG* c. *Haute Autorité, 5 Recueil* (1958–9) 160.

[175] *Meroni et Cie, Industrie Metallurgiche SPA* c. *Haute Autorité, 4 Recueil* (1958) 26–7.

[176] *International Labour Organization and the Conditions of Agricultural Labour*, PCIJ, 1922, Series B, no. 2, pp. 39–40.

[177] *Gouvernement de la république italienne* c. *Haute Autorité, 1 Recueil* (1954–5) 26.

[178] *Bochumer Verein für Gusstahlfabrikation AG, Niederrheinische Hütte AG et Stahlwerke Südwestfalen AG* c. *Haute Autorité, 5 Recueil* (1958–9) 241.

[179] *Firme I. Nold KG* c. *Haute Autorité, ibid.* p. 131.

[180] *Groupement des industries sidérurgiques . . .* c. *Haute Autorité, 2 Recueil* (1955–6) 137.

[181] *Compagnie des hauts fourneaux . . . de Givors . . .* c. *Haute Autorité, 6/1 Recueil* (1960) 551.

[182] A. D. McNair, 'The Functions and Differing Legal Character of Treaties', 11 *BYBIL* (1930) 118.

[183] de Visscher, 'L'Interprétation judiciaire des traités d'Organisation Internationale', 41 *Rivista di Diritto Internazionale* (1958) 177.

[184] See C. W. Jenks, 'Some Constitutional Problems of International Organizations', 22 *BYBIL* (1945) 16.

[185] 4 Wheaton (1819) 413.

[186] Ibid. p. 413.

[187] *Missouri* v. *Holland*, 252 US 416 (1920).

[188] McNair, 11 *BYBIL* (1930) 106: 'I suggest that it is significant that the seed-bed of the traditional rules as to the formation, validity, interpretation, and discharge of treaties which swell the bulk of our text-books, too often written in slavish imitation of their predecessors, was sown at a time when the old conception of a treaty as a compact, a bargain, a *Vertrag*, was exclusively predominant and the dawn of the new multilateral treaty had not begun.'

[189] See Kopelmanas, *L'Organisation des Nations Unies* (1947), p. 295.

[190] See *Annuaire de l'Institut de Droit International* (1952), 2nd part, pp. 366, 391.

[191] Jenks, 'State Succession in Respect of Law-making Treaties', 29 *BYBIL* (1952) 105: 'Just as treaty provisions creating local obligations are to be regarded as having the character of executed conveyances rather than that of contractual provisions which continue to be executory, so obligations under legislative instruments should be regarded as obligations under the law rather than as contractual obligations'; *International Status of South West Africa, ICJ Rep. 1950*, p. 128.

[192] *Competence of the General Assembly for the Admission of a State to the UN*, ibid. p. 23: 'The interpretation of the San Francisco instruments will always have to present a teleological character if they are to meet the

requirements of world peace, co-operation between men, individual freedom
and social progress.'
193 Bebr, 42 *Minnesota Law Review* (1957–8) 855–6.
194 Fitzmaurice, 'The Law and Procedure of the ICJ', 33 *BYBIL* (1957) 208.

CHAPTER 2

1 cf. H. L. A. Hart, *The Concept of Law* (Oxford, Clarendon Press, 1961).
2 See the Southern Rhodesia Act 1965.
3 Of course, even in the US, a decision like *Brown* v. *Board of Education*,
347 US 483 (1954), depended, in terms of its incidence, on contemporary
political factors, and represented but the initiation of a process dependent
to a great degree on support action by federal authority.
4 On Kenya since independence see H. W. O. Okoth-Ogendo, 'The Politics of
Constitutional Change in Kenya since Independence, 1963–69', *Afr. Aff.*,
Jan. 1972, p. 9.
5 *ICJ Rep. 1962*, p. 151. See Leo Gross, 'Expenses of the UN for Peace-
Keeping Operations: the Advisory Opinion of the International Court of
Justice', *Int. Org.*, vol. 17, 1963, p. 1.
6 GA res. 2850 (XXVI), 20 Dec. 1971.
7 e.g. Costa Rica, Iceland, Bhutan, Fiji, Maldive Islands.
8 20 Dec. 1971.
9 24 Oct. 1970. See also GA res. 2878 (XXVI), 20 Dec. 1971; and GA res.
2787 (XXVI), 6 Dec. 1971.
10 20 Dec. 1971.
11 20 Dec. 1971. See also GA res. 2795 (XXVI), on Portuguese territories; GA
res. 2796 (XXVI) on Southern Rhodesia; and GA res. 2871 (XXVI) on
Namibia.
12 Res. 2847 (XXVI), 20 Dec. 1971.
13 See the Judgment in the *Barcelona Traction* Case (Second Phase), *ICJ Rep.
1970*, pp. 3, 32.
14 For action during the 26th sess., see GA res. 2874 (XXVI), 20 Dec. 1971.
15 cf. *Reg.* v. *Metropolitan Police Commissioner, ex parte Blackburn* [1968]
2 QB 118, 150.
16 7 Dec. 1971: 104 in favour; 11 against; 10 abstentions.
17 One may compare the behaviour of the UN organs in relation to the
attempted secession of Biafra. In that situation considerable deference to
the policies of the Organization of African Unity was shown.
18 Gross, 12 *Harvard Int. Law J.*, 436, 439–40.
19 Res. 298 (1971), reproduced in 10 *Int. Leg. Materials* (1971) 1294.
20 Res. 2799 (XXVI), 13 Dec. 1971. See also GA res. 2851 (XXVI). 20 Dec.
1971, on the Report of the Special Committee to Investigate Israeli Practices
Affecting the Human Rights of the Population of the Occupied Territories.
21 GA res. 2835 (XXVI), 17 Dec. 1971.
22 See the Advisory Opinion in the *Expenses* Case, *ICJ Rep. 1962*, p. 151.
23 Secretariat Legal Opinion, *UN Juridical Yearbook 1964*, p. 228.
24 *ICJ Rep. 1971*, p. 16.
25 See the dissenting Opinion of Judge Fitzmaurice in the *Namibia* proceedings,
ICJ Rep. 1971, p. 221.
26 301 (1971), 20 Oct. 1971.
27 *UN Monthly Chronicle*, Nov. 1971, p. 19.
28 See GA res. 2784 (XXVI), 6 Dec. 1971; GA res. 2785 (XXVI), same date;
and GA res. 2786 (XXVI), same date.
29 GA res. 2859 (XXVI), 20 Dec. 1971.
30 GA res. 2826 (XXVI), 16 Dec. 1971; text in Annex.
31 GA res. 2777 (XXVI), 29 Nov. 1971; text in Annex.
32 14 Dec. 1971.
33 See Philip C. Jessup's letter to the Editor, *NY Times*, 16 Dec. 1971.
34 4 Feb. 1972.

CHAPTER 3

[1] *Report of a Study Group on the Peaceful Settlement of International Disputes* (London, David Davies Memorial Inst. of Int. Studies, 1966), p. 125.

[2] Ibid. p. 126.

[3] *The Prospects of International Adjudication* (London, Stevens, 1964), p. 758.

[4] See his speech at the Annual Dinner of the American Society of Int. Law, *Proceed. ASIL 1970*, pp. 286–7.

[5] *The Structure of Impartiality* (New York, Macmillan, 1968), p. 46.

[6] R. A. Falk, *Legal Order in a Violent World* (Princeton, NJ, Princeton UP, 1968), pp. 124–5.

[7] *Statement to the Asian-African Legal Consultative Committee, Tenth Session, Karachi, January 22, 1969*, reprinted in 63 *AJIL* (1969) 689.

[8] *The Place of Law and Tribunals in International Relations* (Manchester UP, 1957).

[9] ' Policy Considerations and the International Judicial Process ', 17 *ICLQ* (1968) 58.

[10] *The Development of International Law by the International Court* (London, Stevens, 1958), p. 4.

[11] *The Prospects of International Adjudication*, p. 760.

[12] S. Rosenne, *The Law and Practice of the International Court*, vol. 1 (Leyden, Sijthoff, 1965), p. 95.

[13] *Competence of the General Assembly for the Admission of a State to the United Nations, ICJ Rep. 1950*.

[14] *Certain Expenses of the United Nations (Art. 17 (2) of the Charter), ICJ Rep. 1962*.

[15] *Customs Régime between Germany and Austria*, PCIJ, 1931, Ser. A/B, no. 41.

[16] *South West Africa (Ethiopia v. South Africa; Liberia v. South Africa), ICJ Rep. 1966*.

[17] R. B. Stevens and B. Yamey, *The Restrictive Practices Court: a Study of the Judicial Process and Economic Policy* (London, Weidenfeld & Nicolson, 1965).

[18] Franck, p. 207.

[19] *Int. Conciliation*, Jan. 1962.

[20] *The Structure of Impartiality*, p. 197.

[21] *Corfu Channel (United Kingdom v. Albania)*. The Court established an expert committee of seven naval officers from the navies of Norway, Sweden, and the Netherlands. This Committee presented a written report and was then asked to proceed to Yugoslavia and Albania to conduct further investigations and experiments with a view to verifying, completing, and, if necessary, modifying the answers given in its report. This the experts did; and also answered further questions put to them by the Court, *ICJ Rep. 1949*, p. 9.

[22] *Temple of Preah Vihear (Cambodia v. Thailand), ICJ Rep. 1962*.

[23] *South West Africa (Ethiopia v. South Africa; Liberia v. South Africa), ICJ Rep. 1966*.

[24] *Barcelona Traction, Light and Power Company, Ltd (Belgium v. Spain), ICJ Rep. 1970*.

[25] *Right of Passage over Indian Territory (Portugal v. India), ICJ Rep. 1960*.

[26] *Sovereignty over Certain Frontier Land (Belgium/Netherlands), ICJ Rep. 1959*.

[27] *Interhandel (Switzerland v. United States), ICJ Rep. 1959*.

[28] *Temple of Preah Vihear (Cambodia v. Thailand), ICJ Rep. 1962*.

[29] *Northern Cameroons (Cameroon v. United Kingdom), ICJ Rep. 1963*.

[30] *Report of a Study Group on the Peaceful Settlement of International Disputes*, pp. 131–3.

[31] 64 *AJIL* (1970) 238–53.

[32] Catherine Senf Manno, 'Majority Decisions and Minority Responses', *Journal of Conflict Resolution*, Mar. 1966, pp. 1–20.

[33] Allott also makes the point that Art. 36 would have to be reworded, and some states might take the opportunity to enter reservations excluding international organizations; p. 139.

[34] See esp. Rosenne, vol. 1, pp. 100–14; B. Akzin, *New States and International Organizations* (Paris, UNESCO, 1955); R. P. Anand, 'The Role of the "New" Asian-African Countries in the Present International Legal Order', 56 *AJIL* (1962) 383, and 'Attitude of the "New" Asian-African Countries towards the ICJ', *Int. Studies* (New Delhi), vol. 4, 1962, p. 119; and G. I. Tunkin. 'Co-existence and International Law', 95 (Hague) *Recueil des Cours*, III (1958) 5–79.

[35] *Systems, States, Diplomacy and Rules* (London, CUP, 1968), p. 222.

[36] A point made by Rosenne, vol. 1, pp. 100–1.

[37] *The Prospects of International Adjudication*, pp. 768–9.

[38] *The Place of Law and Tribunals in International Relations*, p. 9.

[39] For a detailed explanation of what international relations scholars mean by systems, and of behaviour that is systemic or non-systemic, see Burton's *Systems, States, Diplomacy and Rules*, esp. chs 6 and 7.

[40] *The Structure of Impartiality*, pp. 182–3.

[41] Ibid. p. 184.

[42] See Oran Young, *The Intermediaries: Third Parties in International Crises* (Princeton, NJ, Princeton UP, 1967).

CHAPTER 4

[1] *A Study of the Capacity of the UN Development System*, i:iii (Geneva, UN, 1969).

[2] Pierre-Michel Fontaine, 'Regionalism and Functionalism in International Organization: the UN Economic Commission for Latin America' (unpublished Ph.D. dissertation, Univ. of Denver, 1968), pp. 352–3.

[3] W. Laves and C. Thomson, *UNESCO* (Bloomington, Ind., Indiana UP, 1957), p. 49. Huxley's view was not accepted by the conference, which was not prepared to adopt any particular philosophic point of view. Subsequently the French philosopher Jacques Maritain called for a guiding philosophy based on 'common practical ideas'. Ibid. p. 50.

[4] See *Beyond the Nation-State* (Stanford, Calif., Stanford UP, 1964), pp. 127, 445.

[5] Ibid. p. 127.

[6] The Secretary-General's report Problems of Human Environment (E/4667, 26 May 1969) and the preparation for the UN conference in Stockholm in 1972 demonstrated the vigorous and strategic role played by the international secretariat under the leadership of Maurice Strong.

[7] See H. Brandon, *Conversations with Henry Brandon* (London, Deutsch, 1966), p. 25.

CHAPTER 5

[1] A summary of his analysis appears in *Status and Problems of Very Small States and Territories* (New York, UNITAR, 1969), pp. 143–54.

[2] Gambian representatives have been attached to the Senegalese delegation.

[3] Monaco and the Holy See have observer missions. None of these 'ministates' had been a member of the League of Nations.

[4] Andorra, sometimes listed as a ' mini-state ', is a condominium and lacks the attributes of national sovereignty.

[5] In 1972 unsuccessful attempts were made to negotiate a union between Guyana and most of these associated states.

[6] S/9836. See further Stephen M. Schwebel, 67 *AJIL* (1973) 108.

[7] The UNITAR study already cited points out (p. 3, n. 2) that the General Assembly resolution of 1967 establishing a Council for South West Africa (Namibia), though adopted by 85 votes to 2 with 30 abstentions, could be viewed in another light. Members voting for the resolution contributed under 20 per cent to the UN budget and the abstainers contributed 80 per cent.

[8] Ibid. pp. 200–5. See further Patricia Wohlgemuth Blair, *The Ministate Dilemma* (New York, Carnegie Endowment for International Peace, 1967); and *Proceed. ASIL . . . 1968*, pp. 155–88.

[9] See S. A. de Smith, *Microstates and Micronesia: Problems of America's Pacific Islands and Other Minute Territories* (New York, New York UP, 1970), ch. 4.

[10] See e.g. de Smith, 31 *Modern Law Review* (1968) 612, n. 39 (on Mauritius).

[11] Standards at the UN had been still more generous in the late 1940s. The UN acquiesced in France's decision not to supply further information in respect of her overseas territories although (unlike France's overseas departments), they were not fully integrated with the metropolitan country, nor were they internally self-governing or free to secede.

[12] Cmnd. 2865 (1965). See further Margaret Broderick, 17 *ICLQ* (1968) 368. Jamaica and Trinidad, the two largest units in the former West Indies Federation, became independent in 1962; and Barbados, the third largest, in 1966. Guyana was never a unit in the Federation.

[13] Anguilla Act 1971; Anguilla (Administration) Order 1971 (S.I. 1971 No. 1235), replacing the Anguilla (Temporary Provision) Order 1969 (S.I. 1969 No. 371). The British government envisaged that Anguilla would eventually determine its own future. The 1971 Act provided (section 1 (3)) that if the associated state were to proceed to exercise its power under the West Indies Act 1967 of terminating its association with the UK, an Order in Council could be made detaching Anguilla from the associated state. Nothing in the West Indies Act 1967 or in the reports of the constitutional conferences preceding its enactment had adverted to the possibility that the UK might sever part of the territory of an associated state against the will of the government of that state.

Under the 1971 Order, new laws made by the associated state were to apply to Anguilla only if adopted locally.

[14] See further the author's *Microstates and Micronesia*, chs 8–12.

[15] The Carolines (including the Yap, Truk, Palau and Ponape districts) and the Marshalls are the other two island groups within the territory.

[16] The motto of Guam is ' Where America's Day Begins '.

[17] The Marianas are the most prosperous district in Micronesia, and the closest to Guam in ethnic composition, religion, and geographical location. Early in 1971 the premises of the Congress of Micronesia on Saipan in the Marianas were burned down, probably by Mariana separatists. The Congress then moved to Palau in the Carolines.

When Micronesia proceeds to self-determination it is not unlikely that the Marianas will be treated as a special case. See also p. 78 below.

[18] Strictly the Committee of Twenty-four has no competence to pronounce on the affairs of Micronesia because the territory falls within the province of the Security Council and not the General Assembly. However, the Committee is not lightly inhibited by jurisdictional niceties.

CHAPTER 6

[1] See e.g. General Debate statement by the Chairman of the Cyprus Delegation, Ambassador Z. Rossides, *GAOR*, 15th sess., 906th mtg; address by H. B. Archbishop Makarios, President of the Republic of Cyprus, to the General Assembly, 7 June 1962, *GAOR*, 16th sess., 1107th mtg, and to the Belgrade and Cairo Conferences of Non-aligned States, 1961 and 1964, *The Conference of Heads of States or Government of Non-Aligned Countries* (Belgrade, 1961), pp. 170–5, and *Cyprus Today*, Suppl. 28, 15 Oct. 1964, resp.

[2] *GAOR*, 15th sess., 883rd mtg, p. 332.

[3] 'The Strengthening of the UN', Press release SG/SM/51.

[4] For these alternatives see generally A. Cox, *Prospects for Peacekeeping* (Washington, DC, Brookings Instn, 1967), pp. 50–72. The Cyprus case presents a clear illustration.

[5] Such as the Dominican Republic (1965) and Czechoslovak (1968) situations. See e.g. the Introduction to the Secretary-General's Annual Report on the Work of the Organization, *GAOR*, 23rd sess., Suppl. 1A, A/7201/Add. 1, para. 189.

[6] *Documents of the UN Conference on International Organization, San Francisco, Calif.*, vol. 1, doc. 1209, p. 665.

[7] See report of Third Conference on the UN of the Next Decade, held in Dubrovnik, June 1968, under the auspices of the Stanley Foundation (Muscatine, Iowa, 1968).

[8] It is interesting to note that an offer by Bulgaria and Czechoslovakia in 1964 to provide forces on call by the Security Council under Art. 43 of the Charter has not been taken up in view of the fundamental disagreement on the issue.

[9] In Apr. 1966, authorizing the UK to stop, if necessary by force, ships carrying oil to Southern Rhodesia—res. 221 (1966). Likewise res. 232 (1966) of Dec. 1966 imposing economic sanctions.

[10] See e.g. W. R. Frye, *A UN Peace Force* (Dobbs Ferry, NY, Oceana, 1957); *Federal Union's Proposals for a Permanent UN Force* (London, FU, 1957); G. Clark and L. B. Sohn, *Draft of a Proposed Treaty establishing a World Disarmament and World Development Organization within the Framework of the UN* (1962), pp. 78–90.

[11] See Z. Rossides, *Cyprus in the UN* (New York, 1963), p. 12 (General Debate statement, *GAOR*, 17th sess., 1155th mtg, p. 534).

[12] See Z. Rossides, *Cyprus in the UN* (New York, 1962), p. 14 (General Debate statement, *GAOR*, 16th sess., 1039th mtg, pp. 486–7).

[13] Rossides, *Cyprus in the UN* (1963), p. 81 (statement made in 5th Cttee, Dec. 1962). On this aspect see R. and H. Taubenfeld, 'Independent Revenue for the UN', *Int. Org.*, vol. XVIII, no. 2 (1964), 241–68; and see generally J. G. Stoessinger, *Financing the UN System* (Washington, DC, Brookings Instn, 1964).

[14] Press release SG/1520.

[15] Ibid. p. 8.

[16] See the works cited in n. 10 above.

[17] See generally A. Cox, *Prospects for Peacekeeping* (Washington, DC, Brookings Instn, 1967); R. Higgins, *UN Peacekeeping 1946–1967: Documents and Commentary*, 2 vols. (London, OUP for RIIA, 1969–70); D. W. Bowett, *UN Forces: a Legal Study of UN Practice* (New York, Praeger for David Davies Memorial Inst., 1964); R. B. Russell, *UN Experience with Military Forces: Political and Legal Aspects* (Washington, DC, Brookings Instn, 1964); R. N. Gardner, 'The Development of the Peacekeeping Capacity of the UN', *Proceed. ASIL . . . 1963*, pp. 224–34. For a comprehensive bibliography see A. Legault (compiler), *Peace-keeping Operations: Bibliography* (Paris, International Information Center on Peacekeeping Operations, 1967).

[18] Press release SG 1520, p. 3.

[19] For a full treatment of the subject, see D. W. Wainhouse and others, *International Peace Observation* (Baltimore, Md, Johns Hopkins Press, 1966).

[20] For the basic documents see e.g. E. Lauterpacht, *The UN Emergency Force* (London, Stevens, 1960). The pertinent UN documents are summarized in Legault (see n. 17 above), pp. 31–137. Of these, particular note should be taken of A/3943, 9 Oct. 1958 (*GAOR*, 13th sess., Annexes, agenda item 65), entitled ' Summary Study of the Experience Derived from the Establishment and Operation of the Force: Report of the Secretary-General ', esp. ch. 6 (legal aspects) and ch. 7 (basic principles).

[21] See e.g. ' Withdrawal of the UN Emergency Force: Some Questions Answered ', *UN Monthly Chronicle*, July 1967, pp. 87–94, and for a full account see the Secretary-General's Report, A/6730 and Add. 1–3 (*GAOR*, 5th emergency special sess., Annexes, agenda item 5). See also N. El Araby, ' A Case Study of the Withdrawal of UNEF ', *New York University Journal of International Law and Politics*, vol. 1, no. 2, 1968.

[22] For a full treatment of the subject see E. W. Lefever, *Crisis in the Congo: A UN Force in Action* (Washington, DC, Brookings Instn, 1965). See also R. Bunche, ' The UN Operation in the Congo ', in J. Larus, ed., *From Collective Security to Preventive Diplomacy* (New York, Wiley, 1965). The pertinent UN documents are summarized in Legault (see n. 17 above), pp. 118–27. For legal aspects of the operation see E. M. Miller [pseud.], ' Legal aspects of the UN Action in the Congo ', 55 *AJIL* (Jan. 1961); O. Schachter, ' Preventing the Internationalization of Internal Conflict: a Legal Analysis of the UN Congo Experience ', *Proceed. ASIL . . . 1963*; Thomas M. Franck and John Carey, ' Working Paper: the Role of the UN in the Congo ', in Assn of the Bar of the City of New York, Cttee on Lawyer's Role in Search for Peace (2nd Hammarskjöld Forum, 1962), *Legal Aspects of UN Action in the Congo* (Dobbs Ferry, NY, Oceana, 1963); Bowett, pp. 153–261. See also C. Cruise O'Brien, *To Katanga and Back* (New York, Simon & Schuster, 1962).

[23] The bibliography on UNFICYP includes: Andrestinos N. Papadopoulos, *Peace-making and Peace-keeping by the UN: Cyprus, a Case Study* (Nicosia, 1969); J. A. Stegenga, *The UN Force in Cyprus* (Columbus, Ohio State UP, 1968); T. Ehrlich, ' Cyprus, the Warlike Isle: Origins and Elements of the Current Crisis ', 18 *Stanford Law Review* (May, 1966); T. M. Boyd, ' Cyprus, Episode in Peacekeeping ', *International Journal*, summer 1964; Bowett, pp. 552–60; R. Stephens, *Cyprus: a Place of Arms* (London, Pall Mall Press, 1966); L. B. Miller, *World Order and Local Disorder: the UN and Internal Conflicts* (Princeton UP, 1967), pp. 116–48, and *Cyprus: the Law and Politics of Civil Strife* (Cambridge, Mass., Harvard Univ. Center for International Affairs, 1968); C. Foley, *Legacy of Strife: Cyprus from Rebellion to Civil War* (Harmondsworth, Penguin Books, 1964). The earlier relevant UN documents are summarized in Legault, pp. 138–44. See also *The Function of the UN Force in Cyprus—an Assessment* (Nicosia, Public Inf. Off., 1967).

[24] See works cited in nn. 20, 22, 23, and Legault (n. 17) above.

[25] See e.g. *Cyprus: the Problem in Perspective* (Nicosia, Public Inf. Off., 1967); H. J. Psomiades, ' The Cyprus Dispute ', *Current History*, May 1965, pp. 269–76 and 305–6; Stegenga; Ehrlich; Stephens; L. B. Miller; Foley; RIIA Inf. Dept, *Cyprus: the Dispute and the Settlement* (London, OUP, 1959); S. G. Xydis, *Cyprus: Conflict and Conciliation, 1954–58* (Columbus, Ohio State UP, 1967).

[26] See GB, Colonial Off. and others, *Cyprus*, Cmnd 1093 (London, HMSO, 1960) for the basic documents, and *Cyprus: the Problem in perspective* (cited fully in n. 25 above) for the proposals of 30 Nov. 1963 (13 points); also C. Tornaritis, *The Legal Aspects of the Question of Cyprus* (Nicosia, 1965); G. Zotiades, *The Treaty of Guarantee and the Principle of Non-intervention* (1965); T. Zoupanos, *The Invalidity and the Inapplicability of the Treaty of Guarantee in Cyprus*, Conf. 1964 (in Greek); A. J. Jacovides, *Treaties Conflicting with Peremptory Norms of International Law and the Zurich-London ' Agreements '* (Nicosia, 1966); C. Tornaritis and others,

Cyprus To-day, vol. II, no. 3 (1964); A. Chayes and others, compilers, *International Legal Process*, vol. 2 (Boston, Little, Brown, 1969), pp. 1234–312. See also the Security Council and General Assembly debates on Cyprus and esp. statement of the Foreign Minister of Cyprus at the 1098th mtg of the Security Council (*SCOR*, 19th yr).

27 See works cited in n. 25 above.

28 S/5488 (*SCOR*, 18th yr, Suppl. Oct.–Dec. 1963).

29 The 1085th mtg (*SCOR*, 18th yr).

30 S/5514 (*SCOR*, 19th yr, Suppl. Jan.–Mar. 1964), and S/5516 (ibid.). Gen. Gyani of India, former commander of UNEF and UNYOM was appointed; he was later to become the first commander of UNFICYP.

31 For a not unbiased account of the surrounding circumstances, see E. Weinthal and C. Bartlett, *Facing the Brink: an Intimate Study of Crisis Diplomacy* (New York, Scribner, 1967), pp. 16–36. See also P. Windsor, *Nato and the Cyprus Crisis* (London, ISS, 1964, Adelphi Paper no. 14).

32 A letter of 26 Dec. 1963 (S/5488, *SCOR*, 18th yr, Suppl. Oct.–Dec. 1963) from the Cyprus Permanent Representative had already been inscribed on the Security Council agenda.

33 See *SCOR*, 1964, 1095th mtg and following.

34 And thus, indirectly, precluding Turkey from using her alleged right of forcible intervention against Cyprus.

35 On the issue of the validity of the Nicosia Treaties of Aug. 1960, the Council, rightly, did not adopt a position but simply took into consideration in the preamble the position of the parties. See Jacovides, as cited in n. 26 above, pp. 25–6.

36 SC res. 186 (1964).

37 S/5578 (*SCOR*, 19th yr, Suppl. Jan.–Mar. 1964).

38 A/3943 (*GAOR*, 13th sess., Annexes, agenda item 65).

39 e.g. while a certain Eastern European country is said to have offered to participate, this offer was not taken up, presumably because it did not fit within this area of the common denominator.

40 See Cyprus Mission press release No. 6 in reply to Max Frankel's *New York Times* article, 8 July 1964.

41 There have been one Hungarian, one Bulgarian, and several Czechoslovak officials, all of whom, it is the general view, have behaved impartially and conscientiously as UN officials within the letter and the spirit of the Charter.

42 In fact the Secretary General in S/5671, 29 Apr. 1964 (*SCOR*, 19th yr, Suppl. Apr.–June) set out objectives and interim aims of the Force. The instructions in detail which are being constantly sent, whenever the occasion requires them, from UN Headquarters have not been published.

43 By Cyprus in Mar. 1964; by Cyprus and Turkey in Aug. 1964; by Turkey and Cyprus in Aug. 1965; by Turkey in Nov. 1965; by Cyprus in Nov. 1967.

44 S/5653 (*SCOR*, 19th yr, Suppl. Apr.–June 1964); also S/5671 (ibid.).

45 S/5764 (ibid.).

46 S/5950 (*SCOR*, 19th yr, Suppl. July–Sept. 1964, pp. 280 ff.). In para. 220 the Secretary-General stated that 'UNFICYP was not established by the Security Council as an arm of the Government of Cyprus. . . . It respects at all times the sovereignty and independence of Cyprus and the authority of the Government but it acts independently in the discharge of its mandate, in accordance with the resolutions of the Security Council.' In the same report (paras 218 and 219), U Thant said '. . . there has been all along and continues to be what I consider to be a misunderstanding on the part of the Turkish community of Cyprus and of the Turkish Government as to the function and duty of the United Nations Force in Cyprus . . . in their eyes, UNFICYP should have been employing force, wherever and whenever necessary to restore, over the opposition of the Cypriot Government, the constitutional situation relating to the privileges, rights and immunities of the Turkish community in Cyprus. . . . I have not, of course, accepted these positions. . . .'

[47] cf. in this connection the correspondence between Mr Aiken, Irish Minister for External Affairs, and the Secretary-General as regards the Irish government's understandings prior to agreeing to participate in the Force, notably that ' an assurance will be forthcoming from the Governments of Great Britain, Greece and Turkey, that, during the presence of the force in Cyprus, they will not intervene or attempt to intervene by force, or by threat of force, to impose a solution of the problem and, particularly, a solution by partition.' (Letter of 13 Mar. 1964.) See also Mr Aiken's subsequent letter (24 Mar. 1964) in which he stressed that ' if during the presence of the United Nations force in Cyprus the Governments of Great Britain, Greece and Turkey or any of them, should intervene, or attempt to impose by force or by threat of force a solution of the problem, and particularly a solution by partition, immediate steps will be taken to withdraw the Irish contingent from Cyprus.'. UN Press release CYP/4, 13 Mar. 1964.

[48] S/5950, para. 232.

[49] One such occasion arose in Dec. 1967 over implementation of the Athens-Ankara agreement of 27 Nov. 1967 in conjunction with the Secretary-General's appeal (S/8248/Add. 6 (SCOR, 22nd yr, Suppl. Oct.–Dec. 1967). For reasons that cannot be fully explained here it did not result in any change of UNFICYP's mandate.

[50] Under para. 7 of SC res. 186 (1964).

[51] Such renewals took place in June, Sept. and Dec. 1964 (SC res. 192, 194 and 198, resp.); in Mar., June and Dec. 1965 (SC res. 206, 207 and 219); in Mar., June and Dec. 1966 (SC res. 220, 222 and 231); in June and Dec. 1967 (SC res. 238 and 244); and in Mar., June and Dec. 1968 (SC res. 247, 254 and 261).

[52] The main trends were aptly summarized in the statement of the Representative of India in the Special Committee on Peace-Keeping Operations as reflected in A/AC. 121/WGA/SRI: ' There appeared now to be universal agreement that the Security Council had the primary responsibility . . . for the establishment of peace-keeping operations. That was not to deny such authority as the General Assembly had in that field. The differences that existed arose out of the attempts to define the exact authority of the Security Council and the General Assembly respectively. There was sizable support for the view that the General Assembly was vested with considerable residual authority, particularly in situations in which the Security Council failed to act. There was the opposite view, however, that, while the General Assembly had the right, the authority and, indeed, the responsibility to discuss any question, it could not under any circumstances take action within the meaning of Article 11 (2) of the Charter. The proponents of that view extended their definition of " action ", to cover even the dispatch of a single soldier to a trouble spot in the world. There was also a third point of view . . . in the French Government's view, the apportionment of functions between the Security Council and the General Assembly was based primarily on Article 11 (2) of the Charter; that provision could not be limited to the measures provided for in Articles 41 and 42, but also covered any measures involving the creation of a military force, even if the force was created with the agreement of the states covered and even if the actual use of armed force was theoretically limited to certain exceptional cases. Within those limits, the French Government maintained, the Security Council had exclusive authority; the General Assembly could undertake such operations as observation, surveillance or investigation, provided that those operations were not carried out by units placed under military command and that the units were not responsible for their own security. . . .'

[53] *Certain Expenses of the United Nations* (1962), *ICJ Rep. 1962.*

[54] In fact the opinion prevailed in the Special Cttee that it would be futile to try to resolve the basic constitutional issue, and, instead, the emphasis is currently being placed on less controversial and more practical steps in the implementation of the Cttee's mandate. See e.g. *GAOR*, 23rd sess.,

Suppl. 1 (A/7201), p. 76; and A/7455 (*GAOR*, 23rd sess., Annexes, agenda item 32).

55 S/8914 (*SCOR*, 23rd yr, Suppl. Oct.–Dec. 1968).

56 On the role of the law in the context of peacekeeping operations see generally O. Schachter, 'The Uses of Law in International Peace-keeping', *Virginia Law Review*, vol. 50, no. 6 (1964).

57 This is also the view set out in *Repertoire of the Practice of the Security Council*, Suppl. 1964–5, pp. 67 ff. Art. 29 reads: 'The Security Council may establish such subsidiary organs as it deems necessary for the performance of its functions.'

58 See generally Bowett, *UN Forces*, p. 553; Higgins, *World Today*, vol. 20, no. 8 (1964), pp. 347–50; Papadopoulos, *Peace-making and Peace-keeping by the UN*, pp. 27–8.

59 55 *AJIL* (Jan. 1961).

60 See e.g. L. M. Goodrich and E. Hambro, *Charter of the UN: Commentary and Documents* (Boston, World Peace Federation, 1949), pp. 273–6.

61 492 UNTS 58–87; also S/5634 (*SCOR*, 19th yr, Suppl. Jan.–Mar. 1964).

62 e.g. Exchange of Letters . . . between the UN and Sweden . . . , 21 Feb. 1966, 555 UNTS 170–5.

63 ST/SGB/UNFICYP I, issued 25 Apr. 1964, 555 UNTS 132–49.

64 Originally Mr Galo Plaza of Ecuador (who in 1968 became Secretary-General of the OAS), later Mr C. Bernardes of Brazil, and then Mr B. Osorio-Taffal of Mexico.

65 A post admirably filled by a meticulously impartial and cautious Swiss, Dr R. Gorge.

66 Mr C. Ortiz and subsequently Mr L. Moreno, both Mexican, who left behind them the best possible impressions.

67 Up till now a post filled by a national of an Eastern European state.

68 Besides the Secretary-General U Thant, these are Under-Secretary-Generals R. Bunche, J. Rolz-Bennett and (as Legal Counsel) C. Stavropoulos; Mr B. Urquhart, Mr G. Sherry, Mr F. T. Liu, and, I am sure, others.

69 S/6102 (*SCOR*, 19th yr, Suppl. Oct.–Dec. 1964).

70 Hopefully we can see the light of a peaceful solution at the end of the tunnel. What exact form this solution will take can only be the object of speculation, but it is relevant to mention the suggestion by Mr Stephens (*Cyprus: a Place of Arms*, pp. 216–18) to the effect that British bases in Cyprus, or at least that of Dhekelia (which, by most accounts, is redundant), be used for UN forces: that would both assure a tangible UN presence in the island and help to develop the peacekeeping capacity of the UN for future operations elsewhere.

71 Press release SG/SM/76.

72 Res. 377 A (V), para. C.8.

73 See e.g. Lester Pearson's Dag Hammerskjöld Memorial Lecture 'Keeping the Peace', given at Carleton Univ., Ottawa, 7 May 1964, printed in A. W. Cordier and W. Foote, eds, *The Quest for Peace* (New York, Columbia UP, 1965); and P. Martin's Jacob Blaustein Lecture 'Canada's Role in Supporting UN Peacekeeping Efforts', given at Columbia Univ., 26 Apr. 1967, printed in his *Canada and the Quest for Peace* (New York, Columbia UP, 1967); see also A/AC. 121/17, 19 June 1968.

74 See A/AC. 121/11, 20 Mar. 1968.

75 See A/AC. 121/14, 28 Mar. 1968.

76 See A/AC. 121/12, 29 Mar. 1968.

77 See A/AC. 121/13, 29 Mar. 1968.

78 See A/AC. 121/18, 26 June 1968.

79 See A/AC. 121/19, 9 July 1968.

80 See A/AC. 121/16, 29 May 1968.

81 See A/AC. 121/15, 21 May 1968.

82 See generally, P. Frydenberg, *Peace-keeping: Experience and Evaluation* (Oslo, Norwegian Inst. of Int. Affairs, 1964); World Veterans Federation, *The Functioning of Ad Hoc UN Emergency Forces* (Paris, 1963); I, J. Rikhye, *UN Peace-keeping Operations—Higher Conduct* (Paris, Int. Inf.

Center on Peace-keeping Operations, 1967); A. J. Wilson, *Some Principles for Peace-keeping Operations—a Guide for Senior Officers* (Paris, Int. Inf. Center on Peace-keeping Operations, 1967); B. Egge, 'The Ottawa Conference on UN Peace-keeping Forces', *Disarmament* (Paris), Dec. 1965, pp. 210–26.

[83] e.g. SG/SM/76, p. 9.

[84] e.g. see P. Haekkerup, 'Scandinavia's Peace-keeping Forces for UN', *For. Aff.*, July 1964, pp. 675–82.

[85] e.g. see the UK paper (A/AC. 121/16, 29 May 1968) for specific suggestions to that end.

[86] A/5721 (*GAOR*, 19th sess., Annex no. 21) and A/6641, which has also been issued under S/7841 (*SCOR*, 22nd yr, Suppl. Apr.–June 1967). See also N. A. Pitersky, 'On the Establishment of International UN Forces', *Disarmament* (Paris), Mar. 1965, pp. 5–8.

[87] S/7852 (*SCOR*, 22nd yr, Suppl. Apr.–June 1967), 13 Apr. 1967, reflecting the earlier offer of 26 Nov. 1964 (S/6070, mimeo.).

[88] e.g. the apparent slowness on the part of Third World countries to participate more actively in the ear-marking process, for example, is due largely to a lack of wide awareness of the problems involved in addition to their financial and technical limitations.

[89] The case of Cyprus furnishes a remarkable illustration of the variety of methods for peaceful settlement employed in the effort to find a solution: the attempt to forestall the explosion through the offer to negotiate on the local level through the 'thirteen points' proposals of 30 Nov. 1963; the effort to negotiate on the quasi-regional level provided by the London Conference in Jan. 1964; the reference to the Security Council and acceptance of UN mediation in Mar. 1964; the initiative of Mr Acheson acting under the umbrella of, but in fact substituting, the first UN mediator, Mr Tuomioja, to secure an agreement between Greece and Turkey in Geneva in the summer of 1964; there followed the renewed UN mediation effort under Dr Plaza resulting in his report of Mar. 1965; subsequently the General Assembly, called upon to pronounce on the merits of the case, passed the resolution of 18 Dec. 1965; there followed in the spring of 1966 the enlargement of the functions of the Special Representative of the Secretary-General in Cyprus, Mr Bernardes, to include quasi-mediational functions; the next step was the initiating of the secret 'dialogue' between Athens and Ankara which ended abruptly in failure in Sept. 1967; after the crisis of Nov.–Dec. 1967, the Security Council urged that the parties avail themselves of the good offices of the Secretary-General which they did early in 1968. The effort is carried out in Cyprus itself through the 'local talks' to be followed, if they succeed, by a wider round in which the three outside signatories of the 1959–60 accords would also participate. It thus appears that, short of arbitration and judicial settlement, the full range of possibilities has been used in the effort to find a solution, with special reliance upon the possibilities available through the UN and more particularly the Secretary-General's office. On these, see the views expressed by the Representative of Cyprus, *GAOR*, 18th sess., 6th Cttee, 824th mtg, pp. 246–8, and Jacovides, *Treaties Conflicting with Peremptory Norms of International Law and the Zurich-London 'Agreements'*, pp. 24–7.

CHAPTER 7

[1] As a necessary, but essentially secondary, qualification it may be said that there is fully enough scientific evidence available that marine pollution is occurring. What is not yet known is the full and precise effect of particular pollutants, nor is adequate institutional machinery yet in operation to establish such effects. Discussion in various specialized bodies (in particular

the Intergovernmental Oceanographic Commission (IOC) and the Joint IMCO/FAO/UNESCO/WMO/WHO/IAEA Group of Experts on the Scientific Aspects of Marine Pollution (GESAMP), and at the FAO Technical Conference on Marine Pollution and its Effects on Living Resources and Fishing, held in Dec. 1970), regarding methods of ocean monitoring and surveillance, has been directed to filling these gaps. Greater knowledge will make it easier to determine what degree of control and what specific measures should be introduced in particular instances.

2 'The study of marine geology has unlocked the history of the oceans, and it seems likely to make intelligible the history of the continents as well. We are in the middle of a rejuvenating process in geology comparable to the one that physics experienced in the 1890's and to the one that is now in process in molecular biology.' Sir Edward Bullard, 'The Origin of the Oceans', *Scientific American*, Sept. 1969, p. 66. See similarly R. Revelle, 'The Ocean', ibid. p. 55.

3 The 1968 total world fishing catch was 64 million metric tons, almost double the 1958 total of 33 million metric tons. *Yearbook of Fishery Statistics (Commodities) 1968* (FAO, 1970). There was, however, a 2 per cent drop in 1969, and catches of certain species or in certain areas have fallen appreciably: *Yearbook of Fishery Statistics (Commodities) 1969* (FAO, 1970).

4 Comprehensive Outline of the Scope of the Long-Term and Expanded Programme of Oceanic Exploration and Research, UN doc. A/7750, 10 Nov. 1969, annex, pt I, sec. 3. The definition was originally prepared by a SCOR/ACMRR Working Group, and has since been slightly amended. See also the report of GESAMP's first session, Mar. 1969, GESAMP I/11, para. 12. It may be noted that the definition includes the introduction of sounds (e.g. explosions), as well as of substances.

5 It would be interesting to examine the reasons why the notion of an *actio popularis* has not developed further in international law. As regards the protection of the seas, the answer would seem to lie, first, in the general absence of damage hitherto, secondly, in difficulties of proof, and, thirdly, in the reluctance of customary international law, given its basis in state sovereignty, to recognize the right or claim of one state to represent community interests. It may be noted that the possibility of responsibility for harm to such interests has already been touched on by the International Law Commission in its discussion of state responsibility. Report of the International Law Commission on the Work of its Twenty-second Session, *GAOR*, 25th sess., Suppl. 10 (A/8010/Rev. 1), para. 73.

6 The lack, under existing law, of regulatory powers applicable prior to an accident was one of the reasons advanced by the Canadian government in justification of its decision to establish direct unilateral controls over shipping entering Arctic waters. See further below.

7 The oceans provide, together with the biosphere, the reservoirs which take up the carbon dioxide in the atmosphere. Since the concentration of carbon dioxide in the atmosphere is rising with the increased use of fossil fuels, the question is presented of determining the limits of the seas' capacity in this respect (see generally the discussion in *Man's Impact on the Global Environment: Assessment and Recommendations for Action*, Report of the Study of Critical Environmental Problems, Director: C. L. Wilson (Cambridge, Mass., MIT Press, 1970), pp. 46 ff.). For present purposes the possibility of major climatic or other environmental changes, which might threaten human existence, may be distinguished from more limited effects on the oceans and the marine ecosystem, with which this paper deals.

8 The relationship between direct controls (legal, administrative, etc.) and scientific inquiry requires elaboration. Until strong scientific evidence is clear and forthcoming, there is an understandable reluctance on the part of national authorities to take action; in the case where damage to economic interests is immediately discernible (e.g. large oil slicks heading for the holidaymakers' coasts) governmental intervention is fairly speedy, but such instances form, relatively, the exception. As regards scientific investigations

of more complex effects, to provide precise and comprehensive monitoring of the oceans is very difficult—indeed, we are only just beginning to understand how difficult it is, involving, as it does, the question of how the world as a whole, *qua* environment, operates; such inquiries, if under-taken, will also require government support. It may therefore be quicker and easier (difficult though it may be) simply to ban or limit particular practices at source (e.g. the use of certain chemicals), even before the full mechanism for investigating the oceans has been constructed and exact understanding reached. But since most processes conducted on a scale likely to entail serious harm to the marine environment are widespread and involve existing interests, whether such controls will be introduced (and how strictly they will be enforced) will depend on the weight of scientific evidence, and thus the problem moves round in a circle. As a (perhaps) encouraging note, it should be pointed out, however, that the introduction of direct controls may not be dependent on investigations of marine conditions *per se* if, as in the case of air pollution, harm is likely to be done to man directly, irrespective of that done to him or his interests via the seas.

9   Thus increased attention has been paid to assessing world production figures of particular chemicals which result, directly or indirectly, in marine pollution, so as to enable estimates to be made of the volumes reaching the seas. This technique was particularly used in *Man's Impact on the Global Environment*, and its influence is to be found also in the report of the FAO Seminar on Methods of Detection, Measurement and Monitoring of Pollutants in the Marine Environment (FIR : TPMB/70/6 Rev., cited hereafter as FAO Seminar Report) which preceded the FAO Technical Conference in Dec. 1970.

10   Thus the IMCO Legal Committee, which was requested, following the con-clusion of the 1969 Conventions concerning tankers, to examine the legal aspects of pollution from noxious and hazardous cargo other than oil, decided to postpone consideration of the matter until more technical in-formation was available and, in particular, until it had received GESAMP's report on the substances to be considered. IMCO Legal Committee, 9th sess., LEG IX/6, 6 Oct. 1970, para. A.1.

11   The following classification follows that used by the FAO Seminar Report (cited fully in n. 9 above) which, together with the FAO Technical Con-ference and its background papers, constitutes the most exhaustive study of the matter yet made. Specific mention is made in the text, however, of the release of thermal energy, which is referred to separately by GESAMP (doc. II/11, annex V). GESAMP's classification, though scientifically similar, also takes account of the different activities involved.

12   It should be noted that the classes listed are not mutually exclusive. Strictly speaking, halogenated hydrocarbons and petroleum are organic chemicals, but are sufficiently distinct in this context to require separate discussion.

13   Tankers 530,000 metric tons (30,000 in the case of those using the 'load on top' method, 500,000 the remainder), other ships 500,000 metric tons. *Man's Impact on the Global Environment*, p. 267.

14   Ibid. p. 141.

15   World crude oil production is expected to double at least between 1970 and 1980. Thus, since, from a combination of uses man may now be putting in the seas an amount of petroleum hydrocarbons approximately equal to that produced naturally (O. Schachter and D. Serwer, 'Marine Pollution: Problems and Remedies', 65 *AJIL* (1971) 89, and works there cited), by 1980 the seas will be required to deal with twice that volume; on this basis even if, by 1980, there will be no direct discharges from ships, the oceans would be receiving a considerably larger volume of petroleum pollution than at present.

16   This may be for various purposes—to clear channels for navigation, or to obtain gravel or minerals such as tin or aragonite (see n. 123 below).

17   A class of synthetic chemicals which are widely used in industry and agriculture, the best known example being DDT and its associated com-

pounds. They are not easily degraded and this fact, together with the tendency for concentrations to be built up in the marine food chain, results in long-lasting harmful effects upon marine animals and plants, and indirectly on man. For further technical details and references regarding this and the other categories mentioned, see FAO Seminar Report (cited fully in n. 9 above).

18 This includes a number of heavy metals, released during industrial (or similar) processes or eventually disposed of as waste, many of them highly toxic, both for marine life and for humans. Mercury and lead are considered the most threatening.

19 The most complex case, including petrochemicals, pulp and paper mill waste. detergents, tannins, and aniline dyes. The effects produced are equally complex, depending on the quantity and concentration of the matter disposed of, but include the indirect encouraging of marine toxins.

20 Nutrient chemicals (chiefly nitrogen and phosphorus) are necessary for the growth of marine plants; overproduction of phytoplankton, however, may lead to eutrophication, namely the removal of oxygen from the water because of the accumulation of decaying material, which results in the suffocation of marine life (e.g. fish) requiring oxygen. Nutrients are released by man chiefly as domestic and industrial wastes. Steps have already been taken to reduce phosphates in detergents (see further below).

21 The FAO Seminar and Technical Conference, and many of the 140 papers produced for the Conference, dealt with detailed aspects of the release of chemicals in these four classes into the marine environment.

22 e.g. the use of household detergents containing phosphates and nitrogen.

23 Two documents prepared by WMO for GESAMP (GESAMP II/2/4 and II/2/1) describe respectively the role of the atmosphere in hydrological cycles which contributes to marine pollution as a result of run-off from land contaminated by industrial dust or agricultural pesticides, and atmospheric pollution in general and the establishment of a network of stations whereby atmospheric pollution (which contributes to marine pollution) may be measured.

24 As evidenced by the FAO Technical Conference, the preceding Seminar, the 1970 Study of Critical Environmental Problems, and GESAMP's second report, doc. II/11, annex V.

25 Arguably increased radioactivity of the seas caused by fallout should be added as a fourth case (see GESAMP II/11, annex V, table 2). The general opinion, however, has been that, over the long term, as more nuclear power stations are built, the disposal of radioactive wastes will be the major problem as regards this form of pollution.

26 This is particularly dealt with by Schachter and Serwer, 65 *AJIL* (1971) 95 ff. Chlorinated hydrocarbons are used for pesticides (particularly DDT) and, in the form of polychlorinated biphenyls, for purposes (such as insulation and fire retardation) which, unlike the pesticides, do not involve their deliberate release into the atmosphere. No one appears to have found out yet how the PCBs reach the sea.

27 For a full list, and assessment of relative danger, see FAO Seminar Report (cited fully in n. 9 above), pp. 27 ff. After lead (used in anti-knock additives to petrol) and mercury (used in manufacture of PVC), which are classified as the most serious dangers, on a world-wide and local basis respectively, cadmium (used in electroplating), and arsenic are the most serious; arsenic is not, however, airborne. The only other toxic heavy metal now known to be carried by the atmosphere to the seas is vanadium and, possibly, titanium.

Mercury compounds, besides being used in factory processes, are also used for agricultural purposes and carried into the inland water system as run off, or to the seas via the atmosphere. A number of countries (Canada, Finland, Japan, Sweden, and the United States) have prohibited or reduced the use of mercury compounds in agriculture and strengthened controls in order to cut down mercury losses from industrial processes.

28 But not always very effectively: thus it was reported in the press that trees in Norway were growing less because of the effect on the soil and water

there of sulphuric acid carried by winds coming from England. The 'black snow' over parts of Scandinavia was traced to pollutants carried by air currents from the Ruhr, *New York Times*, 11 Jan. 1970. (As against this, it could presumably be said that but for existing controls in the countries where the pollution originates, the effect would be even greater.)

29 Hungary, Sweden, and Denmark have banned its use (Schachter and Serwer, 65 *AJIL* (1971) 97), and other countries are contemplating similar action. A quarter of the DDT produced is believed to be finding its way into the oceans, virtually all via the atmosphere. (*Man's Impact on the Global Environment*, pp. 131 ff.), although amounts are also disposed of as domestic and industrial wastes, or are transported by run off.

30 GESAMP II/11, annex V, p. 18.

31 Issued 12 Feb. 1971. DDT was at one time used against a large number of insect-borne diseases. Alternatives have been found in most cases, but not as regards the control of malaria transmitted by mosquitos or of sleeping sickness transmitted by tsetse flies. Annual DDT production now amounts to between 200,000 and 250,000 metric tons, some 15 to 20 per cent of which is used for the control of disease.

32 Besides the activities of the Council of Europe and of the Organization of Economic Co-operation and Development, the UN Economic Commission for Europe has played a leading part. The matter of environmental protection has also been discussed within the framework of NATO.

33 And the well-known *Trail Smelter* Case (see n. 41 below). This is an important award, but can hardly be left to provide the sole guidance in this area.

34 The approximate order of magnitude with respect to pollution hazards amongst industrial waste products is as follows: pesticides, heavy metals and other inorganic toxic compounds, radioactive substances, petrochemicals, oil, organic waste, detergents, heat, solid objects and dredging spoils. This list shows clearly the range of land activities and industries affected by efforts to reduce marine pollution. See GESAMP report on its first session, GESAMP I/11.

35 Natural resources development and policies, including environmental considerations, Report of the Secretary-General, addendum: River discharge and marine pollution, doc. E/C.7/2/Add.8, 14 Jan. 1971. See also doc. E/C.7/2/Add.7, annex II. (Particular issues raised with respect to the use of international rivers are not discussed in this paper.)

36 A report by the Secretary-General, Marine Science and Technology: Survey and Proposals, E/4487, 24 Apr. 1968, contains a certain amount of general information on this topic (see Parts I, E; II, 2 and 3; III, D; and Annex XIV), based in part on a questionnaire sent to states in 1967. Twelve states only reported activity in monitoring and forecasting marine pollution (Australia, Canada, Chile, Federal Republic of Germany, Finland, France, Japan, Norway, South Africa, Sweden, UK, and US). Further information is to be found in the replies to a more detailed questionnaire sent by IMCO in 1969; see, e.g. the reply of the UK contained in IMCO doc. OP VII/4(b), annex II, 7 Aug. 1969. Reference may also be made to *Water Pollution Control: National Legislation and Policy* (FAO, 1968), which contains references to specific acts of national legislation, and G. Moore, *The Control of Marine Pollution and the Protection of Living Resources of the Sea*, prepared for the FAO Technical Conference (FIR:MP/70/R-15), part 3 of which is a survey of national legislation. Moore illustrates the diverse patterns of national management which have been adopted, including legislation relating to harbours and fishery regulations, and the attempts which are now being made to turn these patches of law and administration into a more coherent system of environment management.

37 e.g. in accordance with a voluntary system operated by the Ministry of Agriculture, Fisheries and Food, the UK dumps toxic wastes in water deeper than 2,000 fathoms outside territorial waters. Denmark stated that 'Danish shipowners have instructed their ships not to discharge imperishable sewage and rubbish into Danish waters'. IMCO doc. OP VII/4(b), annex II.

[38] To date this has been the governing factor, as is borne out by the following statement made by two US experts: 'Historically, waste disposal policies in the U.S. generally have been based on the axiom of maximum permissible levels of water pollution. Indeed, it may be questioned whether there were policies at all. . . . Water quality management policies admittedly followed vague estimates of what happened when pollutants were deposited in estuaries and coastal waters. The practice was to dispose first and to investigate later, an invitation to disaster that requires no documentation for the proof of sinister changes in the estuarine life of many coastal areas in the U.S. is dismally at hand for anyone to examine.' W. Espey and F. Bender, 'Systems Analysis of Galveston Bay: a Major Step toward Controlled Environment', *Ocean Industry*, Feb. 1970, pp. 60–1.

[39] For a case involving Italy and France, see *New York Times*, 19 July 1970.

[40] Or, as it was put by the Secretary-General '. . . in fact a valuable and legitimate use of the near-shore marine environment is as a diluting and assimilating medium for waste materials, provided that these are introduced within the capacity of the environment', E/4487, para. 89. The problem thus becomes, in part, determination of the capacity of the environment.

[41] The *Corfu Channel* Case, *ICJ Rep. 1949*, p. 4; the *Trail Smelter* Award (1941), *UN Reports of International Arbitral Awards*, vol. 3, p. 1063; and the *Lac Lanoux Arbitral* Award (1957), *UNRIAA*, vol. 12, p. 281, might be cited, but this merely indicates the scarcity of precedents. It is of interest that in the *Trail Smelter* Award the tribunal ordered that operations might only be continued subject to a régime of specified controls.

[42] What is the extent of the 'special interest' possessed by a coastal state in the maintenance of the productivity of the living resources in any area of the high seas adjacent to its territorial sea (1958 Convention on Fishing and Conservation of the Living Resources of the High Seas, article 6)? Would the complainant state need to have adopted conservation measures under the Fishing Convention or to show that the fish stocks were of special importance and regularly exploited by its nationals? What would be the *locus standi* of other states using the same fishing grounds more rarely, or which might wish to do so in future? What effect would be attached to action on the part of any Fishery Commission concerned? What if the complainant state (or states) could show only a statistical correlation between a decline in catches and an increase in the amount of wastes dumped? It should also be borne in mind that just as pollution has increased in recent years, so has fishing; thus in the recent dispute over Atlantic salmon, Denmark attributed the decline in catches to pollution, as well as to disease, and the UK attributed it to more intensive fishing. *New York Times*, 19 Mar. 1970. Many of these (or analogous) issues may of course also be posed with respect to injury to fishing interests caused by other forms of pollution.

[43] Much of the discussion relating to liability for injurious acts has usually been devoted to the question of whether responsibility should be based on strict or absolute liability or on proof of negligence (i.e. a duty, on the part of the defendant, merely of reasonable care). Examination of the case of marine pollution, caused by waste disposal at least, suggests that the activity concerned (at least in most instances) is not so dangerous or major accidents so inevitable as to justify the automatic imposition of strict or absolute liability. James Fawcett has argued in the context of outer space activities that there should be absolute liability for the consequences of pollution (*International Law and the Uses of Outer Space*, Manchester UP, 1968, p. 67), and in the case of accidents with respect to oil tankers a similar approach has been taken (see below). In these instances, however, the contingencies to be guarded against are primarily those which may be catastrophic on a wide scale. As regards waste disposal, the danger is not of a sudden large catastrophe, but of a steadily deteriorating situation over a period of years, so that the possibility of preventing 'accidents' exists, provided efforts are made. How energetic would efforts have to be to show reasonable care? It is suggested that a distinction might be drawn between

disposal of the more dangerous pollutants, for which liability might be strict, and disposal of routine waste, with the important qualification that the degree of harm might depend either on the inherent quality of the waste, as in the case of toxic compounds, or on the volume disposed of, almost irrespective of the substance. The essence of the matter will be the capacity of the sea, in the particular area concerned, to absorb (or to continue to absorb) the waste in question, without deleterious effects for other marine users, which in turn will come back to the question of monitoring and surveillance.

It is one of the themes of the present essay that discussion along the traditional legal lines is to some degree barren, or at least secondary: what has to be determined is the capacity of the marine environment to receive coastal and industrial wastes, in various (but increasing) quantities and places, without deterioration, and, when this capacity has been established, to regulate the situation accordingly. Liability, as virtually the sole means of social control should, in other words, be replaced by regulation based on knowledge derived from an established system of international scientific inquiries, and liability reserved essentially to deal with major catastrophes and accidents.

[44] A sevenfold increase in the industrial wastes disposed of in the seas over the next decade is forecast by E. Wenk, 'The Physical Resources of the Ocean', *Scientific American*, Sept. 1969, p. 174. Over a million square miles of shellfish-producing waters bordering the US are now unusable owing to pollution, ibid. The threat of pollution to mariculture has been stressed by FAO; see GESAMP I/11, para. 7.

[45] The increase in estuarine pollution in the US seems to be an irreversible phenomenon, see G. Claus, 'Disposal of Sewage in the Ocean and the Pollution of the Estuaries', in *Proceedings of Conference on International and Interstate Regulation of Water Pollution, March 12–13, 1970* (New York, Columbia Journal of Transnational Law), pp. 245 and 252. The *New York Times* of 27 Oct. 1968 reported plans for a sewage pipeline going 80 miles out to sea from the Trenton-Philadelphia-Wilmington area; while this project has not been proceeded with, it has been suggested that sewage sludge, now dumped 12 miles from the shore, should in future be dumped at sites 100 miles out. *New York Times*, 15 and 21 Feb. 1970.

[46] See e.g. President Nixon's message to Congress of 9 Feb. 1971. A report on ocean dumping was made by the Council of Environmental Quality in Oct. 1970. Schachter and Serwer, 65 *AJIL* (1971) 108, discuss this aspect, including the 'standard setting' role which an international organization could play in conjunction with a system of international registration.

[47] Or even by non-nationals; thus it has been reported that the Netherlands legislation would control the disposal of wastes beyond Dutch territorial waters by non-Dutch ships where the waste has been transported through the Netherlands prior to disposal (Moore, cited fully in n. 36 above, paras 3, 2, 7).

[48] The International Council for the Exploration of the Sea established working groups to study pollution in the North Sea and the Baltic; reports were issued in 1969 and 1970. The International Commission for the Scientific Exploration of the Mediterranean (ICSEM) is examining pollution in the Mediterranean and has requested one of its scientific committees to study, on a continuing basis, the effects of pollution in that sea and the means required to control it. The General Fisheries Council for the Mediterranean adopted two resolutions on pollution in Dec. 1969, providing for the collection of information and establishing an expert group, to co-operate with ICSEM. (Information kindly supplied by Mr Jean Carroz, FAO.) At the FAO Technical Conference, papers were presented dealing with pollution in the Baltic, Mediterranean, and the North Sea.

[49] Thus a joint research programme, aimed at curbing water pollution in the Gulf of Mexico, was recently agreed upon by the states members of the Caribbean Sea and Adjacent Regions Co-operative. *New York Times*, 28 Feb. 1970. The Council of Europe, the Economic Commission for

Europe, and the Organization for Economic Co-operation and Development, have all been active in this sphere. As regards the Council of Europe, see in particular recommendation 626 (1971), adopted by the Consultative Assembly on 21 Jan. 1971, and the accompanying report of the Legal Affairs Committee (doc. 2896).

50 As an indication of magnitude, West German industries are now said to set aside 6 per cent of their new plant investments for pollution control. *New York Times*, 28 Feb. 1970.

51 This has not worked very effectively in the case of the Great Lakes between Canada and the US, but it is doubtful if either country would have been prepared to accept an agency with direct enforcement powers. See F. Jordan, 'Recent Developments in International Environmental Pollution Control', 15 *McGill Law Journal* (1969) 279. H. Landis, General Counsel of the Ontario Water Resources Commission, has argued in favour of a new treaty with the US, giving primary responsibility, so far as Canada is concerned, to the provinces: 'Legal Controls of Pollution in the Great Lakes Basin', 48 *Canadian Bar Review* (1970) 66.

52 See the series of reports and resolutions on international river law adopted by the International Law Association, culminating in the adoption in 1966 of the Helsinki Rules on the Uses of the Waters of International Rivers. The Law relating to International Watercourses has recently been recommended by the General Assembly to the International Law Commission for study. For a general survey of the topic see Natural Resources Development and Policies, including Environmental Considerations, Report of the Secretary-General, addendum: Issues of International Water Resources Development, doc. E/C.7/2/Add.6, 18 Jan. 1971.
For a report on ILA consideration of marine pollution, see the paper by K. Cuperus presented to the FAO Technical Conference, FIR:MP/70/E-54.

53 International Co-operation in Problems related to the Oceans, progress report, doc. E/4836, 2 Apr. 1970, para. 44.

54 480 UNTS 43.

55 Art. 1. Could this be done, other than by tunnelling from the land?

56 See the Secretariat working paper, The Military Uses of the Sea-Bed and the Ocean Floor beyond the Limits of Present National Jurisdiction, A/AC.135/28, 10 July 1968.

57 Committee on the Peaceful Uses of the Sea-Bed and the Ocean Floor beyond the Limits of National Jurisdiction, 12th mtg, 11 Nov. 1969, A/AC.138/SR. 12.

58 See generally, W. Boulanger, 'International Conventions and Agreements on Nuclear Ships' in *Nuclear Law for a Developing World*, IAEA Legal Series No. 5, p. 175, and M. Hardy, 'The Liability of Operators of Nuclear Ships', *ICLQ*, vol. 12, part 3 (1963), p. 778.

59 For an excellent survey see R. Burgio, 'Radioisotopes in the Marine Environment', in *The Decade Ahead, 1970–1980* (Washington, DC, Marine Technology Society, 1969), p. 153.

60 See e.g. R. Edwards and J. Zupanick, 'Floating Powerplant to Support Submerged Offshore Operations', in *First Annual Offshore Technology Conference, 1969* (Dallas? 1969), paper no. 1131, vol. II, p. 481.

61 IMCO doc. LEG.VII/5, 25 Mar. 1970 and LEG.VII/11, 9 Jan. 1970, para. 21. See also ENEA, 4 *Nuclear Law Bulletin*, Dec. 1969, pp. 23–4 and 28–9.

62 e.g. even 'half-lives' of radioisotopes may be thousands of years—although most are not. Disposal in the sea of radioisotopes with half-lives of thirty or more years has been common.

63 *Recommendations of the First Meeting of the IOC Working Group on Marine Pollution* (14–17 Aug. 1967), n. 10 to Table of Major Categories of Pollution.

64 An account of IAEA's activities in this sphere is to be found in various sources; that given above is taken largely from doc. E/4487, annex XI. See also M. McDougal and W. Burke, *The Public Law of the Oceans* (London, Yale UP, 1962), pp. 852–68, and works there cited, for a general discussion of the legal issues.

[65] *Radioactive Waste Disposal into the Sea*, IAEA Safety Series No. 5.

[66] Including those of a legal panel which met four times over the period 1961–3 and which produced two different drafts of a report, reflecting two diverging views on the fundamental question of the permissibility of disposing radioactive wastes into the sea under international law. A symposium held in 1966, however, indicated that outstanding problems have narrowed considerably, E/4487, annex XI, paras. 157–9.

[67] Perfect control of radiation hazards at sea may indeed prove very difficult, and a decade or so may elapse before it is achieved. See F. Wang and M. Cruikshank, 'Technologic Gaps in Exploration and Exploitation of Sub-Sea Mineral Resources', in *1969 Offshore Technology Conference*, vol. I, OTC paper no. 1031, p. 295. See also C. Polvani, 'Radioactive Solid Waste Disposal into the Oceans: Implications and Perspectives', in *Symposium on the International Régime of the Sea-Bed*, Rome, 1969.

[68] *Principles for Limiting the Introduction of Radioactive Wastes into the Seas*, Report of IAEA Panel Meeting, Nov. 1970. It is now envisaged that national authorities should keep records of radioactive waste released in the marine environment. The pertinent data (types of waste and of radioactivity, quantities disposed of, and location of major releases) would be sent annually to IAEA, which would maintain a central register.

[69] Thus in 1967 a group of European states (Belgium, France, Federal Republic of Germany, Netherlands, and the UK) together disposed of 11,000 metric tons of radioactive material in an undertaking organized by ENEA. *Radioactive Waste Disposal Operation into the Atlantic 1967*, ENEA. The use of international 'escorting officers' is of interest, ibid. p. 32 and annex III.

[70] A number of states moreover might claim that the activity itself is illegal. As regards the application of the principles embodied in the conventions on nuclear liability, however, it could be argued that these were adopted to regulate responsibility for accidents due to nuclear power sources, and the hazards presented by the marine dumping of used radioactive materials, of low strength, are not of the same order of magnitude and should be treated differently.

[71] This paper deals with the dumping of military wastes and not with the firing of shells etc., either in tests or during hostile actions. Apart from the case of radioactive fallout the only appreciable marine pollution caused by military activities is the dumping of material—which constitutes a 'significant factor' in the overall situation (GESAMP II/11, annex V, para. 3.8).

[72] e.g. biological and chemical warfare agents, poison gas, heavy metals, as well as explosives.

[73] Report of the Committee on the Peaceful Uses of the Sea-Bed and the Ocean Floor Beyond the Limits of National Jurisdiction, A/8021, para. 25. The Legal Adviser of the US Department of State pointed out that, if the US draft convention (ibid. annex V) had been in force the US action would have been subject to a precise system of international authorization and surveillance.

[74] By way of explanation, it should be pointed out that ships empty of cargo lie high in the water and may move violently in strong wind or in rough sea. Sea water is therefore pumped into the tanks, as ballast; tankers receive their ballast water into the same tanks which carry their cargo, and other vessels (unless they have separate ballasting tanks, which are expensive), receive the ballast water into their fuel tanks. Unless the tanks are cleaned before this is done, the water mixes with the oil residue to form an oily mixture. It is this mixture which forms the pollutant when it is discharged in the course of the ship's operations (when tankers take on new cargo, or other ships are refuelled).

The possibility of routine oil spills so caused should be distinguished from accidental spills on a large scale, as in the *Torrey Canyon* case. Such accidents involving the discharge of the cargo of a bulk carrier may involve oil or other substances (such as chemicals or pesticides). Attention with respect to accidents has so far been concentrated on oil pollution, but proposals have been made for parallel regulation of other ship-borne pollutants also (see below).

75 It should also be noted that Canada, which considered that the Conventions concerned provide insufficient protection for her interests, has decided to take unilateral measures whereby ships entering designated zones extending 100 nautical miles from her Arctic coasts are required to satisfy Canadian regulations with respect to the prevention of marine pollution (see below).

76 UNTS, vol. 327, p. 3 and vol. 600, p. 336. The 1962 amendments entered into force in 1967; the 1969 amendments (which are annexed to IMCO Assembly res. A.175(VI) of 21 Oct. 1969) are not yet in force. It is not proposed to enter into a detailed commentary here on the provisions of the Convention and the various amendments; for an analysis of the 1962 version of the Convention see US Commission on Marine Science, Engineering and Resources, *Our Nation and the Sea*, vol. 3: *Report of the International Panel* (1969), pp. VIII–79 ff.

77 Under the 1962 amendments, the prohibited area extends generally 50 miles from the coast of all countries and may be extended by a state party to 100 miles; special consideration was given to particular regions, such as shallow or semi-enclosed seas like the Mediterranean. Under the 1969 amendments there is a ban on the discharge of oil in excess of a rate of 60 litres of oil for each mile travelled.

78 According to the Report of the International Panel (see n. 76 above), pp. VIII–87, many 'flags of convenience' vessels appear to enjoy practical immunity. However, it is reported that a radar-like sensory device (called a micro-wave radiometer) has now been developed which enables coast guard planes to detect oil dumping carried on under cover of darkness. *New York Times*, 8 Mar. 1970.

79 As a means of preventing oil pollution the use of 'load on top' procedures has probably been far more effective than the requirements of the 1954 Convention, even as amended, although the two need to be looked at together. Of the estimated 530,000 metric tons of oil released in the oceans in 1969 as a result of normal tanker operations, only 30,000 metric tons was attributed to tankers using the 'load on top' procedure, and the remainder to those not doing so. Those using the technique, however, constitute 80 per cent of the world's tanker fleet—thus, a mere 20 per cent of tankers may be responsible for 94 per cent of the direct loss caused by tanker operations. *Man's Impact on the Global Environment*, p. 267. Proceeding from these calculations it has sometimes been suggested that the states which are parties to the 1954 Convention (which are also, for the most part, the states whose tankers use the 'load on top' procedures) should decline to allow the tankers of states which are not parties and/or not using such procedures, to enter their territorial seas or to use their harbours, as a means of bringing pressure on those states, either to sign the Convention or to adopt 'load on top' practices. The difficulty in this respect is that the states in the first category are also, generally speaking, those with the greatest interest in safeguarding unimpeded freedom of navigation, and who would probably not therefore wish to encourage a move towards the institution of new unilateral measures of control over the transit of ships.

80 Or already established, e.g. the International Regulations for Preventing Collisions at Sea, 1960.

81 The International Legal Conference on Marine Pollution Damage, which led to the conclusion of the two Conventions, was held in Brussels between 10 and 29 Nov. 1969. For the text of the two Conventions and the resolutions adopted see the attachment to the Final Act. The 'Public Law' Convention will enter into force when fifteen states have become parties (Art. XI); the 'Private Law' Convention will enter into force when eight states have become parties, including five states each with not less than 1,000,000 gross tons of tanker tonnage (Art. XV).

82 Either individually under the 1969 'Public Law' Convention, or collectively. Thus the North Sea states have entered into co-operative arrangements to

keep one another informed of threats of oil pollution, based on a division of the North Sea into zones for which individual states will be responsible. States parties to the Agreement may call on one another for assistance; in such circumstances a report is to be made to the Contracting parties and to IMCO. The Agreement is not in its terms limited to oil pollution caused by ships. Agreement for Co-operation in dealing with Pollution of the North Sea by Oil, 78 UKTS (1969), Cmnd 4205. The Agreement was signed at Bonn on 9 June 1969 and entered into force on 9 Aug. 1969.

[83] Art. I, 1. The Convention is applicable to any sea-going vessel, other than those used for naval purposes. The 'related interests' referred to are illustrated as including fishing activities, tourist attractions, and the health of the coastal population, Art. II, 4.

[84] Art. V.

[85] In brief, acts of war, act of God, intentional act of a third party, or wrongful act by the authority or government responsible for the maintenance of lights or other navigational aids. Art. III, 2.

[86] One of the principal issues at the Brussels Conference was whether liability should be borne by the shipowner or by the owner of the cargo. Broadly speaking, coastal states that saw themselves chiefly as potential victims favoured the latter, as offering the best means of recourse against a source (the oil companies) able to pay, and oil-transporting states favoured the former. After considerable discussion, the coastal states accepted the position of the shipping states on this point in order to secure their participation in the Convention. Stress was laid throughout the discussion on the fact that whereas the insurers could be readily identified, cargo on a given tanker might be owned by more than one party, and, indeed, ownership could pass from one party to another even during the course of a voyage.

[87] Wherever taken, and including also any further loss or damage caused by preventive measures, Arts. I, 6, and II.

[88] Detailed provisions as regards the position of the insurer and rights of subrogation are contained in Art. V. Claims for compensation may also be brought directly against the insurer or other person providing financial security, Art. VII, 8.

[89] Art. VII, 1.

[90] Art. VII, 11. As a corollary, a contracting state may not permit a ship under its flag to trade unless a certificate has been issued. Art. VII, 10.

[91] Within three years of the occurrence of the damage and in any case not more than six years after the accident. Art. VIII.

[92] Art. IX, which distinguishes between pollution damage and preventive measures as grounds for action, although in Art. I, 6, pollution damage is expressly defined as including the costs of preventive measures and further loss or damage so caused. The matter is presumably spelt out in Art. IX *ex abundante cautela.*

[93] This followed the failure of an attempt to reach agreement on an Optional Protocol which would have empowered parties to the 'Public Law' Convention to apply its provisions to all agents of pollution other than oil. See generally IMCO doc. LEG.VII/4.

[94] IMCO doc. LEG.VII/11, paras 7–10.

[95] GESAMP I/11, paras 14–18, IMCO LEG.VII/4, and GESAMP II/11, annex V.

[96] The proposal must be seen in its context. The two basic principles of the 'Private Law' Convention are the strict liability of the shipowner in nearly all foreseeable cases and the ceiling of $14 million set on maximum liability. The strict liability of the shipowner (and the consequent high costs of insurance coverage) was not what shipowning interests wished, and the limitation on the amount of maximum compensation was not what countries who saw themselves chiefly as potential victims wished; the result therefore was a compromise between these two sets of economic interests. (See also *The Economist,* 6 Dec. 1969.) The object of the international compensation fund would come nearer to a 'social security' approach, whereby compensation would be paid up to a much higher ceiling figure and with as

few exceptions as possible; at the same time the fund would seek to relieve the burden placed on the shipowner under the 1969 Convention, of paying compensation in virtually all cases. The fund would (or might), however, have the possibility of recourse against the shipowner, under the usual principles of maritime law, most notably the requirement of proof of fault (or proof, on the part of the shipowner, that negligence had not been committed) and much lower limits of compensation. There would also be the possibility of the fund recovering, at least in part, sums it had itself paid out, from the tanker owners or other parties closely connected with the maritime carriage of oil in bulk. The tanker owners have in fact already established a fund (TOVALOP: tanker owners' voluntary organization on oil pollution), with a ceiling of $9,600,000 per accident; this fund being intended to compensate governments directly, an 'Oil Companies International Marine Forum' has also been created, with the intention of providing the higher 'cover' with which the IMCO Working Group on the compensation fund is concerned.

97 The Working Group held its fifth and final session in Mar. 1971. A plenipotentiary conference was held in Brussels, 29 Nov.–18 Dec. 1971, which prepared and opened for signature and subsequent accession the International Convention on the Establishment of an International Fund for Compensation for Oil Pollution Damage.

98 See the statements and proposals made by the Canadian delegation at the Brussels Conference, in particular those contained in IMCO doc. LEG/CONF/SR.2 and SR.5, and LEG/CONF/4/Add.3, and the Canadian note, dated 16 Apr. 1970, to the US.

99 An Act to Amend the Territorial Sea and Fishing Zones Act, 18–19 Eliz. 2, c. 68 (Can. 1970).

100 Arctic Waters Pollution Prevention Act, 18–19 Eliz. 2, c. 47 (Can. 1970). For commentaries on the Canadian legislation see R. Bilder, 'The Canadian Arctic Waters Pollution Prevention Act: New Stresses on the Law of the Sea', 69 *Michigan Law Review* (1970) 1, and R. Neuman, 'Oil on Troubled Waters: the International Control of Oil Pollution', 2 *Journal of Maritime Law and Commerce* (1971) 349.

101 In notes of 9 and 15 Apr. 1970, the US protested against the Canadian proposals, in particular the exercise of control over US vessels on the high seas. In a State Department statement of 15 Apr. 1970 stress was laid on the danger that the Canadian example would be taken as precedent by other states seeking to introduce other unilateral changes in existing law. In its reply of 16 Apr. 1970 the Canadian government, which had changed the terms of Canada's acceptance of the compulsory jurisdiction of the International Court of Justice before introducing the bills so as to exclude disputes that might arise as to their legality, declined to accede to a US proposal that the case be submitted to the International Court. The Canadian Premier, Mr Trudeau, speaking in the Canadian House of Commons, declared that 'we will not go to court until such time as the law catches up with technology'. In the meantime the US tanker Manhattan, which passed through the Northwest passage in 1969, has complied with a series of safety modifications required by the Canadian government and deposited a large bond before undertaking further tests in Arctic waters. *New York Times*, 19 Apr. 1970 and *Times*, 5 May 1970.

102 Though perhaps some similar cases can be found, e.g. Denmark in relation to Greenland, the areas beyond the northernmost coasts of Norway (including Spitzbergen) and the Soviet Union, and the Antarctic, without considering examples where states might make special claims based on other geographical features (e.g. island archipelagos).

103 These may consist of petroleum (oil or natural gas) or hard minerals, such as submarine phosphate or manganese nodules and crusts, situated either as surficial deposits or as deposits within bedrock. The methods of exploitation are drilling, in the case of petroleum, or various dredging or similar systems in the case of hard minerals.

[104] The Declaration of Principles Governing the Sea-Bed and the Ocean Floor, and the Subsoil thereof, beyond the Limits of National Jurisdiction, adopted by the General Assembly on 17 Dec. 1971 (108 in favour, none against, 14 abstentions), affirms the existence of such an area (res. 2749 (XXV)).

[105] Art. 5, para. 1.

[106] Art. 5, para. 7. On 1 Apr. 1970 forty-one states were parties to the Convention. Would these provisions, observed by all states exploiting their continental shelf, whether or not parties to the Convention, now constitute part of the general principles of law or a customary obligation?

[107] Nevertheless complaints have been made that states could be more careful than they are. Thus the Permanent Representative of Norway, speaking in the First Committee during the twenty-fourth session of the General Assembly, questioned whether, as regards the international area, the international community would be satisfied ' with certain lax approaches used today in oil drilling by various countries to the effect that the more or less haphazard work manuals of a drilling platform are accepted as the only safety code and anti-pollution code applicable to the oceans of the world ', A/C.1/PV.1676, Nov. 1969, p. 33.

[108] Government Measures pertaining to the Development of the Mineral Resources of the Continental Shelf, A/AC.138/21, 27 Jan. 1970, para. 57.

[109] Including the cost of control and total removal of the pollutant, Code of Federal Regulations, Title 30, chap. II, section 250.43, *Federal Register*, Vol. 34, No. 161, 22 Aug. 1969, p. 13547, and section 11 (f), Water Quality Improvement Act of 1970, Report No. 91-940, H. of Representatives, 91st Congress, 2nd sess.

[110] Water Quality Improvement Act of 1970.

[111] See generally the report of the Secretary-General, Marine Pollution and Other Hazardous and Harmful Effects which might arise from the Exploration and Exploitation of the Sea-Bed and the Ocean Floor, and the Subsoil thereof, beyond the Limits of National Jurisdiction, doc. A/7924, 11 June 1970.

[112] Note also para. 14 of the Declaration: ' Every State shall have the responsibility to ensure that activities in the area, including those relating to its resources, whether undertaken by governmental agencies, or non-governmental entities or persons under its jurisdiction, or acting on its behalf, shall be carried out in conformity with the international régime to be established. The same responsibility applies to international organizations and their members for activities undertaken by such organizations or on their behalf. Damage caused by such activities shall entail liability.'

[113] See e.g. the proposal by a group of Afro-Asian states, contained in the Interim Report of the Economic and Technical Sub-Committee of the Sea-Bed Committee, A/AC.138/SC.2/L.6, annex III, 24 Mar. 1970. The nature of the future international regime would also affect the means of implementation of any rules adopted, an issue which is merely noted here. An international body with wide functions might e.g. be empowered to inspect operations and to impose fines or to take further measures if regulations (including those relating to pollution control) were not complied with. The US draft convention (see n. 73 above) would provide a full international regulatory mechanism for dealing, *inter alia*, with pollution; see Arts 1 (1), 9–12, 19 (2), 23, 27, and 40 (j) and (k).

[114] See the proposals for study put forward by the USSR, ibid. annex II.

[115] Originally, it would appear, by the Netherlands. See the proposal contained in A/AC.135/1, pp. 23–4, cited in Study on the Question of Establishing in due time Appropriate International Machinery for the Promotion of the Exploration and Exploitation of the Resources of the Sea-Bed and the Ocean Floor beyond the Limits of National Jurisdiction, and the Use of these Resources in the Interests of Mankind, footnote 26 (the study is annexed to the Report of the Sea-Bed Committee to the 24th sess. of the General Assembly, A/7622).

[116] At least as regards matters not covered by international regulations (e.g. questions relating to criminal law and jurisdiction).

[117] See the proposal contained in A/AC.138/SC.2/L.6, annex I, para. 17. It is also possible to envisage the adoption of minimum international regulations (subject either to the consent of states members of the international authority or to the adoption of special conventions), to complement national legislation; see the statement by the representative of France, A/AC.138/SC.2/SR.20, 19 Aug. 1969, pp. 68–9.

[118] A/AC.138/SC.2/SR.29, 13 Mar. 1970, p. 11.

[119] See e.g. statement of the representative of Iceland, A/AC.138/SC.2/SR.31, 17 Mar. 1970, p. 14, and in the First Committee, A/C.1/PV.1678, 6 Nov. 1969, p. 46. Reference has been made in this connection to Art. 6 of the Convention on Fishing and Conservation of the Living Resources of the High Seas. Contrary views have also been expressed, however; for a summary, see the report of the Legal Sub-Committee, A/7622, Part 2, para. 72.

[120] The programme of work of the Legal Sub-Committee included the elaboration of legal principles relating to the 'question of pollution and other hazards, and obligations and liability of States involved in the exploration, use and exploitation' of mineral resources in the area beyond national jurisdiction, A/7622, Part 2, para. 5. The matter was particularly discussed during the third session of the Sea-Bed Committee, held in Aug. 1969. Note also para. 11 of the Declaration of Principles (see n. 112 above).

For developments in the Sea-Bed Committee since the adoption of the Declaration of Principles up to Mar. 1973, see M. Hardy, 'Offshore Development and Marine Pollution', *Ocean Development and Int. Law Journal*, vol. 1, no. 3 (1973), and idem, 'Sources of Marine Pollution', in R. R. Churchill and others, eds, *New Directions in the Law of the Sea*, vol. 3 (London, Brit. Inst. of Int. and Comp. Law, 1973), where the recent activities of other UN bodies, including IMCO, are also dealt with.

[121] For a summary of the views expressed see A/7622, Part 2, para. 70. See also the statement of the Yugoslav representative, who distinguished between damage to the property of the operator or of individuals, and that which might be done to the common interest or to the economy of the nearest coastal state. He suggested that the concept of liability for the activities in question should be strengthened to provide not only for compensation but also for criminal prosecution of those responsible. A/AC.138/SC.1/SR.22, 22 Aug. 1969. Although the proposal for criminal prosecution has a forerunner in the 1884 Convention for the Protection of Submarine Cables (which renders the intentional or negligent breaking or damaging of submarine cables punishable by the appropriate signatory power), it is not evident why the nature of the injury, as having been done to the common interest, should of itself justify criminal proceedings, except possibly in the case of intentional or negligent acts—but these are not those most likely to occur.

[122] On this aspect (and generally) see the statement of the US representative in the Economic and Technical Sub-Committee, A/AC.138/SC.2/SR.5, 17 Mar. 1969.

[123] Intensive dredging in particular areas, equivalent to strip mining, could do long-lasting damage to marine flora and fauna; see the criticism of a proposal to mine 5·2 million acres off the Bahamas for aragonite (a pure form of calcium carbonate), *New York Times*, 6 Apr. 1970. The fact of the matter is that no one knows at present what the effect of such undertakings may be; the Bahamaian venture may become the largest operation for the exploitation of marine hard minerals so far undertaken. See F. Wang and M. Cruickshank, 'Technologic Gaps in Exploration and Exploitation of Sub-Sea Mineral Resources', in *1969 Offshore Technology Conference*, vol. I, OTC Paper 1031, p. 291, where it is pointed out that knowledge of the effect of dredging and associated processes 'on the benthonic biological régimes and their susceptibility to environmental changes is almost completely unknown.'

[124] V. McKelvey and F. Wang, *World Subsea Mineral Resources: a Discussion*

to *Accompany Miscellaneous Geologic Investigations Map 1–632, Second Printing*, Dept of the Interior, US Geological Survey (1969), p. 9.

[125] Working Paper presented by the US, A/AC.138/SC.2/L.6, annex IV, para. 9.

[126] See the list of topics for study suggested by certain states, ibid. annex I, para. 19. And what would be the ceiling of liability?

[127] Proposals for study put forward by the USSR, ibid. annex II, para. 1. Para. 11 of the Declaration of Principles begins with the assertion of the responsibility of states for the acts of those under their jurisdiction, but then qualifies this by reference to the international regime to be established; the matter thus still stands open.

[128] From accidents that is. The need for ships to receive information with respect to the site of drilling installations, and the institution of shipping lanes, is a separate issue now being handled by IMCO; see IMCO res. A.VI/Res.180, of 28 Oct. 1969.

[129] Assuming that strict liability was generally applied with respect to oil pollution caused by mineral exploitation, arguably mineral operators should receive compensation only in the event of intentional or negligent conduct on the part of a neighbouring operator. (This idea is derived from certain suggestions put forward by L. F. E. Goldie, 'Liability for Damage and the Progressive Development of International Law', 1965 *ICLQ*, vol. 14, part 4, p. 1189, with respect to accidents between space vehicles.) However, what about damage to marine operators engaged in activities within national jurisdiction, caused by operations in the international area, or vice versa? The complications appear endless.

[130] This would appear to be at least as likely to occur as a result of intensive dredging, conducted continuously, as through the occasional escape of oil following drilling; the fact that both activities may be conducted at the same time, on an ever larger scale, increases the need that appropriate safeguards be adopted in due course against the possibility of a gradual deterioration in the marine environment.

[131] This arose out of the request by the General Assembly, in resolution 2467 D (XXIII) of 21 Dec. 1968, that IOC co-operate with the Secretary-General of the UN in the preparation of the comprehensive outline of the scope of a long-term programme of oceanographic research. The programme was drawn up after a series of inquiries and meetings, in particular of a joint working party nominated by the Scientific Committee for Oceanic Research, the Advisory Committee on Marine Resources, and WMO. The programme is contained in A/7750, 10 Nov. 1969, from which quotations are taken.

[132] This would comprise 'the collection of samples from various environments and biota, their submission and analysis at analytic centres, the transmission of the results of analyses to oceanographic data centres and the evaluation, interpretation and publication of the results on a regular basis'. Ibid. project 3.7.

[133] See e.g. Summary Report of the Third Meeting of the IOC Group of Experts on the Legal Status of Ocean Data Acquisition Systems, SC/IOC. EG-1/7, 20 Dec. 1969. The proposal remains under discussion. This work, aimed essentially at defining the legal status of ODAS and protecting them from depredation, has been done in collaboration with IMCO. A conference of governmental experts was convened by UNESCO and IMCO in Feb. 1972.

[134] Reported in GESAMP I/11, 17 July 1969.

[135] Report of 2nd sess., GESAMP II/11, esp. annexes V and VI.

[136] Report of First Session of the IOC Group of Experts on Long-Term Scientific Policy and Planning (GELTSPAP), section concerning Marine Pollution. SC/IOC-Inf. 171, 4 Dec. 1970.

[137] Issued under the title *Man's Impact on the Global Environment* (cited fully in n. 7 above). The study was produced by some forty scientists and others who met in July 1970 for an intensive, one-month interdisciplinary examination of the complex problems (including ocean pollution) coming

under that heading. The results of their work are likely to provide much of the intellectual motor for endeavours in this field for some time to come; the 'carry over' (in part of individuals, but in considerable part also of ideas) at the FAO Seminar and Technical Conference, for example, was marked, and also influenced the 1972 Conference on the Human Environment, to aid which the study was made.

138 IMCO Assembly res. A 176(VI), 21 Oct. 1969. The expression 'other equipment' has been defined by the IMCO Maritime Safety Committee to include pipelines from drilling rigs and platforms for conveying gas or oil to the shore, but excluding pipelines from shore installations. IMCO doc. OP VIII/6.

139 Report of IMCO Sub-Committee on Marine Pollution, 8th sess., OP VIII/11, 15 Sept. 1970.

140 Marine Science and Technology: Survey and Proposals, E/4487, 24 Apr. 1968. Parts I E, II A 2 and 3, and III D, together with annex XIV, deal with various aspects of pollution and its prevention. The report also gives information, in annex XI, paras 153–173, of the relevant activities up to that date of IAEA.

141 GA res. 2414 (XXIII), 17 Dec. 1968.

142 Part A of res. 2467 (XXIII) established the UN Sea-Bed Committee, whose consideration of the question of marine pollution arising out of mineral exploitation was previously referred to.

143 See the Secretary-General's Report, A/7924, 11 June 1970 (cited fully in n. 111 above).

144 Res. 2566 (XXIV), 13 Dec. 1969.

145 Problems of the Human Environment, E/4667, 26 May 1969, para. 59.

146 Described ibid. annex F.

147 Res. 2750 C (XXV), 17 Dec. 1970.

148 It may be noted that at its second session (8–19 Feb. 1971) the Preparatory Committee decided, *inter alia*, to establish two Intergovernmental Working Groups, one on marine pollution and the other on environmental monitoring. That on marine pollution was asked to report on: (i) the extent to which general guidelines and criteria can be established; and (ii) specific actions which might be taken as regards (a) particular substances, (b) an appraisal of international arrangements, in particular those on a regional or sub-regional basis, and (c) an appraisal of the action which the Conference might take to improve the enforcement of existing instruments and to encourage the implementation of further instruments in this field. Report of the Preparatory Committee, 2nd sess., A/CONF.48/PC.9, para. 42.

149 In the words of the Secretary-General, 'Investigation and control of marine pollution . . . is a matter on which international action on both regional and global scales is now becoming urgent', E/4487, 24 Apr. 1968, para. 278.

150 e.g. for a global network which would monitor changes in the earth's environment, such as those caused, *inter alia*, by pollution; this proposal was considered by the congress of the International Biological Programme, held in Sept. 1970. The creation of an international environmental agency has been proposed by R. Baxter, at the Columbia Univ. Conference on International and Interstate Regulation of Water Pollution, 13 Mar. 1970, and by G. Kennan, 'To Prevent a World Wasteland: a Proposal', *For. Aff.*, Apr. 1970, p. 401.

151 See J. Sherman, 'Space Craft Oceanography—Its Scientific and Economic Implications for the Next Decade', in *Space Exploration and Applications*, vol. I (UN, 1969), p. 645, and Development of Natural Resources: Natural Resources Satellites, Report of the Secretary-General, E/4779, 4 Feb. 1970.

INDEX